Princeton Theological Monograph Series

Dikran Y. Hadidian

General Editor

50

EUROPEAN PIETISM REVIEWED

FREDERICK HERZOG

EUROPEAN PIETISM REVIEWED

FREDERICK HERZOG

PICKWICK PUBLICATIONS
San Jose, California

Published by

Pickwick Publications
215 Incline Way
San Jose, CA 95139-1526

Printed in the United States of America

Herzog, Frederick
    European pietism reviewed / Frederick Herzog.
        p.   cm. -- (Princeton theological monograph series ; 50)
    Includes bibliographical references.
    ISBN 1-55635-042-2
        1. Pietism. 2. Europe--Church History. I. Title. II. Series.

BR1650.3H47 2003
273'.7--dc21
                                            2003051183

Printed in the United States by Morris Publishing
3212 East Highway 30
Kearney, NE 68847
1-800-650-7888

CONTENTS

Philipp Jacob Spener

Jean de Labadie

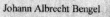

Johann Albrecht Bengel

Gottfried Arnold

August Hermann Francke

Nicolas Ludwig Graf von Zinzendorf

Friedrich Christoph Oetinger

J.F. OBERLIN
Pasteur à Waldersbach au Ban-de-la-Roche

Johann Friedrich Oberlin

LOWELL ZUCK'S PREFACE TO
FREDERICK HERZOG'S
EUROPEAN PIETISM REVIEWED

A very favorable view of Pietism is that of Trond Enger in the Oxford Companion to Christian Thought. He describes it as "the most intense and profound attempt in the history of the church to realize the power of early Christianity that has therefore never ceased to inspire."

Frederick Herzog, writing from a critical Pietistic perspective in 1968, summarized his conclusions in this work by saying that "the recent resurgence of pietistic movements in America might do well to remember their German forebears whose noble spiritual aspirations lost their momentum by an uncritical alliance with the secular realm of government."

Herzog, known mostly for developing an original liberation theology out of the Civil Rights struggle of the U.S. South, proves with this never published work that a critical spirituality sensitized him to grasp the social problems of his time from a firm theological and historical perspective.

In an effort to bring the work up to date I have made slight corrections and additions in the Introduction and translated texts and notes. Frederick Herzog himself updated his original 1968 introduction in the 1980's, as printed here. No modern English translation of the Francke text exists elsewhere, and the Labadie and Oetinger selections have never been translated before, we think. Kristin Herzog is the Oetinger translator, and the "Genealogy of the Well-Grounded Thoughts of a Theologian" accounts for the special value of this publication. The "Editor's Introduction" to Francke's work as well as that to the Oetinger selection are a combination of my work with that of Herzog, and I have made slight additions to the footnotes. I have added many additional titles to the bibliography, almost all of which have been referred to in the text.

My own summary thirty-three years later, after continuing Frederick Herzog's choice of notable Pietist documents by de Labadie, Francke, and Oetinger, with his comments largely intact, suggests that in the light of the 9/11 terrorist attacks upon the U.S. the three major world religions, Judaism, Christianity, and Islam, with their divine revelational perspectives, sometimes tend toward murderous delusional judgments of continuing danger to civilization among many of their followers, in continuity with their mixed past historical behaviors.

Insofar as Pietism in each of those religions supplements their revelational understandings with mystical, experiential encounters with God, it is possible that a more peace-effecting spirituality might counter fundamentalism in its dangerous forms. I believe that Pietist perceptions of divinely initiated experiential religion, leading to renewal actions, realistically questioning excessive rationalism or emotionalism in favor of recovery of scriptural perspectives, as well as openness to science and technology, can be true interpretations which are powerful and effective in the world today.

Interpreting Pietism remains controversial. Thirty years ago Horst Weigelt discerned six different German interpretations of Pietist origins: the usual German view of renewal amid Lutheran orthodoxy, Albrecht Ritschl's disapproving Franciscan revitalization of mysticism perspective, an opposite approving view of Evangelical mysticism, a different origin in English Puritan and Dutch Precisianism, a specific English Puritan influence, Emanuel Hirsch's approval of Pietism as gravedigger of orthodoxy and transition to Enlightenment, and a final multiple-origin view which is still prominent among interpreters.

Pietism is understood usually as a reform movement initiated by Philip Jakob Spener within German Lutheranism. He emphasized individual conversion, "living faith" and the fruits of faith. The name is derived from the *collegia pietatis* (informal devotional meetings) first organized around 1670 when Spener was pastor in Frankfurt. Spener was influenced at Geneva by the French Catholic convert to the Reformed faith, Jean de Labadie, who later became a Pietist Separatist. Labadie's 1667 *Reform of the Church through the Pastorate* provided a model for Spener's later *Pia Desideria*, though Spener always resisted separatism.

Whether separatist or not, Pietism can be understood in a wider context in different countries and churches during the 16th, 17th and 18th centuries as piety among Puritans and Methodists in England, further reformation in the Reformed Netherlands, Jansenists in Catholic France and Belgium, and the Spiritualists and Pietists in Protestant Germany.

In a more doctrinal context Pietism may be seen resulting from conflict between the doctrine of salvation through grace and God's requirement of individual holiness. It thus also goes back to ascetic, mystical and monastic desires for holiness appearing in early and medieval Orthodox and Catholic Christian traditions as well as among 18th century Hasidic Jews and 10th century Moslem mystical Sufis. It is also powerfully represented in all sorts of religious movements in the 21st century world.

Frederick Herzog's introduction wisely summarizes fairly traditional varieties of mostly German Pietism, explaining first its context and original recovery of a "theology of the heart", a term used by the French Protestant mystic, Pierre Poiret. August Hermann Francke, whom Spener recruited, was a brilliant organizer and teacher who made the newly founded University of Halle the intellectual center of Pietism. The university and other institutions organized by Francke at Halle sent out lay and clerical leaders to influence the ruling class of Protestant Germany, especially Prussia, and the younger generation of pastors. Instead of Spener's eschatology of hope and expectation of better times, Francke developed an active approach to seeking reform in the world. His method of conversion and education came to dominate Pietism, as Bible study, missions and church-related social institutions brought him worldwide fame and influence.

Nicolaus Ludwig Graf von Zinzendorf was one of Francke's students who in a joyful way tried to gather all of God's children into a non-confessional fraternal society. Its ecumenism paradoxically became the renewed Church of the Unity of the Brethren (Moravian Church). While Herzog sympathizes somewhat with Zinzendorf's semi-separatist tendencies, he criticizes Francke for compromising his own strong influence by serving Prussian state interests (especially military) too much.

The most unusual document which Herzog's wife, Kristin, translated in the 1960's is Friedrich Christoph Oetinger's *Genealogy*. A Württemberg pastor, Oetinger was a student of the powerful biblical scholar Johann Albrecht Bengel, who helped make Pietism thoroughly at home in that state-church. Herzog suggests that Oetinger more than any of the other Pietists, especially Francke, was free from compromise with state claims in making a this-world-oriented faith-statement that was pious, truthful, and practically compelling. While this claim is difficult to support, the little-known Oetinger belongs among the most winsome, penetrating, and relevant Pietists worthy of study in today's world, in spite of his own peculiar speculative tendencies.

Herzog claims that "only Friedrich Christoph Oetinger saw the need for a theology which bases the community of the church upon truth, is aware of the inroads of secularism, and is able to keep a critical distance in regard to the machinations of secular governments." I think that a more accurate assessment of Oetinger would be that he, like his master, Bengel, awaiting the Parousia in 1836, could only reject the absolutist state. On the other hand, he took into account the mystical and intellectual giants of his age (Boehme, Paracelsus, Leibniz and Newton), developed a religious interpretation of all creation, and also saw a reality beyond the scientific, psychic or historical realms, a wholeness mediated powerfully in the Bible. Strange as are many aspects of this old type of Pietism to modern sophisticates, their wisdom and relevance for helping to cope also with our own problems is striking.

When one moves beyond Europe to the wider world, especially North America, one thinks immediately of relating Pietism to what Americans call the Great Awakening. William G. McLoughlin in 1978 described three and perhaps four Great Awakenings (though some historians deny there were any): the First from the 1730's led by a spellbinding revival preacher from England, George Whitefield; the Second around 1800, more elitist, featuring Charles Finney, later a professor at Oberlin College; the Third with the fiery Billy Sunday, spawning in liberal reaction the Social Gospel of Walter Rauschenbusch, and, McLoughlin thought, a Fourth, around the 1960's, featuring the more mass-communication-ready Billy Graham and a host of more popular beats and Jesus people.

In 2000 the 1993 Economics Nobel prize winner, Robert W. Fogel, stepped down from his cliometric precision stance into a questionable agenda for today, the fourth (religious/secular) great awakening. Overlooking the massive Wesleyan/holiness/Pentecostal strain in American evangelical religion, Fogel opts for dominance of a renewed secular Calvinism without frugality, welcoming enthusiastic religion as a bulwark for family values. Behind his argument is an economic explanation that the Industrial Revolution impoverished the poor until the bounties of accomplished industrialization helped the whole population. He now waits for the present cycle of electronic revolution to benefit all instead of the few, and in the meantime thinks that improved access to spiritual assets will turn us into disciplined secular Calvinists.

The problem with this approach is that it suggests taking religion with little ultimate seriousness, a common problem for many of us. Yet the Fogel joy over "60 million Americans engulfed in enthusiasm" does seem to indicate that present-day Pietism has something dangerous and powerful going for it.

I want to express my appreciation for having had the opportunity to add to a significant work on Pietism by a serious, path-breaking advocate of its most worthy aspects. This work is Frederick Herzog's last, excellent contribution to responsible theological, historical interpretation, opening the possibility for a more truth and justice-filled world.

A careful examination of the historical precedents for pietistic faith and worldliness which Herzog has so seriously undertaken and judged here, making use of his wife's excellent Oetinger translation, might alert, warn and possibly invigorate a frightened while complacent populace who could benefit from considering the origins of many of their faiths.

Lowell H. Zuck
St. Louis, Missouri
January 2002

FREDERICK HERZOG'S SUMMARY
OF HIS MANUSCRIPT

EUROPEAN PIETISM REVIEWED, 1968

History gives evidence that the same political reef upon which the Lutheran Reformation became shipwrecked also caused the Pietistic movement of the 17th and 18th centuries to founder. Whereas Luther's reform was exploited by the German princes in their struggle with the Roman pontiff, so the Pietistic movement was exploited by the burgeoning Prussian kingdom in their power struggle with the German nobility. In both cases, spiritual reform gave way to secular expediency. Philipp Jakob Spener never attempted to challenge Luther's doctrine of "two kingdoms" and wanted to understand the church as wholly obedient to the state. August Hermann Francke openly courted the support of the Prussian monarchs and contributed to the military ascendancy of that kingdom. Nicolaus Ludwig Graf von Zinzendorf opted for a separated community which sought to ignore the relation of the church to the greater society. Only Friedrich Christoph Oetinger saw the need for a theology which bases the community of the church upon truth, is aware of the inroads of secularism, and is able to keep a critical distance in regard to the machinations of secular governments. The recent resurgence of pietistic movements in America might do well to remember their German forebears whose noble spiritual aspirations lost their momentum by an uncritical alliance with the secular realm of government.

INTRODUCTION
Frederick Herzog

PIETISM SPIRITUALITY

Pietism spirituality will best be understood
and defined by reliving its history.

"One only has to visit a Pietist forge or shoe repair shop. There
sits the master, next to him at his right the Bible, at the left—frequently
at least—the whiskey bottle. Not much work is going on. Most of the
time the master reads the Bible, occasionally takes a drink, and now
and then sings a hymn with his workers. Yet the main thing going on is
criticizing the neighbor."[1] So Friedrich Engels in his description of his
hometown Wuppertal. For one of the founders of Communism in the
early nineteenth century, Pietism had left a bad taste in his mouth. We
still think of Pietism more in terms of what Engels was rebelling
against: second, third, or fourth-generation Pietism. It smacks of religious narcissism and legalism.[2] In the beginning, however, it was an
event of considerable momentum, a dynamic force not unlike the Reformation. Only later did it turn into religious mush—the butt of theological jokes.[3]

Initially Pietism was an expression of the liberation of Christians
from backwardness and oppression in post-Reformation Orthodoxy. It
is best understood on the foil of the Reformation which had sought to
free human beings from monastery walls and the confessional. But no
one had satisfactorily answered the question of what exactly to do with
the newly found freedom.

While the Reformation had concentrated on training people for
being better churchmen and churchwomen, Pietism concerned itself
with the spirituality of Christian formation. Only recently did it occur
to Christians that churchmanship or churchwomanship and spirituality
were two sides of the same coin and that they pave the way toward the
liberation of humankind to true personhood.

The contemporary church is trying to figure out what Christianity
might still contribute to humankind becoming more human. Pietism reminds us of a few traps on that road, but also demonstrates significant
possibilities. It distinguished itself by introducing *ecclesiolae in ecclesia*, little churches in the big church, often referred to as conventicles.
Yet the Pietist band was never a mere banding together of individuals.

They were people covenanting for accomplishing common goals: the reformation of the pastorate or the renewal of the diaconate, for example. They were centers of renewal in Christian formation. Yet it did not take long before some fell into traps of shallow spirituality, traps that also lie in wait for us today.

Church renewal is an inevitable dynamics of Christian commitment to the church. *Ecclesia semper reformanda*—the church is always to be reformed. The idea did not begin with the segment of history we now call the Reformation. But to focus the renewal of the church on the clergy, as the first Pietist, Jean de Labadie, proposed, before long led to the appearance of the "Divine," the ""geistlicher Herr," or "the Reverend." The stress on the diaconate eventually produced the "professional servant." Professionalism of spirituality has always been a special temptation of Pietism, contributing heavily to religion as "opium of the people.""

Today we long for a steeled spirituality that can stand up to the madness of the nuclear age in a society exploiting nature and humankind. Pietism promoted the stimulation of the religious affections. It resulted in people feeling good about themselves. But this is not the same as discipleship. Today we need to make a sharp distinction between piety as affection and piety as resistance, the piety of emotion and the piety of discipleship. The ultimate end of Christian spirituality is the evocation of the resistance spirit, so that God's justice may prevail in the world.

In our time we strongly sense the clash between the sheer religious and the secular. Pietism was already caught in the clash. The secularization of society is characteristic of our age. Halle Pietism already began consciously to tackle the incipient problem. Was the church going to confine itself to the merely religious realm? Or was it going to assume responsibility for society as a whole? Would it have to join forces with the state?

Albeit only for a brief time, in this regard Pietism no longer thought only of the reformation of the church, but also of the reformation of society. At least in one of its strands, in Halle Pietism, it went beyond the Lutheran Reformation which had no well-developed plans for world-transformation.[4] Yet the professionalism of servanthood soon made the scheme founder, so that its idealistic aspirations were never fully tested in the rough-and-tumble of politics.

When pietism arrived in North America it appeared almost exclusively in the form of religious affection.[5] The history of Pietism shows that there are alternatives. In one of its forms, in Württemberg Pietism, it began a thought project. It suggested that without careful analysis of the spiritual dynamics shaping piety, we can hardly see what it might still be able to deliver to an increasingly secular world. Though it did not produce an ideal solution, it succeeded in articulating all that Pietism was able to yield—its strength and its limits.

THE UNFINISHED REFORMATION

Reformation thought of the sixteenth century, animated by the notion of *ecclesia semper reformanda* (the church is always to be reformed), realized that the reformation of the church is never finished.[6] The great achievements of the Reformation are well known. Central was the courage to give faith its rightful place among Christians. "Dogma was no longer binding doctrinal law, but the confession of faith in grace. Saintliness was no longer self-torture, but ethical discipline in thought and action. Cult was no longer magical apparatus, but edification in the Spirit. The constitution of the church was no longer divine order, but temporal form for the sharing of Christ's words....The church was now an object of faith, no longer the ruler supreme over all of life."[7]

Though we have come to think of the German Reformation as a great change in the life of the German people, the fact is that it brought only partial change. Luther had not been able to attain a total reform of the church. Especially worship and life remained much the same as before.[8] Philip Jakob Spener (1635-1705), the founder of German Pietism, was convinced that "in the Reformation by far not everything was accomplished that should have been accomplished."[9] Luther's primary contribution was the proclamation of the pure Gospel doctrine. Although Spener did not deny Luther's attainments in the new forming of the church, he felt that Luther's life had been too short to complete the work of the Reformation. Besides the reformation of doctrine there was still the reformation of life. The newly discovered truth needed to be "implanted in the hearts of the people" much more thoroughly. So Spener concluded "that we have to introduce an edifying discipline in the church."

The Pietism dynamics Spener articulated are still with us. While on the Reformation age dawned the thought of what Kierkegaard later called the need of every generation to begin all over again with Christ, the church as an institution did not catch on to it in a broad sense. The Reformation reach was much farther than its grasp. Not everything envisioned was attained. But the spreading of the dynamics of renewal was an important step. Pietism took up that banner and offered the "discovery" to a new generation of Christians, obviously also not in a perfect way.

Even so, what comes through loud and clear in Pietism is the renewal dynamics of the Reformation. We need to be careful, though, not immediately to idealize some of its forms, like the renewal of the pastorate or the reshaping of the diaconate. From the outset we need to see also the drawbacks of Pietism.

Obviously historical limitations had prevented the consummation of the Reformation.[10] While for Luther personally the major issues had been religious, he entrusted the political fate of his movement to princes, initially for protection, but later on also for shaping organizational structure. For the princes themselves, the issues almost from the outset had been primarily political and economic.[11]

Reformation in a number of German territories soon also meant secularization, that is, transfer of church property to the princes. Acquisition of such property was often the best reason for wealth-obsessed and power-hungry princes to turn Protestant. Thus some people quickly shifted from lofty faith questions supposedly at the center of the Reformation dynamics to the confiscation of property. Already in those days when one said "Bible," one meant cotton. The fact of the movement no longer depended on Luther and the Protestant ministry, but on magistrates, dukes, and kings.

Did the leaders of Pietism ever fully sense the real causes of the corruption of the church they were so vehemently opposing? In retrospect we today perhaps can better see that the dilemmas Pietism was facing had a lot to do with the secularization handed down to it by the Reformation.

Most of the leaders of the Reformation became entrenched in political positions in order to secure their gains. Luther, in his later years, was overcome by considerable resignation. He warned against "experiments," though he also claimed that people plainly did not want to change, even with the Gospel in their hands. The students at Wittenberg, for example, seemed to Luther as they had always been—disobedient, boisterous, and without discipline. The great change Luther had hoped for did not happen. People did not join him in his experience of repentance and new life.

Trying to interpret the origins of Pietism, Albrecht Ritschl was not quite correct when he stressed that Luther did not directly intend a reform of the Christian life, but only of doctrine and worship, or faith and order.[12] He was correct, however, in claiming that Luther in whatever he wished to accomplish was hemmed in by the princes.[13] The growth of the power of the princes in the affairs of the church was one of the major developments that led to the emergence of Pietism, however little Pietism itself may have been conscious of the problem. The Reformation simply had not come to grips with the relationship between the political and the religious spheres. To the extent that princes shaped the end result of the Reformation, interest in spirituality dwindled.[14] This laid the actual ground for the subsequent attacks of Pietism on the corruption of the church.

The historical origins of Pietism, however, are complex and cannot exclusively be explained by developments in Germany. It did not spring from German Lutheranism like Athena from the head of Zeus. It had antecedents. In its pedigree appears Dutch Precisionism[15] as well as English Puritanism.[16] The Reformation had been a European event, not merely a German thunderstorm. In Switzerland, Calvin had been able to build his Reformation on the insights of Luther and Zwingli and their achievements. Mainly under Calvin's influence Holland turned Reformed. England under Henry VIII, as far as Reformation is concerned, experienced largely a change of ecclesiastical structure. So it comes as no surprise that the "post-Reformation reformation" began in England where only minor changes had occurred in faith outlook and ecclesiastical structure.[17]

It is less obvious why Holland, which had experienced a more thorough Reformation than Luther's Germany, began much earlier to reform the Reformation. Probably the impact of "post-Reformation reformation" influences from England were a significant factor. Dutch people like Willem Teelinck (1579-1629) crossed the channel for theological studies. And English folk like William Ames (1576-1633), some on their own initiative, some on account of persecution, came to Holland to instruct and to preach. In this give-and-take it was natural that concerns of the Puritan Reformation should quickly take hold in Holland.

Spener mentions reading Puritan divines in his early youth. This does not, however, indicate that German Pietism began exclusively under the aegis of Puritanism or Precisionism. German Spiritualism, Radical Reformation concerns, and even Catholic piety, contributed to the new movement. The Reformation had freed the human mind from ecclesiastical tutelage. It began to drink freely from whatever fountain offered itself to quench the thirst for understanding the spiritual life. Pietism dynamics banked considerably on a first flourishing of what we today call the ecumenical spirit.

From the array of forces one dare not forget Reform-Orthodoxy in Lutheranism whose literature represents a further link between the Reformation and Pietism.[18] It was a movement that tried to counteract the stifling effects of the orthodox tradition.

Since Luther had stressed Gospel doctrine so much, Orthodoxy considered its main task the conservation of doctrine. In a time when the gains of the Reformation were invariably threatened by Roman Catholicism and altercations among Protestant princes, a theology emerged that rightly sought to maintain the integrity of what had been delivered to the church by the saints of the Reformation. It soon turned into rampant intellectualism. Says Ritschl: "In the merely intellectual formulation of the doctrines of the Gospel that total view of Christianity that would correspond to the Reformation had not yet found expression."[19] Concentrating on the intellectual grasp of the Christian faith, Orthodoxy deepened the isolation of religion from everyday affairs. Worse yet, it certainly did not curtail the control of the church by princes and magistrates.

In the light of the foregoing, Martin Schmidt's definition of Pietism affords a first vantage point to view the movement as a whole: "Pietism is that deepening movement of the later seventeenth and early eighteenth century that set itself the goal of a new Reformation, because the first, in its transition to Protestant Orthodoxy, had ground to a halt in the institutional and dogmatic."[20] Is this definition comprehensive enough? Might one not also speak of a Dutch Pietism or a Puritan Pietism? Max Weber is one of the voices reminding us of the possibilities for a broader definition: "Pietism split off from the Calvinist movement in England and especially Holland. It remained loosely connected with orthodoxy, shading off from it in imperceptible graduations, until at the end of the seventeenth century it was absorbed into Lutheranism under Spener's leadership."[21]

We already called attention to the pedigree of Pietism that reaches back to England via Holland. It is thus instructive to see someone argue for an even more inclusive concept, as F. Ernest Stoeffler has done: "All experiential Protestantism during the post-Reformation period can be treated as an essential unity. It constitutes a movement which, if seen in its full range, penetrated all of Protestantism during the seventeenth and eighteenth centuries, and its influence has been felt wherever Protestantism appeared."[22] For viewing the entire range of Pietism dynamics it is indeed helpful to regard Pietism as a homogeneous entity covering much of Western Europe. Similarly, it makes eminent sense to keep in mind the experiential tradition mediated through the Middle Ages and the Reformation to Pietism and the so-called modern age.

The experiential tradition and Pietism are not completely separate entities for sure. Yet for purposes of this book it will be wise to limit ourselves to Pietism as German Pietism. Moreover, when Cotton Mather (1663-1728) corresponded with August Hermann Francke (1663-1727) he was confronted with a unique configuration of historical forces that as Pietism were distinct from Puritanism both English and North American. When Heinrich Melchior Mühlenberg (1711-1787) was sent from Halle, Francke's place, to what would become the United States, where he represented the "Luther" of at least the Pennsylvania Lutherans, he imported the Pietist modification of the Reformation that has remained the hallmark of American Lutheranism to this day. Whenever we in the States today speak of Pietism it is its German expression we have in mind.

We need to underscore that German Pietism was a peculiar attempt to continue the Reformation. While it drew on English and Dutch precedents, it was burdened by Luther's peculiar struggle. Neither in England nor in Holland had there been a figure like Luther whose personal faith struggle had become the paradigm. German Lutheranism at its core *is* Martin Luther. German Pietism is not far off that center. Its relationship to society and the state also remains unsolved. All goes back directly to Martin Luther: "The Lutheran saint, in his pursuit of the invisible kingdom of heaven, turned away from politics and left the kingdom of earth, as Luther himself wrote, 'to anyone who wants to take it'."[23] Stoeffler's distinction between pietistic and political Puritans makes a lot of sense. The word pietistic is here apropos. Yet in Germany Pietists of the political Puritan stripe never existed because of Luther's verdict about church/state relations.

While some Pietists of the Halle stripe briefly wanted to change the world, it was not through programmed political action, and certainly not through revolution. Puritan tendencies differ in that regard.[24] Therefore we will put less strain on the epithet Pietist if we do not use it for the Puritan. While the sentiment of piety certainly is a common bond between Puritans and Pietists, its concrete shape in action differs. Though the relationship between the Dutch shape of piety and German Pietism is less fraught with complications,[25] the peculiar Lutheran tendencies in piety are not part of the original Dutch mix.

THE CONSERVATION OF THE
REFORMATION (Orthodoxy)

In order yet better to understand the origins of Pietism we have to take a good look at Lutheran Orthodoxy—the generation that followed the Reformers. At its best, the sixteenth century in middle-Europe had been the age of a *vital* faith. Yet the Reformers themselves had already summarized it in confessional writings, such as the Augsburg Confession. The seventeenth century codified its principles. Professors and pastors competed with one another in their codification efforts.[26] Here the Reformation became a heritage conserved airtight. Characteristic features of Orthodoxy were polemics against other Protestant denominations, Roman Catholicism, rationalism, and a mystical spirituality rejecting the institutional church.[27]

All the while the political fate of the people shaped up according to the dictates of the powers that be. The nobility sought to prove its superiority over the common folk in lavishness of apparel and other status symbols. Many churches built special pews for the nobility.[28] During the Eucharist Christians often approached the communion table according to rank, the nobility first. In 1672 members of the Saxon nobility demanded baptism of their children in the home, claiming it would be humiliating for a noble child to be baptized with the same water as the child of a commoner. Obviously the priesthood of all believers went begging. The church had turned into a mere copy of the social pecking order.[29] Protestant Christianity reflected the political fate rather than the *living* faith.

Secure in their social order, theologians began to build their theological castles in the air. Conserving the principles of the Reformation in systems of thought brought a sea change. Justification by faith was no longer as important as the Scripture principle of *sola Scriptura*.[30] Orthodox polemics did not care about personal faith. If there was a "personal interest" it was in an absolutely valid external authority. Medieval craving for a safe, objectively grounded truth, surviving the Reformation, incarnated itself in the "papal" office of the Scriptures.

The doctrine of the Holy Scripture was developed with a vengeance and a precision that went far beyond the Reformation. A definite body of doctrine had to secure the Scriptural truth. Only on grounds of objective certainty could one be sure of justification. Gradually the basic Reformation witness was abandoned. The assurance of personal salvation retreated far behind the assurance of the truth of a doctrine. Assurance of salvation could now easily be understood as assent to a body of correct doctrine.

In any case, live trust in God, *fiducia*, was no longer primary.
God's activity was seen as deposited in the biblical word which as a
means of grace was sufficient unto itself. Orthodoxy concerned itself
with secondary causes at the neglect of a vital relationship to God: "It
shows to what feeble state the religious pulse had fallen in the theology
of the day, that the doctrine of the active operation of the Holy Spirit
should have become strange and incredible. The subject of both the
first work against Spener, viz., that of C. Dilfeld, and the first work of
Löscher, the last advocate of this orthodoxy, was 'Enthusiasm.' In this
respect, then, Spener opens the living fountains of primitive Christianity and of the Reformation."[31]

Our picture of Orthodoxy, however, should not suggest that Pietism appeared, as it were, out of the blue in Lutheranism. A reform-
orthodox representative by the name of Theophil Grossgebauer (1627-
1661), for example, already criticized Orthodoxy for promulgating a
merely *verbal* justification. Instead he called for regeneration—a new
life with God. The faith of churchfolk in his day he called pseudo-faith
bereft of the experience of justification.[32]

Karl Holl claimed that Pietism did not add a single new thought to
Reform-Orthodoxy. All it did was to create new forms.[33] In any case,
before Pietism appeared, Reform-Orthodoxy already read Puritan theologians such as Joseph Hall, Lewis Bayly, and Daniel Dyke.[34] The way
of Pietism was therefore well prepared for in the very movement it began so vehemently to battle. The transition from Orthodoxy to Pietism
is complex. Thoughts of reform continued to float around after the Reformation in England, Holland, and Switzerland, as well as in Germany,
but Orthodoxy proved incapable of translating the dynamics of reform
into its own time and context. It was merely a question of time that the
scattered energies for reform would crystallize in a vigorous movement.[35]

We need to be fair to Orthodoxy. On some levels, it was an inevitable occurrence. The teachings of the Reformation had to be guarded
in the face of attack. It developed a strong catechetical approach,[36] produced great hymn writers, and provided the refuge of faith in times of
trial such as the Thirty Years' War.[37] Its collapse in many respects
proved its weakness to protect itself against new secularizing tendencies making headway in society.

It is impossible to close one's eyes to the weaknesses of Orthodoxy. Its greatest drawback was probably its surrender to abstract
thought. In the eyes of the Pietist, this was a denial of Luther, especially the "young Luther." The Pietists stressed "life" over "doctrine" and
"power" over "office." Faith again was *living* faith in keeping with the
Reformation. The power of faith was active in love and not in confessional squabbles.[38]

Whoever wishes to benefit from Pietism dynamics today needs at
least to keep in mind two drawbacks that the movement inherited from

Orthodoxy.

1. The *theoretical heritage*. Christianity was seen as an idea-deposit of truth in creeds, confessions, and theological systems. For the believer the important thing was assent to ideas and to act upon them only in reaction to their appropriation.

2. The *political heritage*. Orthodoxy's lack of resistance to the interference of the state in the affairs of the church was equally debilitating. Some Reform-Orthodox people realized that the state usurped powers not its own.[39] Grossgebauer, for example, observed: "It is a terrible thing that the authorities should usurp the power and authority of the churches, taking away from the brotherhood." But the criticism in the end amounted to only halfhearted protest, since it did not address itself to the major autonomy of the secular realm. Certain attitudes were critiqued. But the principle of the empire was not questioned. Pietism did not change anything in that regard. Also in Pietism Christians easily reconciled themselves to two loyalties and thus serving two masters.

In this regard, Pietism almost from the outset began on the wrong foot. Its praxis, often referred to as *praxis pietatis*, did not generate its own steam. It took over from Orthodoxy the notion that theory precedes praxis. Obviously a wide-ranging tradition of Christian reflection lies behind this notion. But it had found expression in Orthodoxy with a vengeance. On the other hand, Orthodoxy saddled Pietism with a lack of praxis at least in one important area of life, the political. We are still burdened with this paradigm in all of Protestant thought. One of the reasons for presenting the Pietist materials is to show how our Europe-imported faith is deeply imbued with a wrong theory-praxis relationship. Emphasizing piety does not at all mean changing basic thought patterns of faith.

THE REFORMATION OF
THE REFORMATION (Spener)

Philip Jakob Spener was the person destined to consolidate the tendencies toward reform in German Lutheranism in his *"Pia Desideria or Heartfelt desire for a God-pleasing Reform of the true Evangelical Church. Together with Several Simple Christian proposals Looking Toward this End."* The volume initially appeared as preface to a new edition of John Arndt's *True Christianity*[40] in 1675, later printed as a separate publication. It was the "official" beginning of Pietism.[41] Arndt's treatise, introduced gratefully by Spener, had already become the most popular devotional handbook for the new Pietists.

What many had felt and said in one way or another, Spener was able effectively to communicate, evoking a wide response. In Spener's book one can immediately discover the direction and concern of the new movement. From the outset, it is bent toward deepening religious affection. The socio-political situation created by the Reformation is left essentially untouched.[42]

In the outcome of the Reformation, the responsibility for the structure is lodged finally in the state. The "empire" determined whether a church would be Catholic, Lutheran, or Reformed. Pietism did not resist. Rather, it gave birth to conventicles that conformed to political structures in almost every instance.

Spener's reform piece has three major points: 1. An overview of corrupt conditions in the church. 2. The appeal to the potential for improved conditions. 3. The proposal for correcting the bad conditions. Spener lodged the realization of church reformation in the reformation of individuals. He does not find the main fault with the organization of the church as such, but with the way individuals behave in it and thereby distort the very character of the church.

He begins with a description of the corruption in government, clergy, and the people. As to government, he points to the usual debaucheries attendant to court life and the seeking of self-advantage among the magistrates.[43] The clergy do not fare much better. The lives of ministers reflect a "worldly spirit, marked by carnal pleasure, lust of the eye, and arrogant behavior, so that it is evident that they have never taken even the first practical principle of Christianity seriously, namely, denial of self."[44] The people can hardly be better than their leaders. Lawsuits, begging, drinking and the like are widely prevalent. Under these circumstances the Christian spirit will not thrive. "Most people hardly know any other way of helping a needy neighbor than reluctantly to toss a few pennies to a beggar once in a while."[45]

Spener was convinced that "God has promised his church here on earth a better state than this."[46] He wants to point out "what is best for the church."[47] His program is not a means for creating conventicles separate from the church. Spener believes that God has promised the church a form not as corrupt as the present one. Primitive Christianity functions as model for an improved form, enabling Spener to offer a number of "Proposals to Correct Conditions in the Church."

1.   The first proposal is a *more extensive use of the Word of God* among us.[48] Beyond daily or frequent preaching from the pulpit there ought to be diligent reading of the Scriptures by the head of the household or by someone designated for this task. Besides preaching services, "the ancient and apostolic kind of church meetings"[49] are to be reintroduced in which according to I Corinthians 14:26-40 Christians exchange with one another their understanding of the Word of God and try to answer spiritual needs in dialogue with one another for their mutual edification.

2.   Next Spener counsels "*the establishment and diligent exercise of the spiritual priesthood.*"[50] Jesus Christ makes all Christians priests. They are bound to act as such, though the regular and public performance of the spiritual functions has been "entrusted to ministers appointed for this purpose."[51] While under the papacy the functions of the universal priesthood "were assigned solely to the clergy,"[52] it should be understood that principally every Christian is called by "the grace that is given him to teach others, especially those under his own roof, to chastise, exhort, convert, and to edify them, to observe their life, pray for all, and insofar as possible be concerned about their salvation."[53] Without such interaction, the professional ministry cannot accomplish its work effectively. If Christians could be found who would assist in the work of the professional ministry, "finally the church would be visibly reformed."[54]

3.   In the third place, Christians are reminded that "*it is by no means enough to have knowledge of the Christian faith, for Christianity consists rather of practice.*"[55] Here lies the core of Pietism, the strong emphasis on *practice*. It involves what we today know as spiritual direction. Spener counsels that "it may be useful if those who have earnestly resolved to walk in the way of the Lord would enter into a confidential relationship with their confessor[56] or some other judicious and enlightened Christian and would regularly report to him how they live, what opportunities they have had to practice Christian love, and how they have employed or neglected them. This should be done with the intention of discovering what is amiss and securing such an individual's counsel and instruction as to what is to be done."[57]

4. The fourth proposal deals with specific actions: the Christian tasks in *"religious* controversies with unbelievers and heretics."[58] We take note here of Spener's great concern for the protection of the spiritual life: "We must first take pains to strengthen and confirm ourselves, our friends, and other fellow believers in the known truth and to protect them with great care from every kind of seduction. Then we must remind ourselves of our duty toward the erring."[59] Steps to be taken are prayer, good example, demonstration of how the errors conflict with God's Word, and finally "practice of heartfelt love toward all unbelievers and heretics."[60] Disputation is never enough to maintain the truth among believers or to impart it to unbelievers.[61]

5. Since Spener believes that the professional ministry bears the greatest responsibility in reforming the church, he is especially concerned that the training of the ministers in *"in our schools and universities"*[62] be changed. He considers it of great importance "that the office of the ministry be occupied by men who, above all, are themselves true Christians and then have the divine wisdom to guide others carefully on the way of the Lord."[63] Spener scores the unchristian academic life where "the devils of ambition, tippling, carousing, and brawling"[64] prevail. "Students should unceasingly have it impressed upon them that holy life is not of less consequence than diligence and study, indeed that study without piety is worthless."[65] Spener goes so far as to suggest that it 'would not be a bad thing if all students were required to bring from their universities testimonials concerning their piety as well as their diligence and skill."[66] He does by no means wish to exclude training in theological debate. But, on the whole, it would be desirable "that disputations be held in the German language, so that students may learn to use the terminology which is suited to this purpose, for it will be difficult for them in the ministry when they wish to mention something about a controversy from the pulpit and must speak to the congregation in German, although they never had any practice in this."[67] But controversy should always be kept within bounds, "and the whole of theology should be brought back to apostolic simplicity."[68] Instead of spending time on idle controversies they should use their time in reading the *Theologia Germanica*, Tauler and Thomas à Kempis. "Since theology is a practical discipline"[69] . . . and does not consist only of knowledge, study alone is not enough, nor is the mere accumulation and imparting of information.[70] So under the leadership of a professor small groups could meet for seminars oriented in practice, such as comforting the sick or learning how to preach, as introduction to teaching. This is a point of Spener's reform program that probably connects him with Jean de Labadie's (1610-1674) notion of reforming the church through the pastorate.[71] It becomes quite clear that Spener puts great stock in the reform of theological studies. The introduction of *collegia pietatis* at the university leading to the *praxis pietatis* was a radical

break with past practice.

6. As the last counsel for improving the church, Spener encourages a change in the customary style of preaching. Proclamation ought not to be an opportunity for showmanship, an occasion where the preacher displays scholarship, knowledge of foreign languages, and feats of rhetoric. The sermon should edify the inner life of a person. Spener points to sermons by Johannes Arndt (1555-1621) as models.

The *Pia Desideria* is not only Spener's personal program, but the program of Pietism.[72] Its historical impact surpassed all other proposals for reform in the seventeenth century. That was partly because of its comprehensive grasp of the predicament, issuing in clear reform proposals rather than in mere gripes. Spener did not promote a change of mere peccadillos, but a radical renewal of the religious life as a whole. Spener's followers grew in numbers after the publication. Since 1677 one spoke of Spenerians and soon also of Pietists. Before long Pietism was involved in long drawn-out battles covering the entire scale from value conflicts to power conflicts in the church.[73] Spener reflects all of this in the course of his life. There were clear-cut public arguments and public actions. But there was also much power-play behind the scenes.

If one compares Spener's program with the writings of the early Luther one cannot but notice that Spener is a follower and not an inventor. He does not relive the Gospel in a pristine way, something that led Luther to the formulation of new doctrine. Spener certainly makes regeneration a big deal. But he does not question the body of teaching of the Reformation, the way Luther questioned the teachings of the Roman Catholic Church. Regeneration was enabling one to have genuine piety, a new relationship with God on grounds of justification. Yet the regeneration had not been a topic suppressed by the Reformation, though obviously justification received top billing. Orthodoxy did not suppress regeneration either. Therefore Spener was able practically to treat the doctrinal body of thought produced by the Reformation as a deposit of truth. Piety was religious affection evoked by regeneration as part of the doctrinal expectation of the Reformation—at least that is the way Spener saw the logic of his proposals. The *praxis pietatis* which he wanted his *collegia Pietatis* to be engaged in was an application of regeneration, a consequence of Piety.

There is no reason to score a person like Spener who was up against tremendous obstacles. Yet we can note where history produced some "delaying tactics" that kept the church from grasping the truth of the matter with which it was struggling. Luther in trying to understand Romans practically relived the genesis of the justification doctrine. *Praxis* gave rise to thought, as it gave rise to piety. Pietism, together with Orthodoxy, turned that pristine experience around. Rationalism and the rise of the historico-critical method tried to make up for the lack of showing the "genesis" of praxis. But both proceeded in an iconoclastic mood that was always ready to throw out the baby with the bath, so that regeneration as well as justification would be shucked as obsolete myths. In any case, we today still face the task of coming to grips with the genuine hope of Pietism and to offer a more creative translation of its basic contribution. We still need sainthood, but we can do without the professional saint. We still need servanthood, but the professional servant usually perverts the true service of God.

VARIETIES OF PIETISM

Similar to the Reformation, which generated several streams of Protestantism—Lutheran, Reformed, and Radical groups—Pietism also contributed to the variety of Protestantism. It did not "spawn" denominations as such, but various corporate expressions of piety. This was, however, more because of geographical and sociological than of doctrinal differences.[74] There are many aspects of these varieties of Pietism that make for an interesting story. Our major concern will be with Pietism as an expression of religious affection in various contexts where initially at least its genesis in the doctrinal system of Protestantism remained unreflected and, as a consequence, its social and political stance remained largely uncritical. Only in Württemberg Pietism did the reflection on its genesis begin with small first steps in the direction of a socio-political critique.

1. *Spener as "Founder."* While we have already reviewed Spener's programmatic statement of Pietism, we still need to consider the immediate impact he made which stands out as one of the peculiar forms of Pietism.[75] Among his demands, the most effective was the call for the *collegia pietatis*.[76] One could form them almost anywhere. They also had a great potential for keeping people together. Yet the gathering of the core Christians within a single congregation also involved certain dangers. As "covenant groups," *ecclesiolae in ecclesia*, they could easily become alienated from the worship of the local congregations. As piety bands, *collegia pietatis*, they enjoyed a quiet development only for a short time. As early as 1677 the Frankfurt police department checked on the newfangled meetings. In January 1678 the Darmstadt consistory sent notice to its ministers warning them against the *collegia*. It was the first "edict" against the Pietists.

An intense struggle developed. One gets a fair picture of its breadth if one considers that the library collection of controversy materials for only the years 1690-1699 at Göttingen University contains more than five hundred items (without any claim to completeness).[77] Charges against the "bands," *collegia*, range from spiritual pride, heresy, and simulated perfection, to new revelations and chiliastic aberrations. While the Pietists were also attacked as enemies of the state, this pertained realistically only to the radicals among them. Spener himself underscored the divine authority of the powers that be and the duty of obedience towards them. Yet he also stressed freedom of conscience in the affairs of religion—something his enemies used to accuse him of doctrinal indifference.

While Spener supported social reform, he would not—in view of the Sermon on the Mount—condone violent change.[78] He did question government power in that he theoretically wanted the landed nobility to function as countervailing power to the prince in the state legislature. Yet practically Spener's struggle in the end contributed to the loss of power among the landed nobility acting in concert with orthodoxy. When attacked by orthodoxy he appealed to the Berlin State government for support. Therefore government interference also worked against the nobility. Because of the coalition of the nobility with orthodoxy whatever weakened orthodoxy also weakened the nobility. So Pietism prevailing over Orthodoxy meant in the end also the prince triumphing over the nobility.

Spener's social reform ideas expressed themselves particularly in an articulate anti-poverty program. Already in his Strasbourg days he had objected to spontaneous almsgiving as promoting mendicancy. Later in Frankfurt and Berlin[79] he developed specific suggestions to combat poverty. State and society as well as the church were responsible for the poor.

Already in Spener the professional saint emerged, a peculiar form of human being torn between the demands of religious affection on the one hand and the demands of society and the state on the other. Spener's good common sense kept him from becoming a spiritual odd-ball. But the presuppositions were there for both buttoned-up piety as well as a romanticism of the affections.

2. *Halle-Pietism*. It was August Hermann Francke (1663-1727), Spener's young friend and follower, who translated the Pietism program into a vast network of influence and outreach. The orphanage he founded in Halle in 1695 grew into an economic enterprise of giant dimensions. The poor and uneducated were offered a new opportunity hitherto unheard of.[80] With many foreign connections, it became a seedbed by producing new leaders for Prussia who shaped their country in more ways than discipline and thrift. Francke was co-author of the tutorial curriculum for Frederick William I. His influence was also felt in the army. Thus in continuing the course already charted by Spener, Pietism in Halle by leaps and bounds became more deeply involved in the state. Francke's personal disposition tended towards a more dramatic expression of religious affection. His association with Pietism began with a peculiar kind of conversion,[81] the *Busskampf*, a penitential struggle. He expected people to become renewed in a similar vein, especially his students.

Halle became the source of many far-reaching activities of Pietism, for example, Bible distribution and care for Protestants "in the dispersion" (the so-called Diaspora), especially in Eastern Europe and the colonial United States (Georgia and Pennsylvania). The clergy (since 1729 ministers in Prussia were required to study for at least two years at Halle University) and the sons of the nobility educated at Halle spread the Gospel of Pietism all over Europe. The most eminent among them was Zinzendorf who, however, soon turned away from Halle and founded a new form of Pietism among the emigrant Moravians at Herrnhut. The conflict between Halle and Herrnhut determined the further history of Pietism in important ways. But Halle made a distinct contribution in the reformation of the church by the diaconate. The Halle orphanage became the womb of the "professional servant" notion of Protestantism which found its premier expression in the deaconesses and deacons of the later Home Mission enterprise.

3. *Moravian Pietism.* The more one moves away from Halle-Pietism the more wider social concern recedes. Zinzendorf (1700-1760) soon developed a stance very much his own, centered in the shaping of the beloved community. On August 13, 1727, he led the Herrnhut community in a communal revival experience, immediate relationship to the Savior being the key emphasis. It became the characteristic aspect of Moravian piety. While the Moravians retained the general Pietistic pattern, they added many innovations, for example, lovefeasts. They also were especially strong in missions. As a whole, their basic distinction lies in the formation of the independent piety-community. Yet after Spener and Francke had established the models of the professional saint and the professional servant, what we get in Moravianism are modifications of the basic pattern, yet expressed in a covenanted life spent completely in community.

4. *Württemberg Pietism.* While Pietism had been introduced to Württemberg by several representatives, notably J. V. Andreä, only in Johann Albrecht Bengel (1697-1752) and Friedrich Christoph Oetinger (1702-1782) did it arrive at an effective dissemination of Pietist ideas. Bengel created classical hermeneutic and exegesis models and promoted a biblical apocalypticism which became the basis of all later calculations of the second coming of Christ. Oetinger joined biblical theology, mysticism, and natural science in a new vision of Christian thought. While his influence on Schelling is widely acknowledged, it remains a moot question to what extent Hegel received impulses from Oetinger. *The Christian Faith* (1831) by Friedrich Schleiermacher is usually considered the basic methodological break with the method inherited from orthodoxy. But Oetinger was alert to the genesis of Christian piety and thought. His autobiography is therefore perhaps the most important contribution Pietism made to the advance of Christian experience. He sensed that professionalism in sainthood and servanthood was getting Protestantism nowhere. The Christian undertaking had to be grasped in each generation anew also methodologically.

5. *Reformed Pietism*. Thus far we have looked only at Lutheran expressions of Pietism. Reformed Pietism, as compared with Lutheran Pietism, appeared geographically in rather limited areas, the lower Rhine region and Bremen, for example. In the lower Rhine region, Gerhard Tersteegen (1697-1769) worked for the renewal of the church in a mystical-spiritualistic way.[82] He was the major Pietist among the Reformed who widely retained the hard-core Calvinistic-orthodox line or a biblicistic version of covenant theology as represented by Coccejus.

6. *Separatist Pietism*. Besides the denominationally faithful Pietists there were those who took a more individualistic or personal tack. In Lutheranism the separatists often stood under the influence of Jakob Böhme (1575-1624). Beyond most of the usual Pietist themes, separatist Pietism stressed spiritual marriage with the heavenly Sophia, demanding virginity of the body and promoting universal salvation. Among the Lutheran Pietists Gottfried Arnold (1666-1714) was the one most strongly under Separatist influence.

The continuing Dunkers or Church of the Brethren, one of the three American historic peace churches (along with the Mennonites and the Quakers), originated among radical Pietists in 1708, when the "New Baptists" separated from Lutheran and Reformed churches in Hesse, Germany.

As to the origins of Pietism, certain separatist tendencies among the Reformed in Holland contributed to the separatist bent that has always been part of the *collegia pietatis* since they had been adopted as the method of church renewal. Through the person of Jean de Labadie, father of Separatist Pietism, a French Catholic convert to Calvinism and then Separatism, Spener had become very much aware of the separatist tendencies and tried to counteract them. Each expression of Pietism contributed to the full picture of a movement that by the end of the nineteenth century had turned into a world-wide phenomenon. Yet we want to confine ourselves to formative influences, especially those that can help us to understand our own sense of religious affection. As a historical phenomenon, Pietism of course was also subject to the "unintentional." History always turns out differently from what we anticipate. Yet the unintended often becomes more normative than what was programmed. We need to watch out that we do not get misled by the unintended as the normative.

AN UNDERGROUND CHURCH? (Collegia)

The initial conflict over Spener's program soon could have led to an oppressed church, a church of the underground. While *Pia Desideria* was published in 1675, the Frankfurt *collegium pietatis* dates back to 1670. There is some indication that a 1669 sermon by Spener evoked the whole enterprise.[83] But Spener's spreading influence is tied to the publication of his church reform essay. We pointed out before that the generation following the Reformation puzzled over what they should do with the newly found freedom. Pietism launched out in the direction of exploring the religious affections. But initially at least it kept tying its explorations in this regard to the structure of the church as well. The creation of the Frankfurt *collegia pietatis* can be understood on these dual grounds only.

What followed in at least the next hundred years was a constant tug-of-war between various Pietism approaches struggling between the poles of personal piety and church structure. Would piety have to live a kind of underground existence leading to an underground church undermining the established church? Or should piety try to turn into an establishment faith taking over the big organizational church? Or should it issue in a separate community basically distancing itself from any established church?

We will carefully examine these three channels through which Pietism sought to move ahead in society. While Pietism along these lines turned into the single largest movement in the Protestant church in Germany between the Reformation and our day, it did not open a new era in the history of the church. Taking its cue from the Reformation and other movements, mysticism for example, it translated antecedents into the new circumstances.[84] Only in the person of Oetinger will we encounter the discovery of a quite new spiritual world.

In the Frankfurt *collegium pietatis* we have the attempt of some laity to make sense of the church. It did not arise at the urging of Spener, but at the insistence of two church members. The idea occasionally surfacing that Spener developed it, recollecting a suggestion of the Strasbourg reformer Martin Bucer, seems unwarranted.[85] The Frankfurt *collegium* was a voluntary group that dealt with faith issues as countermeasure to a happy-go-lucky life. Before long women were included.[86] The label "Pietist" was first used in Darmstadt in 1677. Spener did not like the name, just as Luther had objected to the word "Lutheran." But by the time a decade had passed, it stuck. A little later, in 1689, a professor by the name of J. Fehler made the point:

> The city knows by now: My name is Pietist.
> What is a Pietist? He studies every day
> God's Word and holy will
> And lives it in every way . . .
> I will confess, I feel no shame
> That Pietist is now my name.[87]

What had been a name of dishonor soon became a badge of honor.

Initially Pietism seemed not very dangerous, a reinvigoration of the church desired by many. After a change in government in 1679, the territory of Hesse-Darmstadt opened itself to Pietism. In 1688, Giessen became the first German university to employ a Pietist as professor. As Pietist ideas began to spread widely, orthodox theologians quickly went to work and called for sanctions against the new ideas. By 1690, the territories of Kursachsen, Hanover, Braunschweig, and the city of Hamburg seemed to have been "cleansed" of the new movement. Yet while being persecuted in some territories,[88] it gained ground in others. It quickly spread to Switzerland, Scandinavia, the Baltic countries, and also to North America.

A serious conflict arose in Leipzig (1689-1691), where August Hermann Francke and friends introduced the Pietist meetings at the university and ran into opposition from the university administration.[89] After Francke was expelled from the city he fled to Erfurt where he soon met new opposition.

Among the major Protestant territories in Germany only Prussia did not participate in the suppression of Pietism. In 1691, Spener was called to Berlin as pastor of the prestigious Nicolai Church. Through the influence of his type of Pietism, Berlin gradually developed into the intellectual center of Protestant Germany. In Berlin it was decided to found the University of Halle in 1694. At Spener's behest, August Hermann Francke was invited as one of its first professors. Halle thus became the intellectual seedbed of the Pietist movement in Germany. It was from Halle that Pietism fought its decisive battle with orthodoxy.[90]

Pietism lost its opportunity to become an "underground church" as soon as it was sanctioned by the Prussian state. Yet it never could get rid of the "smell" of separatism, a movement dangerous to the ecclesiastical status quo. Many of the suspicions against Pietism grew out of the somewhat beclouded relationship between Spener and Jean de Labadie (1610-1674), the French Jesuit turned Protestant and later Separatist. Spener had met de Labadie in Geneva in 1660-1661 and listened to a number of his sermons. Allusions have often been made to the effect that Spener already in Geneva became acquainted with gatherings of Christians that anticipated the collegia pietatis. Studies by Johannes Wallmann make it clear that the burden of proof lies with those who make such claims.[91] No such collegia pietatis have ever been discovered in Geneva by historical research. It does not follow, however, that

Spener could not have been influenced by de Labadie. He even translated de Labadie's *La Pratique de L'Oraison et Meditation Chrétienne*, publishing it in 1667 shortly after he arrived in Frankfurt. But this does not lead us any closer to any alleged *collegia pietatis* in Geneva.

The suspicion of Spener's dependence on de Labadie, expressed as early as 1670, may well point to de Labadie's last years in Holland.[92] De Labadie left Geneva for Holland in 1666 to assume a pastorate in the Reformed Church of Middelburg. Three years later, in 1669 (that is, one year before the appearance of the Frankfurt *collegium pietatis*), after having been "excommunicated" from the Reformed Church, he organized a congregation of his own. As word of this separatist phenomenon spread, it was probably assumed that, having shown interest in de Labadie earlier, Spener with his Frankfurt *collegium pietatis* was following a paradigm.

Sensing the precarious situation he was being maneuvered into, Spener wanted to avoid even the appearance of separatism. He kept insisting that the Frankfurt meetings were in response to members of his congregation and remained under pastoral supervision. Among those to whom he responded was Johann Jakob Schütz (1640-1690), a lawyer, a man greatly desirous of spiritual fellowship who temporarily shared leadership in the *collegia* with Spener. A correspondence between Schütz and Anna Maria van Schurman (1607-1679) reveals a considerable dependence of Schütz on Labadist ideas.[93] Through mediation of Schütz, it may well be that Spener was influenced by de Labadie in the writing of the *Pia Desideria* at least in two respects: (1) The reform of the theological studies through introducing *collegia pietatis* at the universities. (2) The reform of the local congregation through introducing Bible study groups in terms of 1 Corinthians 14 under direction of the pastor.

While these two points as such do not amount to separatism, the possibilities that they originated in the separatist de Labadie camp could not be effectively denied, and they contributed to the notion that Pietism inherently was separatist. Johann Jakob Schütz in any case ended up as a separatist propagating independent meetings for the truly spiritual life. He is remembered as the founder of the first separatist movement in Lutheran Pietism,[94] taking his place next to de Labadie, who originated separatism in the Reformed church. It was also never forgotten that Schütz had been Spener's close friend during his Frankfurt years and a co-founder of the *collegia pietatis*.

There seemed to exist little desire to precipitate becoming an oppressed group. As political conditions had shaped up in Germany at the time, the Protestant churches were tools of the territorial princes who would not tolerate separatist deviation from the established creed. Pietism might have had the chance to develop piety not primarily as religious affection, but as resistance to the powers that be. Yet Pietism chose to stress religious affection and aligned itself with the status quo.

A PIETIST ESTABLISHMENT (Halle)

Largely due to the patronage of the Prussian state, Pietism, initially forced underground in many places, was not cast in the role of a resistance movement that could have stood up against church and state. The years 1690-1692 were critical.[95] Spener, who had meanwhile moved to Dresden, had a falling out with the Saxon Prince and with Orthodoxy as well. We already mentioned Francke, who was banished from Leipzig and was expelled from his post at Erfurt a year later. Persecution of Pietists began also in Hamburg and other places.

Elector Frederick III of Prussia came to their rescue when on March 21, 1691, he called Spener to Berlin as pastor of the Nicolai Church. Since then Prussia became the refuge for persecuted Pietists. It was not that Prussia had a special religious predisposition for persecuted Pietists. But it felt that it could employ the new progressive approach for the education of a more enlightened citizenry. To that end, it recruited a number of progressive thinkers. Christian Thomasius, a teacher of law who had defended Francke in Leipzig, was called to the newly founded University of Halle even before Francke, escaping imprisonment in Leipzig by this move.

The Halle situation itself was complex. Until 1680 not a single Reformed person had been allowed to become a Halle citizen. It was strictly a Lutheran town. The citizenry of Halle did not offer a single building for the opening of the University of Halle. Backing Pietism was a move designed by Prussia to create a subservient Lutheranism in the city.[96]

The day Francke arrived in his new parish, January 7, 1692, the Prussian government had issued a decree forbidding sermons against the Pietists. Yet Francke soon found himself embroiled in a controversy with his church and the Halle authorities over his radical views on church discipline. He was unwilling to admit anyone to Holy Communion who had not shown the proper expressions of repentance. For arbitration of that conflict, Francke appealed to the Prussian government. With the assistance of an officially appointed arbitration commission, an agreement was reached November 27, 1692, although the principal opposition of Orthodoxy had not been allayed. Only with the backing of the state had Pietism in Prussia weathered the first storm.

Francke began quickly to channel the newly freed Pietist energies into diaconic efforts. The effects of the Thirty Years' War were still visible everywhere. Poverty and immorality went hand in hand. In Glaucha, among two hundred dwellings there were thirty-seven pubs.

Francke's predecessor at Glaucha, the Reverend Johann Richter, is said
to have been among the top drunks of the place. Francke charged Orthodoxy with complete failure in social action: "The Moritz church in
town has used several thousand 'dollars' (Thaler) to build a steeple. It
is of no use to the town, except under the pretext that one can extin-
guish a fire from there in case the church burns." Another church in
Halle, Francke complained, had an endowment of 30,000 dollars (Thaler), another of 11,000 dollars: "What good could be made of this
among the poor! The houses of stone become rich, and the temple of
God, that is, the poor, one lets perish."[97] Francke tried to change all
this. He started a school for the poor and an orphanage to meet the great
needs. He was concerned to address the spiritual and intellectual as
well as the physical dilemmas. Before long the ultimate goal was the
education of all classes in terms of Pietist renewal.[98] Francke sought to
incorporate the best ideas available for remaking persons and society.[99]

We do not ever want to forget, Francke was able to carry out his
reforms only with the backing of the Prussian government. In order to
make progress more quickly, he asked for a form of tax-exemption. After it had been granted in 1697, difficulties developed with the tax col-
lector. Again, only the personal intervention of the Elector stopped the
opposition.

A year later, the Francke institutions received special privileges,
the most important of which was their being placed directly under the
jurisdiction of the Elector. Yet the opposition continued, especially
among the guilds and the citizenry of Halle because of the economic
competition of Francke's pharmacy and publishing business. During
1699-1700 Francke's position became exceedingly difficult. He again
went to Berlin, and the Elector once more took Francke's side. Gradually it became clear that "Francke scrupulously used the most extreme
view of territorialism in church law in order to promote his own
ends."[100]

The battle between Halle clergy and Francke was finally settled
by an official commission. Francke was found "not guilty." His utter
selflessness was underscored. During these first years at Halle he had
not received any salary for his teaching at the University. It needs to be
underscored, however, that without the support of the Berlin government he probably "would have been defeated by the concerted attack of
Orthodoxy, the Provincial Diet, the regional government, and the Halle
magistrate.[101]

The diaconic service Francke envisioned was a great renewal possibility. Yet it became immediately embroiled in the power struggle of
the state. The conflict between Pietism and the other groups was very
much in the interest of Prussia. *Divide et impera*! Absolutism was developing in Berlin and elsewhere. Part of Prussia's policy of absolutism
was the evisceration of the power of the nobility and the creation of a
subservient citizenry. Prussia was also interested in Francke's econom-

ic ventures.[102] In order to realize his reform programs, he advocated the elimination of the old social order. The "sumepiscopacy" of the Elector could be expanded only at the cost of the rights of the nobility and the local magistrates in church affairs. Pietism at Halle gave a blank check to the absolutist aspirations of the Prussian Elector.[103] It became a key part of the establishment in no uncertain terms.

One might say that Pietism almost from the very beginning did not provide a fair chance for genuine discipleship to assert itself. On the one hand, it was creating the model of the "professional saint," and on the other hand, it turned the diaconic servant into the "professional servant." Much of the dilemma was due to the inability of the initial promoters of Pietism to pay attention to the actual genesis of Christian experience.

ANOTHER COMMUNE?

Zinzendorf

While in Halle an established piety gave aid and comfort to the Prince, in Herrnhut under Count Zinzendorf a different type of Pietism made its way, partly in conscious opposition to Halle. Herrnhut had not been planned by Zinzendorf or anyone else. It just "happened." In granting refuge to a band of persecuted Moravians on his estate, Zinzendorf appropriated a communal expression of Christianity that had already existed for more than two hundred years. He certainly did not engineer a new church. But his peculiar personality traits soon injected themselves in the shaping of a new corporate life. While Moravian communal life stands out as model in several respects, it was initially at least heavily taxed by "professional sainthood" consciously or unconsciously still pursued. In any case, it also did not lend itself to a new intellectual examination of the basic character of Christianity.

More than two hundred and sixty years before the Moravians touched base with Zinzendorf, they had formed the *Unitas Fratrum* in the Kunwald valley (1457), one hundred miles northeast of Prague. It was a band of peasants, nobles, scholars, and priests who were reformers before the Reformation. Some think of them as the first Reformation, with Luther providing us with the second Reformation. The fact is that they had organized themselves in opposition to Roman Catholic oppression of Christian freedom: "This pilgrim band of the Hussite tradition had come to Kunwald to secure that peace and freedom in which, under the leadership of Christ and the standard of the Bible, they might worship according to their conscience, and share unhindered fellowship with kindred souls."[104] While the group did not intend to become a separate church, it was forced into separatism by Roman Catholicism and the government, both of which were determined to destroy the new movement.

A first synod was held in 1467 at which priests were chosen and subsequently ordained by a Waldensian bishop. Persecution followed persecution, but the community spread and prevailed. By 1500 there were at least 100,000 members alone in Bohemia. At the time of Luther's Reformation the *Unitas Fratrum* sought close contact with the reformers, yet continued its separate existence. In 1722 word reached a persecuted Moravian family that Count Zinzendorf was offering them refuge in his newly acquired Berthelsdorf estate. Together with a few friends they made their way to the new promised land. Before long others arrived, and a small "colony" grew in the countryside which was baptized Herrnhut, "Watch of the Lord."

From these small beginnings the community, under Zinzendorf's watchful eye and initiative, grew into a significant enterprise spanning large parts of the world in missions and evangelism. Initially Zinzendorf had "no clear conception of the historic role which the ancient *Unitas Fratrum* had played as a distinct branch of the Christian church, and he aimed only at forming the Brethren into an *ecclesiola* within the Lutheran church; but they insisted more and more on retaining the ancient constitution and regulations of their Church.[105] Tensions between the aspirations of Zinzendorf and the Moravian tradition in varying degrees and at different times shaped the history between the benefactor and his refugees.

Zinzendorf terminated his civil service career at Dresden and since 1727 devoted himself full-time to the new enterprise. Banned several times from Kursachsen because of "conspiracy" with the Moravians, he developed a far-flung Christian activity eventually bringing him to England and even North America. Since the shadow of suspicion always accompanied his activity as self-appointed clergyman, he eagerly sought official recognition of his work from universities and church leaders. In due course he usually got what he wanted. For example, the University of Tübingen approved the new Moravian community, The University of Stralsund certified his orthodoxy. He certainly never aspired to become a separatist. Yet a break between him and many established churches became unavoidable, also between Halle Pietism and Moravian Pietism. For one, the aggressiveness of Herrnhut evangelism offered stiff competition to Halle. What is more, in becoming part of the establishment Halle tended toward a more legalistic kind of Pietism while Zinzendorf predicated his entire enterprise on a theology of the heart.

According to Erich Beyreuther, Zinzendorf did not wish to outdo Halle Pietism which had been able to steer the *ecclesiolae in ecclesia* into institutional normalcy. Yet at the same time many Christians harbored a great longing for deeper fellowship: "The spiritual brotherhood in the loosely knit . . . form of a Bible study group under a local pastor no longer satisfied many."[106] The Enlightenment was making an impact on the church, and many Christians felt a great need for close mutual support in keeping the Christian faith alive. The Moravian community seemed to be a model for such support.

Because of the well-known Moravian persecution history, Herrnhut Pietism was in a much more precarious position in relationship to the state than Halle Pietism, which from its very beginnings had become an instrument of the state for achieving its goals of absolutism.[107] In order to stabilize the position of Herrnhut, Zinzendorf sought to find government support, especially that of the king of Prussia. In fact, it was on account of the backing of the Prussian king that Zinzendorf was ordained a bishop.[108]

Yet from those whose support Zinzendorf wanted most to enlist he received the heaviest critique—the Swabian Pietists Bengel and Oetinger. Among Bengel's objections was the critique that Zinzendorf curried favor with the high and mighty. The tension between the humble walk of a diaconic congregation and the straining for recognition among the powers that be revealed glaring inadequacies of Zinzendorf's theology. In Bengel's view, the whole Herrnhut undertaking did not meet the real needs of the day.

The Enlightenment was already taking its toll, and the authority of the Bible *as a whole* was seriously being questioned. So it seemed to undermine theological integrity when a selection of Zinzendorf hymns published in London was prefaced with the remark: "You will early observe, that they have no affinity at all with that old Book called the Bible: the Illustrious Author soaring as far above this, as above the beggarly Elements of Reason and common sense."[109] Bengel judged that the theological method of the Herrnhut Moravians relegated everything to the heart. He stressed that the New Testament did not view the heart as unquestionably good. So he sharply countered the Moravian, "I feel it," with his "Bible truth demands it." Any community spirit has no right to elevate itself above the Scriptures. Zinzendorf seemed to have made the crucified Christ the entire content of the heart's experience from which Christians were to derive faith, love, and hope, and the whole Christian way of life. This way the *community becomes the living Bible*,[110] assuming more power over its individual members than St. Paul could claim over the Corinthians.[111] " The sufferings of Christ and his wounds become the one article of the Christian faith. So at least the impression is given that disregarding God the Father, we basically sin against the Son who appears to reconcile us with himself and not with the Father.

Zinzendorf seemed extremely one-sided to Bengel. The new approach was like suddenly extinguishing in a big hall all lights but one. One could still see something, but extremely little. Bengel underscored that Christian freedom is not a matter of sheer faith preferences. It contains a measure of faithfulness to the totality of the originative events of the faith. It is incomplete in a gathering of the absolutely likeminded and like-feeling. As little as Christian reality could come to full flower in the Bible study groups as *ecclesiola in ecclesia* (Spener) or in an established *ecclesiola* as a pious tool of the state (Francke), could it find fulfillment in an emotional separatism (Zinzendorf).

Martin Greschat explains the church/state relations of these Pietist traditions as follows: With Spener as prelate at St. Nikolai in 1691 in Berlin, and Francke at the University of Halle, Absolutism and Pietism in Brandenburg-Prussia were working hand in hand against the alliance of the Estates with Lutheran Orthodoxy. Zinzendorf in a different individual way mixed a pre-absolutist imperial tradition with a nontraditional newly organized community or religious society. But in

Württemberg, Pietism seeking freedom with little success played the
opposition of the Estates against the Absolute prince.[112]

SACRED PHILOSOPHY?

Oetinger

At the climax of the Pietist movement stands a theologian who internalizes the various Pietist gropings and aspirations once more and who in his own person tries to separate the Pietist wheat from the Pietist chaff: the Swabian pastor Friedrich Christoph Oetinger (1702-1782). In him we can observe, in a nutshell, as it were, the ups and downs, pros and cons, possibilities and limitations of the movement. Early in his life as a student he encounters in the inspired, the heirs of the French Camisards, the underground church. Though strongly drawn to this frank and stalwart band of Christians, he also realizes that this is a dead-end road for Christian witness in his day. In the person of the daughter of Johann Jakob Schütz who initially had been Spener's co-worker in Frankfurt he encounters the separatist Pietists. Later Oetinger visits Halle, observing life at Francke's institutions and even teaching at Halle University. But he is unconvinced that Christian witness must inevitably express itself in an array of diaconic deeds and enterprises. He claims: "Bengel [in Württemberg] built an orphanage just as much as Francke [in Prussia]. Francke received money from God for the orphanage. Bengel received ideas to build wisdom on seven pillars."[113] Finally, Oetinger's confrontation with Zinzendorf and his Herrnhut commune reveals to us the reasons why a mere Christian counter-commune could not satisfy those who sought the welfare of the whole church.

Oetinger might have become a separatist. He had the potential to become a diaconic leader. And he was often tempted to join a Christian commune. But all these possibilities he rejected to become a pastor of "regular" Württemberg churches. He considered it his task to be of service in the church where it was called for. If Pietism was at all a viable option for the church as a whole it had to permeate the totality of the Christian community and its tasks. And it had to do this not all tied up in knots, but almost playfully.

Thus we see Oetinger at work, not at all pushing himself or others to produce pious people, but occupying himself with the great questions of his day, trying to tackle what needed tackling in the church.

The front over against which he saw himself battling for truth was represented by rationalism, enlightenment, mysticism, and "pietistic Pietism," all selling short the Reformation heritage. At the center of his wrestle lies the battle with Leibniz-Wolffian ideas. Although theology for a goodly while already had felt the inroads of secular thought,

Oetinger's struggle was not a sheer defense operation against modern
trends, but primarily a genuine interest in rationally clarifying the specific nature of the Christian faith. It had to be *logically* clear to him in
what sense the Christian faith was a viable alternative also for thought.
Oetinger saw the critical difference between his position and that
of Leibniz in his view of the basic structure of the world. Leibniz ultimately had reduced everything to the monad, the simple substance. But
for Oetinger simple substance and life do not mix. It appears a completely false view to him "that there should be a unitary *simplex* which
would contain life in itself."[114] Central for Oetinger is life itself, and
the structure of life. Thought is not primal, neither is Being, but life and
movement. In nature things do not move from the uniform to the multi-
form, but from the composite to the simple. Thus Oetinger replaces unity by "binity" as primordial principle. The two-foldness found in life is
polar. In the struggle of opposites, *per nisus contrarios*, life originates.
In a more abstract way, he can speak of the Yes and the No in things.
Less abstract, he will speak of the contrast between light and darkness.
Quite concrete finally is the contrast of fire and water. These various
contrasts or opposites are most adequately grasped in Oetinger as the
polarity between spirit and matter, both battling each other in countless
ways. Time and again Oetinger discovers new illustrations to point out
the battle concretely, as, for example, in the positive and negative poles
of electricity. The struggle always results in a circular movement which
he finds most beautifully expressed in "the wheel of birth" of James
3:6. Two opposite central powers are the beginning of the "wheel of
birth" and produce the movement of things.

Much of what Oetinger develops reminds one of the pre-
Socratics, especially Heraclitus. The main influence, however, was Jakob Böhme, who afforded him the first insight into the *idea vitae* according to which life is produced by opposites. While for Böhme the
contrast between good and evil was dominant, Oetinger is not interested in it. His basic focus is the origin of life in the opposites of spirit and
matter, in terms of which he seeks to overcome Leibniz's monad. Oetinger abandons all concepts of the simple, since for him the simple is
the static which has no life. Life is only in movement. As a consequence, also the concept of Being is unacceptable. There is no Being
apart from becoming.

Opposed to the abstractions of the philosophy of his day, philosophy was for Oetinger something sacred. Thus he could speak of his effort as *philosophia sacra*, sacred philosophy.[115] He claimed that, although he was not a professor, he was a philosopher of sorts. Not the
reasoning faculty of Descartes was his organ of insight—in fact it was
against the *cogito ergo sum* of Descartes that he launched his attack—
but the *sensus communis*. Sensibility (*sensus*) is not ratiocination, but a
feeling "radar" for omnipresent wisdom. Knowledge is not inborn in
man, but sensibility is. The *sensus communis* in human beings is the

higher counterpart of the animal instinct. Thus life is not primarily per-
ceived via the detour of thought, but is sensed in virtue of the *sensus
communis* The latter also functions as community principle, appealing
to human beings to understand themselves as members of society, so
that *the sensus communis* even functions as society-conscience.

From the *sensus communis* Oetinger moves to the *cognitio centralis*, the central cognition, an ability that does not pertain merely to
the *ratio*, but to the whole person. It is first of all a grasp of the whole
of life. Only from the whole, Oetinger believes, can a person move to
the detail. "As compared with the overemphasis on ratiocination characteristic of the school philosophy of his day, Oetinger with his central
cognition had to appear revolutionary."[116] The crucial criterion of
Oetinger's thought is life in its multiplicity and uniformity. This results
methodologically in a phenomenology which radically differs from the
methodology of the school philosophy oriented in the model of mathematics. For Oetinger, thought begins with life as experienced. Consequently experiment—which in his day was bound to be particularly the
alchemistic experiment, representing the beginning of modern chemistry and physics—takes a significant place in his thought and life.

In Oetinger's phenomenology, bodiliness becomes the key concept. He cannot imagine soul or spirit without a body. Thus "corporeality is the end of all of God's ways." The soul is not only not viable
without the body, it cannot even be thought of without it.

It is not surprising that Oetinger's views should have had considerable influence in philosophy as well as theology. We made mention
of this influence upon Schelling which Schelling himself readily acknowledged. In 1938 Robert Schneider proposed the thesis that it was
possible to discover also in Hegel ideas of Oetinger as themes and
structural principles, although Schelling's work could be more readily
understood as a continuation of Oetinger's thought.[117] Recent research
has not borne out this contention. Martin Brecht and Jörg Sandberger
have stressed that, since the most tempting ideas in this respect have to
be supported by evidence from biographical material and this evidence
is not forthcoming in matters of the Oetinger-Hegel relationship,
Schneider's view is a hypothesis at best.[118] There is no record of Hegel
studying Oetinger at any time of his life. Brecht and Sandberger do not
wish to deny the possibility of a relationship of Hegel to Württemberg
Pietism. Obviously within the context in which Hegel grew up Pietist
ideas were in the air. All that Brecht and Sandberger wish to emphasize
is that there is no evidence for the influence of Pietism on Hegel's
thought.[119]

More important than the question of Oetinger's influence in philosophy is the acknowledgement of his actual influence in the church of
his day. It was perhaps his most important contribution that he was able
to join his personal struggle for truth to the church. Ultimately for this
reason his philosophy was *sacred* philosophy, true philosophy. The

mind dare not be afraid to ask the most radical questions. If it is truly led by faith, it is faith that presses it on to the most radical use of reason. And yet it is impossible for the Christian faith to ask the radical questions in an individualistic way.

The Christian faith is tied to the faith community. Its quest within the community, however, has a peculiar aspect. In his debate with Zinzendorf's commune, Oetinger believed that the Herrnhut Pietists were stressing the importance of the personal factor in the Christian relationship to Christ too much.[120] The ground of the Christian community was not Zinzendorf's "I love! I love!," but God's truth. Zinzendorf seemed to put love above truth, whereas for Oetinger brotherly love was the result of the grasp of truth. Oetinger also believed it wrong to regard the church primarily as a community of evangelization. Only the Christian community that is grounded in truth can effectively evangelize. Thus the church for Oetinger was primarily the community of human beings in relationship to truth.

Moving a bit beyond his mentors Francke's and Bengel's activities seeking to transform the world through born-again charities (combined in Francke's case with military and other concessions to Prussian state goals), Oetinger in Württemberg sought in somewhat utopian terms to better politics through reforms, even though his jurist state official friend, Johann Jakob Moser, had been imprisoned for five years by the absolutist Duke Karl Eugen for similar efforts. Oetinger wrote that the world order, at the time of the coming Golden Age, will give way to love (Zinzendorf after all!): "The eyes of the subjects will see the king in his beauty (Isa. 33:17). The law will no longer serve as power exercised by violence, but as free government."[121]

Oetinger was biblical without being a biblicist, scientific without being a rationalist, and philosophical without being a secularist. He did not reject the church. In Oetinger, Pietism yielded its ripest fruit. Once it had fallen off the tree, the high season of Pietism was over. Only shriveling leaves kept hanging on.

PIETISM TODAY

Within a short time span in the second half of the twentieth century, we have experienced in the United States a historical "rhythm" not unlike that movement, not content-wise, but formally speaking. In the fifties in the U.S. we went through the stage of the critique of ecclesiasticism, best represented by Peter L. Berger's *The Noise of Solemn Assemblies*. This paralleled the Labadie-Spener stage. In the sixties we moved into the time of action. This somewhat paralleled the Francke stage. The seventies began with a new interest in communes among the Jesus People and others. This parallels the Zinzendorf enterprise in a number of ways. It is possible that some Oetinger type of thinking emerged in the eighties and nineties, as secular and religious people continued to struggle toward truth concerning responsibility and justice in social and political affairs.

The one thing which the Jesus people, as a movement expressing piety, might have learned from the Pietist movement was the political dilemma of Pietism. Piety at first glance may seem unpolitical. As it made a big splurge in Germany after the Reformation it did not turn out that way. One of the purposes of this introduction has been to point out the need to look behind the verbal expressions of piety and to discover its political limitations or ramifications. Central to our understanding are the church-state alliances Spener and Francke (also Zinzendorf to a certain extent) entered into in their effort to make the Pietist cause prevail. Though Separatist Pietist groups like the Dunkers and Mennonites provide a helpful New Testament alternative in regard to church/government relations, their communal isolation was even more severe than the Moravians'.

The ultimate political subservience of Pietism began as a marriage of convenience between religion and the state. The latter was looking for a partner in cutting down the feudal system which had been sanctioned by Protestant Orthodoxy. Pietism was looking for a powerful shield behind which it could feel safe in case of attack. Initially its goals went far beyond those of the state: there were ecumenical aspirations and missionary hopes pertaining to the world as a whole.[122] But ultimately it was especially Prussia that made the Pietist establishment its loyal servant.[123] Initially Francke thought of Halle as a world center radiating new transforming powers into the world as a whole.[124] And it did become a world center in education, missions, ecumenicity, Bible translations, and *diakonia*. But politically it ended up as a provincial appendage of Berlin, receiving its orders from the king.

Thus the thesis that Pietism was the origin of socialism, as Calvin-

ism was the origin of capitalism (mentioned in note 25), needs to be
viewed with caution. What Pietism produced was a caritative socialism
at best. What is more, Francke's Pietist establishment ultimately became aligned as much with emerging German capitalism as with the
Prussian state. Eduard Winter has observed: "Beginning capitalism was
supported in numerous economic enterprises of Halle Pietism. Francke
and his associates, completely caught up in the perspective of mercantilism, operated in terms of big business and industrial management.
They recklessly applied the new laws of economics, so that they often
felt scruples as to whether or not their policies were commensurate with
the pure Christianity they proclaimed. But they rescued themselves
from this conflict of conscience, which they often clearly grasped, with
the comforting reassurance that it was all necessary for the growth of
their benevolent religious foundations and was thus acceptable."[125]
Winter wonders whether much of Pietism in Halle was not a matter of
the early bourgeoisie asserting itself.[126] Also Hinrichs sees that it was
exactly in the area of economics that Francke was led to numerous
compromises.[127] This ought to be taken into account, however, in any
thesis about the relationship between Pietism and socialism.

     One also needs to point out that Francke, for example, refused to
accept illegitimate children in his orphanage, since he thought he had
learned that it was impossible to make them over into completely equal
members of society.[128] His lack of scruples in using orphans as labor
power in the manufactures belongs to this same context.[129] If one takes
such factors into account, Hinrich's distinction between Calvinism as a
religion of entrepreneurs and Pietism as a religion of civil servants[130]
appears more felicitous than the thesis that Pietism relates to socialism
as Calvinism to capitalism.

     As a hypothesis, it seems more plausible that Pietism became in-
fluential in the formation of socialism via the chiliastic idea. Fritz Gehrlich proposed that chiliasm was injected into the mainstream of Protestant thought by way of Johann Albrecht Bengel (1687-1742),
Oetinger's great teacher and friend.[131] The pedigree from Pietism to socialism would here run from Bengel through Lessing, Kant, Fichte, and
Hegel to Marx and Engels. Gehrlich sees Bengel's crucial thought in
the divine dispensation which is expressed in a historical process run-
ning from the beginning to the end of the world. Bengel thus could
have provided the impetus for the notion of historical process, at least
in terms of the religious view of a divine education of the human race.

     As interesting as the hypothesis of a relationship between Pietism
and socialism is, however mediated, it has not been documented thus
far on grounds of careful research in the sources. It is still based on
speculation. While all this guessing or speculating is going on, our attention is not drawn to the actual socio-political drawbacks of the Pietist movement that contributed to the increasing tendencies towards au-
thoritarianism, nationalism, and finally totalitarianism.

Crucial for the socio-political outlook of Pietism remained the Halle establishment in terms of its relationship to the Prussian state. The most decisive case in point in this relationship is the service Halle rendered in the growth of the Prussian military establishment. It ought to be understood that Prussia was merely one of the many territories engaged that time in seemingly interminable military adventures. Obviously Europe was not a pacified continent for a long time. Pacifism was not a viable option in the general consciousness of that day. Even so, there were critical possibilities built into the Pietist movement itself that unfortunately were soon killed off. Already Spener complained that the princes abused their *ius episcopale* to such an extent that *Caesaro-papism* (the arbitrary decision and action of the princes in the affairs of the church) "belonged to the severest sins in Germany."[132] As indicated before, Pietism did not bring change in this respect, not even in Spener himself.

Francke's relationship to the military makes it all the more obvious how much Caesaropapism had won out. When it so happened that a lone wolf preacher expressed some radical views against the military establishment, the Prussian king let it be known that "preachers . . . should encourage the people . . . to become loyal subjects in relationship to the authorities."[133] He let especially Francke know that he was his loyal friend and would continue to protect him; but he should continue to turn out preachers and not meddle in politics. Francke yielded and took to the task of trying to gain influence in the army, that is, "to permeate it with Pietist sentiment and Pietist reform tendencies."[134] Until that time the army had not been too keen on making common cause with Pietist pastors. Now Francke sought—and gained—an entrée to high-ranking circles of officers. Soon military dash and piety seemed no longer irreconcilable.[135]

A strangely religious view of the military began to gain ground. It was especially through military chaplains that Pietism sought to extend its influence among the military. Finally a considerable portion of the ministry first went through the ranks of military chaplaincy. Obviously this had an impact upon ecclesiastical life as a whole. "The spirit of rigid military discipline . . . found an entrance into the church."[136] What this practically amounted to for Francke, however, was that he became distracted from his reform plans for the world and was drawn more deeply into the network of the Prussian state which more and more increased its expectations of the Halle institutions in regard to personal and practical support.[137]

It cannot be the purpose of our historical review to give publicity to new Evangelicalism or the Jesus People.[138] The point of paralleling Pietism and Jesus People is to suggest the continuing relevance of the Pietist topic. What can new expressions of piety learn from the history of piety? One thing is for sure: piety needs to resist societal expectations and governmental claims that tend to gobble up human beings as individuals. Unbeknownst to themselves, however, some promulgators of the new piety tend to fall into the same trap as the promulgators of the old piety. This need not necessarily lead to the growth of a patriotic piety.[139] But it often does. All around in the churches it may well result in the perpetuation of uncritical piety. American Protestant piety has been influenced by German Pietism in numerous ways, especially through powerful and effective Methodism.[140] On the American Continent pietism has been absorbed much too uncritically thus far. Our study of German Pietism seeks to make a contribution to the growth of a *critical* piety.

This suggestion that critical piety in our day will take its cue from a person like Oetinger merely indicates that Oetinger, in tying piety to the church as community of *truth*, introduced that dimension of a critical possibility that today offers the best hope for a viable expression of piety.[141]

NOTES

1. Karl Kupisch, *Vom Pietismus zum Kommunismus* (Berlin, 1953), 32.

2. Waldo Beach, *The Christian Life* (Richmond, Va., 1966), 16, has succinctly articulated the more current use of the term: "We do not refer to the historical movement within the evangelical churches in Germany and England which combined a warm emotional fervor with a serious moral discipline. We refer rather to what this movement turned into with the third and fourth generation: a narrow, prim legalism that shriveled faith into a self-conscious assurance of 'being saved' and the Christian life into a list of prohibitions." Cf. Gibson Winter, *The New Creation as Metropolis* (New York, 1963), 22f.

3. The gradual deterioration of Pietism has been recognized for a long time. Suffice it to appeal to only one testimony from the nineteenth century. I. A. Dorner, *Geschichte der protestantischen Theologie* (München, 1867), 646f.: "After the death of A. H. Francke ... Pietism ... fell into a spirit of legality, which soon showed its infectious power, and had, after the manner of law, a very disintegrating effect upon popular life, by that spiritual pride and unloving temper, that judgement of and separation from, others, which it is ever wont to introduce."

4. See August Hermann Francke, *Der Grosse Aufsatz* (Otto Podczeck, ed., Berlin, 1962).

5. Peter C. Erb (ed.), *Pietists* (Ramsey, NJ, 1983), claims that in North America among Pietism's descendants knowledge of God "was reduced to an 'emotional experience' undergone at conversion and in devotion" (25).

6. The idea was not discovered by the Reformation. See Richard Friedenthal, *Luther: Sein Leben und seine Zeit* (München, 1967): "'Reformation' was a persistent concept of church history and an ever-recurring necessity" (50).

7. Hans von Schubert, *Grundzüge der Kirchengeschichte* (Tübingen, 1921), 218.

8. This did not mean that in the churches that had been partly reformed the desire for more reformation was immediately emerging. Cf. Albrecht Ritschl, *Geschichte des Pietismus* (Bonn, 1880), I, 81. Referred to as GdP hereinafter.

9. Friedrich Wilhelm Kantzenbach, *Orthodoxie und Pietismus* (Gütersloh, 1966), 144f.

10. Peter C. Erb, *Pietists*, 2.

11. For the following see Richard Friedenthal, op cit., 557-642. One needs carefully to note the complex developments in Luther's own thinking at this point. Cf. Karl Holl, "Luther und das landesherrliche Kirchenregiment," in *Gesammelte Aufsätze zur Kirchengeschichte* (Tübingen, 1932), i, 339ff. The involvement of the princes in the work of the Reformation was for Luther altogether an emergency situation. For him the prince was merely an emergency bishop. His church authority was to be possible only insofar as he also was a member of the church. But the princes, almost immediately, did not understand their spiritual authority on those grounds. Beginning with a decree of the Elec-

tor in 1527 it became clear that the prince did not know the difference between secular and spiritual authority, since he in fact exercised the latter in terms of the former. Holl stresses that while Luther never gave up speaking of the work of the prince in the church as an emergency measure, his good intentions did not help any here. He ought to have protested earlier against the self-understanding of the princes. Later it was too late; the power of the actual circumstances was stronger than Luther's theory.

12. Gdp, I, 35.
13. Ibid., 80f.
14. Cf. Friedenthal, op. cit., 623ff.
15. Wilhelm Goeters, *Die Vorbereitung des Pietismus in der Reformierten Kirche der Niederlande bis zur labadistischen Krisis* (Leipzig, 1911). Complete agreement as to the Dutch influence on Pietism has never been reached. As one representative instance of disagreement, cf. Heinrich Heppe, *Geschichte des Pietismus und der Mystik in der Reformierten Kirche. namentlich der Niederlande* (Leiden, 1879), 7, and Paul Grünberg ed., *Hauptschriften Philipp Jakob Speners* (Gotha, 1889), 2.
16. August Lang, *Puritanismus und Pietismus* (Neukirchen, 1941). Lang in some respects already anticipates Stoeffler's thesis referred to in note 22. See Lang, 126ff.
17. Cf. GdP, I, 93.
18. Kantzenbach, op. cit., 132.
19. GdP, I, 93.
20. RGG3, V, 370.
21. Max Weber, *Die protestantische Ethik* (München and Hamburg, 1965), 115.
22. F. Ernest Stoeffler, *The Rise of Evangelical Pietism* (Leiden, 1965), 8.
23. Michael Walzer, *The Revolution of the Saints* (Cambridge, MA, 1965), 26.
24. Ibid., 12f.
25. It is impossible in a brief introduction to the history of Pietism satisfactorily to take into account the various theories that have been expounded on the subject. But we do need to note the hypothesis of a very distinct difference between Pietism and Puritanism in regard to the acquisition of wealth. It has been most bluntly stated by Erich Beyreuther, *Geschichte der Diakonie und Inneren Mission in der Neuzeit* (Berlin, 1962), 41: "Historical research sees in English Puritanism the beginning of capitalism, in German Pietism the beginning of socialism." To the best of my knowledge, the thesis was first expounded, though less bluntly, by Carl Hinrichs, *Friedrich Wilhelm I. König in Preussen* (Hamburg, 1941), 561: "The elements of Pietism are conversion and regeneration in the service of the social improvement of the world and man. As is well-known, Anglosaxon Puritanism has had similar features. But here in the end social progress resulted in the increase of wealth, for in Puritanism the proof of regeneration is found in individual success, in the blessing God bestows upon the regenerate. What is lacking here is a sense of accountability for the inner redemption of the neighbor, a result of the doctrine of predestination according to which God has decided the destiny of the individual from all eternity: the poor, the unsuccessful, is at the same time the rejected of God, and material gain is a sign of the election. The Anglosaxon sanctifies labor "for himself," the German labors "for others." "In England, with Puritanism capital-

ism begins, in Germany we find [the beginnings] of socialism." But Hinrich's thesis is too simple. Pietism, too, coincides with the beginning of German capitalism. Cf. note 122.

26. Cf. Karl Berger, "Orthodoxie," *RE*, 14, 497f.

27. RGG3, IV, 1719ff.

28. For example, the Protestant church in Brockhagen (Westfalia), renovated in the 1960's, still retains the nobility pew hovering high above the people.

29. Klaus Deppermann, *Der hallesche Pietismus und der preussische Staat unter Friedrich III*. (I), (Göttingen, 1961), 13.

30. Dorner, op. cit., 541ff.

31. Ibid., 635f

32. Karl Holl, *Die Bedeutung der grossen Kriege für das religiöse und kirchliche Leben innerhalb des deutschen Protestantismus* (Tübingen, 1917), 39. For the entire movement of Reform-Orthodoxy, see Hans Leube, *Die Reformideen in der deutschen lutherischen Kirche zur Zeit der Orthodoxie* (Leipzig, 1924).

33. Ibid., 72.

34. Ibid., 38.

35. Heinrich Bornkamm, *Mystik, Spiritualismus und die Anfinge des Pietismus im Luthertum* (Giessen, 1926), 17.

36. Karl Berger, op. cit., 498

37. For a balanced view of the actual ministry during that time, see Heinrich Schmid, *Die Geschichte des Pietismus* (Nördlingen, 1863), 29ff.

38. Ibid., 49ff.

39. Karl Holl, op. cit., 70.

40. English translation, John Arndt, *True Christianity* (Philadelphia, 1868).

41. For the best introduction to Spener's *Pia Desideria* in English, see Theodore G. Tappert's interpretation in the work cited in note 43.

42. Deppermann, op. cit., 45ff.

43. Philip Jacob Spener, *Pia Desideria* (translated, edited, and with an introduction by Theodore G. Tappert; Philadelphia, 1964), 43.

44. Ibid., 45

45. Ibid., 61f.

46. Ibid., 76.

47. Ibid., 86.

48. Ibid., 87

49. Ibid., 89.

50. Ibid., 92.

51. Ibid.,93

52. Ibid.

53. Ibid., 94.

54. Ibid., 95.

55. Ibid.

56. Bonhoeffer, in *Life Together*, again brings up the matter of confessing in a rather matter-of-fact way. It is not a completely odd thing which Spener here proposes for Protestants.

57. *Pia Desideria*, 97.

58. Ibid.

59. Ibid.

60. Ibid., 99
61. Ibid., 102
62. Ibid., 103
63. Ibid.
64. Ibid.
65. Ibid., 104.
66. Ibid., 108.
67. Ibid., 109.
68. Ibid., 110.
69. *Theologia habitus practicus est*, a common assertion of orthodox theologians in the seventeenth century (Theodore G. Tappert).
70. *Pia Desideria*, 112.
71. For the relationship of Spener to Labadie see Kurt Dietrich Schmidt, "Labadie und Spener," in *Zeitschrift für Kirchengeschichte*, 46 (1928), 566-583; and Johannes Wallmann, *Philipp Jakob Spener und die Anfänge des Pietismus* (Tübingen, 1970), 300ff.
72. RGG(3), V, 373.
73. For an impression of the drawn-out struggle see Heinrich Schmid, *Die Geschichte der Pietismus* (Nördlingen, 1863), 42ff.
74. See Carl Hinrichs, "Der Hallische Pietismus als politisch-sociale Reformbewegung des 18. Jahrhunderts," in *Preussen als Historisches Problem (Berlin, 1964), 171 ff.*
75. RE, XV, 778f.
76. Ibid.
77. Paul Grünberg, *Philip Jakob Spener* (Göttingen, 1906), 269-279, in the Spener bibliography offers an opportunity to note at a glance the vast literature accumulated around just one man.
78. For Spener's views of social reform see Willi Grün, *Speners soziale Leistungen und Gedanken. Ein Beitrag zur Geschichte des Armenwesens und des kirchlichen Pietismus in Frankfrut a.M. und in Brandenburg-Preussen* (Würzburg, 1934).
79. RE, XVII, 609-622.
80. For Halle Pietism and the other Pietisms see RGG3, V, 374ff., which I follow closely. For the social concern of Francke see my essay "Diakonia in Modern Times: Eighteenth-Twentieth Centuries," James I. McCord and T. H. L. Parker (eds.), *Service in Christ: Essays Presented to Karl Barth on his 80th Birthday* (London, 1966), 135-150.
81. Johannes Wallmann, op. cit., 89f., stresses the difference between Francke and Spener in the matter of conversion. Also see my essay "August Hermann Francke: Francke's Conversion," *Mid-Stream*, 8:3 (Spring, 1969), 41-49.
82. For the contrast of a man like Tersteegen to Francke or Zinzendorf see August Langen, *Der Wortschatz des deutschen Pietismus* (Tübingen, 1954), 17.
83. Johannes Wallmann, op. cit., 266f.
84. Carl Hinrichs, *Friedrich Wilhelm I.*, 562, makes a strong point that it was actually Francke and not Spener who moved into new avenues in terms of the attempt to transform the world.
85. As opposed to RGG3, V, 370ff.
86. Johannes Wallmann, op. cit., 262.
87. RGG2, IV, 1250.

88. Klaus Deppermann, op. cit., 47. From 1678-1734 no less than 43 edicts were promulgated against Pietism.

89. RE, XV, 799.

90. It is important to keep in mind the politics that undergirded the Pietist movement ever since. Lutheran pietism did not weaken, but strengthened secular church government in Brandenburg-Prussia, although in terms of its origins it should have become the most determined opponent of Caesaropapism. Klaus Deppermann, op. cit., 49.

91. Johannes Wallmann, op. cit., 142.

92. Ibid., 273.

93. Ibid., 283-306.

94. Ritschl, GdP, II, 156.

95.. Eduard Winter, Halle als Ausgangspunkt der deutschen Russlandkunde im 18. Jahrhundert (Berlin, 1953), 9.

96. Carl Hinrichs, Friedrich Wilhelm I., 563.

97. Francke to Spener, September 28, 1696. Klaus Deppermann, op cit., 88.

98. Carl Hinrichs, Friedrich Wilhelm I., 563.

99. Ibid., 564. Here we have the starting point of modern ideas of sociopolitical orientation.

100. Klaus Deppermann, op cit., 128.

101. Ibid., 139.

102. Eduard Winter, op cit., 3. Prussia had to outdo Kursachsen. Manufactures and mining had already been developed in the Kurfürstentum Sachsen exceedingly well. Consequently there appeared economic as well as intellectual competition between the two territories, especially in the areas where Prussian and Kursachsen interests clashed most sharply.

103. Cf. Erich Beyreuther, Zinzendorf und die Christenheit (Marburg, 1961), 40: "Strongly christianized Halle Pietism served the state.... One could depend on the church and state loyalty of the Halle Pietists." For a substantial exposition of Frederick William I's use of Pietist religion in the service of Prussian economics, pedagogy and militarism, see Richard L. Gawthrop's Pietism and the Making of Eighteenth Century Prussia. New York, 1993, pp. 150-284.

104. A. J. Lewis, Zinzendorf the Ecumenical Pioneer (London, 1962), 35.

105. Ibid., 51.

106. Erich Beyreuther, Zinzendorf und die Christenheit, 141.

107. Eduard Winter, op. cit., 278f.

108. Erich Beyreuther, Zinzendorf und die Christenheit, 156.

109. Johann Albrecht Bengel, Abriss der sogenannten Brüder-gemeinde in welchem die Lehre und die ganze Sache geprüfet (Stuttgart, 1751), 14.

110. Ibid., 30.

111. Ibid., 524.

112. Martin Greschat, ed., Orthodoxie und Pietismus (Stuttgart, 1982), 28.

113. Johannes Herzog, Friedrich Christoph Oetinger (Calw and Stuttgart, 1902), 1937.

114. Elisabeth Zinn, Die Theologie des Friedrich Christoph Oetinger (Gütersloh, 1932), 12. For the following see 13-24.

115. Wilhelm-Albert Hauck, Das Geheimnis des Lebens (Heidelberg, 1947), 14.

116. Ibid., 63.

117. Robert Schneider, *Schellings und Hegels schwäbische Geistessahnen* (Würzburg-Aumühle, 1938), 153.

118. Martin Brecht and Jörg Sandberger, "Hegels Begegnung mit der Theologie im Tübinger Stift," *Hegel-Studien,* 5 (1969), 47ff.

119.. See also Martin Brecht, "Vom Pietismus zur Erweckungsbewegung," *Blätter für württembergische Kirchengeschichte* 68/69 (1968/1969), 370.

120. Otto Herpel (ed.), *Friedrich Christoph Oetinger: Die heilige Philosophie* (München, 1923), 118.

121. Quoted from Blair R. Reynolds and Eunice M. Paul, tr., *The Mystical Sources of German Romantic Philosophy*, by Ernst Benz (Allison Park, PA, 1983), 45.

122. Carl Hinrichs, *Friedrich Wilhelm I.*, 562.

123. Klaus Deppermann, op. cit., 153.

124. Carl Hinrichs, *Friedrich Wilhelm I.*, 563.

125. Eduard Winter, op. cit., 7.

126. Ibid., 42.

127. Carl Hinrichs, *Friedrich Wilhelm I.*, 582.

128. Klaus Deppermann, op. cit., 116.

129. Eduard Winter, op. cit., 24.

130. Carl Hinrichs, *Friedrich Wilhelm I.*, 574.

131. Fritz Gehrlich, *Der Kommunismus als Lehre vom tausendjährigen Reich* (München, 1920), 151.

132. Paul Gruenberg, *Philip Jakob Spener* (Göttingen, 1905), II, 116.

133. Carl Hinrichs, "Pietismus und Militarismus im alten Preussen," *Archiv für Reformationsgeschichte*, 49:1/2 (1958), 290.

134. Ibid., 294.

135. Ibid., 302.

136. Ibid., 310.

137. Ibid., 321.

138. Essays and articles have appeared on it from *Time* to *Der Spiegel* and show its popular appeal just as Pietism had in its day.

139. Cf. Koppel A. Pinson, *Pietism as a Factor in the Rise of German Nationalism* (New York, 1934); Gerhard Kaiser, *Pietismus und Patriotismus im literarischen Deutschland* (Wiesbaden, 1961).

140. See Arthur Wilford Nagler, *Pietism and Methodism* (Nashville, Dallas, and Richmond, 1918), 142ff.

141. A very good contribution has been made by Peter C. Erb who very clearly delineates some of the relationships of Continental Pietism to spirituality currents in the U.S. Here is one example: "Pietism was a source for much of John Wesley's spirituality and through him (and members of the nineteenth-century Pietist renewal in Germany), it touched North American nineteenth-century revivalism and the Evangelical movement of the twentieth century. Contemporary North American Evangelicals in particular, as they grapple with their recent and relatively sudden realization of political and social influence and as they continue to move haltingly toward theological self-identity, are increasingly required to study their Pietist ancestors so as to understand the sources of their spirituality and the clearest existing analogues of their piety." (Pietists, 2).

DOCUMENTS

WITH

INTRODUCTIONS

The Reformation

Of the Church by the Pastorate

Contained in Two Pastoral Letters

By

Jean de Labadie

1610-1674

Minister of Jesus Christ

Addressed to some of his intimate friends
and zealous pastors

Middelburg, 1667

EDITOR'S INTRODUCTION

The selections from Jean de Labadie's major writing, *The Reformation of the Church by the Pastorate*, are from pp. 1-101. They cover only a small segment of the extensive argument. But they give an impression of the direction of de Labadie's thought. His work antedates the writings of the German Pietists. While scholarship has not reached agreement on the exact nature of de Labadie's influence on Spener, it is a fact that Spener visited de Labadie in Geneva while the latter was a pastor there. It is also certain that Spener translated and published de Labadie's tract, *La pratique des deux oraisons, mentale et vocale* (1656), in 1667. So for a number of reasons it is of interest to learn what thoughts de Labadie introduced that might have contributed to the formation of the Pietist movement.

Pietism began its attack upon Christendom with a radical critique of church and society. The most widely felt impact was Philip Jakob Spener's *Pia Desideria*. His critique of corrupt conditions in the church covers almost half of his volume. A similar approach can be observed already in many of the Lutheran Reform-Orthodox writers. So when Spener began to combat the corruption of the church in detailed description he fell in line with a "tradition" that went back also to a man like Labadie.

The selections thus offer a model of the Pietist critique of church and society. Even in their brevity they will indicate not only the almost infinite ingenuity of finding ever new aspects of Christian and general human corruption, but also trust in the possibility of renewal and the thoroughly biblical argumentation for both.

The work was conceived as two letters to associates, friends, and sympathizers. The notable intellectual, Anna Maria van Schurman (1607-1678), who held a position of leadership among them and who after de Labadie's death corresponded with Johann Jakob Schütz of the Frankfurt Pietist group, figured significantly in the decision to put the reform ideas into writing. De Labadie appeals to her urging and stresses how much the actual composition was related to circumstances in her life.

In order to understand the spirit of the two letters one has to keep in mind the life of the author. Jean de Labadie was born in 1610 in Bourg, near Bourdeaux, France, as a scion of nobility. Educated in a Jesuit school and having committed himself to the Jesuit order, he later became a secular priest because of a weak bodily constitution. Gradually he developed the notion that his task was to restore primitive Christianity. In 1650 he converted to Protestantism and became a professor of theology and pastor in Montauban, where he immediately sought to renew the Reformed Church. In 1659 he became pastor in Geneva, Switzerland. His zeal in reforming the church continued. In 1666 he went to Middelburg, in Holland, again as pastor of a Reformed Church, where before long he formed a separatist group on the model of the primitive church. As a consequence, he was banned from the city. *The Reformation of the Church by the Pastorate* was written in Middelburg. After leaving the city in 1668 he found asylum in various places, always gathering around him Christians of the true faith until his death in Altona, Germany, in 1674.

If one considers in what turmoil de Labadie must have spent most of his brief sojourn in Middelburg, it seems obvious that the work could not have been the product of careful scholarly reflection. It often seems as though he had been dictating on his feet. He himself was aware of this drawback and apologizes, as it were, for faults in style and logic. But since he was using his mother tongue, French, it is safe to assume that he was able to say what he wanted to say.

Apart from being an introduction to the critique of the church prevalent in early Pietism, the selections also confront the reader with the thinking of a man who has always been considered representative of the separatist strain in Pietism of which it has not been able to rid itself even to the present day. In its initial conception in German Protestantism, Pietism, however, was meant to be neither separatist nor establishment, but regenerative of the church as a whole. This was also the basic intent of de Labadie, as the following selections will show. It was of the reformation of the church that he wished to speak.

This work which was influential on Francke's *Definitio studii theologici* of 1708 reveals an implicit faith in the office of pastor which gives no hint that within two years Labadie would abandon all established forms of church government, with a ministry similar to that of a physician: examining the patient, making a diagnosis and prescribing the necessary remedy. These remedies are enumerated with a yearning and an optimism, since he detects signs of awakening and of spiritual thirst in many circles, with pastors of rightful zeal being raised up by God. *The Reformation* reveals, alongside many scripture references, a wide reading of spiritual writers, notably Cyprian, Basil, Jerome, Bernard of Clairveaux, Salvian, Richard of St. Victor, Tauler, à Kempis and the "Augustinus," all of which he recommends as spiritual reading for young people! None of these references appear in the following selections.

Labadie's labors actually soon led to deformation and schism. He is a challenge and a warning at the same time. The critique of church and society seems overdrawn in a number of places. It was, for example, his opposition to reading Latin authors or to viewing a certain kind of art that reflects almost a fascination with corruption. Overstrained, the bow was bound to snap.

The editor has deleted a few passages where there was too much redundancy and reduced an excessive number of italics. The major point of the selections is to mediate an impression of the kind of critique of church and society that stood at the beginning of the Pietist enterprise.[1]

JEAN De LABADIE

The Reformation of the Church by the Pastorate

Very dear friends and honored brothers in God our common father, and in our common eldest brother Jesus, in whom we are united as children of God and as brothers, by the union of the Holy Spirit.

If I continue to write to you as a group on a subject of common interest the reason is no longer your mutual interest alone but that of many virtuous people who with you not only approve my having done it but who also want me to continue it. They wish that, in order to give you and themselves more complete satisfaction, I should write you more fully and add a second letter to the first which shall not, like the first, treat in a few hasty words points which need to be treated very deliberately and at length.

The generous share you have given of your wealth and your personal well-being to a number of people by making it public property is the reason why the public wishes you and, at the same time, itself, a better share and, at the very least, a larger one, by requesting me to write more extensively on this subject. Since I seek its consolation as well as yours I yield to your orders and its desires. Therefore, without even giving you the trouble to make me speak your language, which I am grieved not to know, or to appear in an alien disguise, I shall forthwith express my views in my own language. What is more, I shall do so under my own name and appear personally to the public in order that it may know me by the two things by which people are known best, by their names and their words, which I do not conceal.

Since people guessed that it was I who had written a certain Pastoral Letter which appeared in Flemish and since, even when I had clad myself in a strange garment, my style betrayed me and my voice gave me away somewhat as in the case of Jacob, I can no longer hide myself, and furthermore, I have no such desire. On the contrary, by revealing my name I wish to reveal my heart and my thoughts as well as my words on points which are too plain not to be seen and too visible for me not to be revealed by them to everybody.

I am taking these points up again one after the other in this letter in the order of their appearance so as to express them better and more carefully, as I was requested to do by the shepherds and lambs who have long been sighing for *The General Reformation of the Churches by the Pastorate.*

First Heading

The Need for a General Reformation

I begin with the first heading, which is no other than *the need for this reformation in the entire Christian world.* In order better to understand it we must examine its deformation or its lapse in the matter of grace, spirit, zeal, morality, discipline, and every kind of virtue whose features have been replaced and abolished by the vices.[2]

Where are those churches which St. Paul so often calls the Assemblies of Saints (Rom. 1; 1 Cor. 1) which help each other and greet each other like saints? Those bodies of Christ, those Churches which he destines for Him like virgins for marriage? (2 Cor. 3; Eph. 1; Phil. 1; 4:21f.) Finally those against which Jesus has only very little reproach, as he observes regarding the Churches of Asia which he praises for much goodness? Certainly one scarcely sees any such in Europe and there are very few in which great evils cannot be detected.

I know well we can be told that we are very great accusers, but are we without grounds? That we are discontented fathers, hard to please, but do we complain wrongly? And have we no reason to say that Christianity in general has lapsed? That Christians have lost their pristine fervor and that they have become mere bodies, vicious and mundane bodies, mere Christian phantoms?

Second Heading

More Individual Proofs of a General Corruption Among Christians

In order to prove it we need only to take a look at our houses of worship in order to see how empty they are on working days, although just as many sermons are preached and prayers said as on Sunday in many places. We have only to consider also how empty and devoid of grace and piety people's hearts seem when the churches are most attended and full. People pray without thinking and without respect. They sing sacred tunes in a truly meaningless manner. They confess their sins without repenting and without any commitment to improve. Instead of weeping for their sins they confess them as if they were singing a song. They read the Bible without paying attention to its meaning and, more than that, without hearing in it the voice of God. Often they even drown out the Bible and God. Man's voice silences the voice of God and often makes it useless and ineffectual to say the least.

Isn't it also true that people talk in church as if they were at home?

That they are noisy as if they were in the street? That they stroll there as if they were in the woods? That they sleep as if in bed? That they rave at church in broad daylight as if in a dream at night? Shall we say that the preaching is aimless too, whether from the point of view of the preacher or his listeners? Certainly the latter often complain that one preacher is as dull and lifeless as the rest and that everything coming from the pulpit is badly neglected and careless. That one preacher puts them to sleep bodily by his lamentation or his singsong style while another does so by his monotonous manner or his way of preaching as if he were reading, the latter by his slowness of speech, the former by a lack of the vigor and zeal needed to express things forcefully and with a certain spiritual energy.

But the worst is that church sermons sometimes lull people's souls into the sleep of sin by a teaching which is either complimentary or indulgent, which weakens the Gospel by taking away its rigor; which never preaches anything but salvation and grace even to dissolute and impenitent persons; which does not dare to correct in public those who sin publicly (1 Tim. 5:20); which says peace when there is no peace for the impious, says God (Is. 48:22; Jer. 6:14); which merely whitewashes the wall without rebuilding it (Ezek. 13:10ff.); which washes the outside of the cup but not the inside and bandages thoughtlessly the mortal wound of Babylon and Zion (Mt. 23 :25). If that is the case we must not resent that the accused accuse us provided they do so justly and mend their own ways as we desire. For this we shall give them not only admonition, but the example of mending our own ways.

Since we seek the improvement of the Christian world let us continue to see its wrongdoing more as guilt than as punishment and its sins as prevailing much more in other places than in sacred ones, outside rather than inside the churches. Let us enter into the most important places after the churches, that is, the palaces of the great called the courts of justice or of the nobility. Alas, although everything speaks only of justice, how little is meted out to the poor, to widows and orphans? How much injustice is done in the name of justice which often wields the sword as well as the pen unjustly?

How often judges are litigants and litigants judges, particularly when the litigants have corrupted them? Don't judges, who are pictured as having neither eyes nor hands, have them both to see and to take unlawful presents and payments in order to give personal consideration and to judge and condemn or absolve according to the dictates of their hatred or affection? Do they not often punish crimes in others which they not only tolerate in themselves, but absolve and reward with honor and pleasure? Do they not permit their household, parents, and friends to do things which they punish in strangers, and spare the blood of some when they shed and waste that of others?

But often they like even better to bleed people's purses than their bodies, solid gold and its yellow being more pleasing than a liquid whose red always causes a certain horror. It is easier to take people's wealth than their lives, and consequently, how much are the judges accustomed to take away from the litigants in order always to reserve a great deal for themselves? The most liquid part of the litigant's wealth is for the judges, and a bit of writing on parchment which they give in closing a lawsuit often serves to take away what the judges help them to gain.

While some judge so badly, how much worse others plead their cases, that is, the sly and clever lawyers who lengthen and drag out suits with more effect than bad surgeons and doctors enlarge or prolong wounds or illnesses? Isn't it the custom to say that they know the art of making lawsuits immortal? As a matter of fact, how many suits we see which have lasted for ages and yet continue day after day? Whole cartloads are not enough to transport the bags of documents with which the offices of court clerks and solicitors are lined more than the storehouses and depots are with supplies of food, weapons, and war materials.

Pleading suits is an action in which clients are killed or robbed with impunity. This lawsuit war is really waged for the purpose of filling the hungry mouths of the officers of justice. No other war ever employed so much cunning or took so many prisoners, as this legal war is not merely satisfied to ransom, but is stripping people of their belongings and always sending them back naked. O how much duplicity and injustice lawsuits bring about! How many false documents! How many false records and contracts! Yet everything is permissible and acceptable provided one has friends in court, as they say. Nobody is ever wrong or loses his suit if he pays well. Arguments of counsel and judgments are venal because either magistrates or hearts are.

Higher and, to say the least, more worldly courts than those of law are no less corrupt and, because they have scarcely anything to do with crimes, are no less guilty; on the contrary they are more guilty because they are hardly ever punished for what they do. How much cheating and dissimulation are the rule in these courts? What a lot of complaining in them about betrayals and traitors! How much human bread is consumed and what a thirst for the people's blood there is which is almost never quenched, at least among political followers?

The Christian world has more toll collectors than the Roman, men of evil ways, much less convertible than Zaccheus or Matthew. Is there anything more fierce than a noble who has the heart of a lion rather than of a Christian when he is bloodthirsty and quarrelsome? Is there anyone who swears more insolently then a reckless gentleman? Where do we find any of them today who are noble-hearted and modest? Don't our brave men display their bravery by attacking heaven, blaspheming the name of Christ and not even fearing God? It would be small matter to find religious ignorance in princely courts if atheism did not often reside there too, sometimes openly, sometimes secretly, if not the theoretical, then at least the practical kind as life and conduct reveal it.

Courts are so political, on the one hand, that one can hardly keep from calling them deceitful, and, on the other hand, so dissolute that today the words of Jesus about the courts of Herod and Caesar can easily apply to the courts of a number of the great nobles, because people went about there languidly and elaborately dressed. They displayed no austerity and wore no hairshirts, and had no thought of living austerely in solitude like John the Baptist. On the contrary, what lavishness there was at light suppers on fasting days and at banquets; in linen, dress, lace—what dissolution in the bodies of those who wear them and are covered by them! What filth there is under those adornments, what dirt hidden under such shining immaculateness!

But why should luxury and lust not accompany each other at courts since they certainly do so elsewhere and persons not provided with the facilities to be found in palaces and among the high nobility? Is it only in noble mansions that we have gambling and dances? Do we not see them in private houses and often see people in those houses better dressed than at court although they are not princesses nor even nobles? What a high level vanity has attained in our age! How far all kinds of Christians are from Christian humility! To the very nails of the sanctuary, I mean to persons who are the least or the most ecclesiastic, there is not one who does not wish to be made of gold like the nails of the ancient tabernacle.

As a matter of fact, who does not sometimes perceive luxury in his own family? Gold and silver on the head, the body or the clothing of his children? Why, do we not see these metals also on mothers, or, at least, rustling velvet, dazzling fabrics, and diamonds still more brilliant? The simplest tradeswomen wear them, although their husbands are neither jewelers nor the kind of people who have to make their wives noticeable through jewels. What shall we say? Are these jewels perhaps acquired through fraudulent dealings? Do they perhaps cost nothing but the trouble of theft or dishonest acquisition?

As you see, I pass from the public places of courts to those of trade where you cannot deny that there is a great traffic in wickedness. Markets are nothing but public places for cheating and stages for theft. The great gathering of people you find there is sometimes nothing but an assembly of cheats in which each one strives to be the shrewdest and to outdo his companion. Do sleight-of-hand artists and jugglers know more tricks than salesmen and buyers these days? Who among them is a man of his word and not of a hundred falsehoods? Who does not swear and perjure himself even for a sou or something of low value? Is there any simple soul who is not tricked or even any wise one who is not cheated? . . .[3]

I pass over in silence the false weights and measures which are not always made of lead or of wood but are in the fingers with which clever salesmen weigh and measure in many places where poor buyers pay and buy without even getting the fabric, the meat, or the commodity which they are entitled to take with them. How many there are who adulterate these commodities and who sell nothing in its pure state, not wine, nor oil, nor liquid of any kind, altering everything they sell and selling for good quality what they have spoiled?

Are there perchance any places where people do not cheat and where they do not steal without being considered thieves? Those where wheat is sold, ground, kneaded, and made into bread, where men are dressed, shod, fed—are they free of cheating and theft? Aren't passers-by and foreigners fleeced in Christian hostelries on the pretext of showing them hospitality? Don't taverns and the public lodging places of shameless and public persons take in drunkards? And don't the hidden ones at least have fairly well-known secrets?

Can we complain enough of the excesses which are committed in such places and are more or less tolerated everywhere? How many are there where chastity is bought and sold like bread and wine and every kind of flesh? How often elsewhere is it stolen or violated or even given for nothing? How widespread lewdness has become among Christians today and, what is more, adultery? And other sins which many people look upon as necessary diversions and excusable and natural appetites? . . .[4]

We see and find moral filth everywhere both at an early and at an adult age in any sex or social position even to the one people regard as the most innocent. How much more corrupt, then, are the advanced and mature ages? Or better still the most seasoned age, although not the coldest? How keen the Christian youth of this time are for their fleshly pleasures at a time when their blood is fairly boiling and burns like a red hot coal? How few young people there are who are chaste and do not lose their virginity before their time! How many shipwrecks of chastity and the chaste there are on dry land, although incontinence is compared to water and is said to derive from it! What need is there to condemn this great vice and to teach young and old to avoid it!

Another vice, namely, intemperance of the appetite, nourishes it by contaminating the body too much. The flesh consumes too much flesh not to become very carnal. People drink too much wine not to be over-supplied with blood, to have a surplus, and a corrupted one, which is as effervescent as wine is buoyant. What excesses it inspires in almost every Christian land, whether it is native there or whether it is brought in as a foreign product!

It is doubtless a shameful thing that Christianity, which is by its nature sober and moderate, has become intemperate and gluttonous....[5]

There is no ... hurry to teach [the children], or make them learn, the Bible, its truths, or its maxims which are very different, whether in prose or verse, from those of Cicero, Horace, or the tales of Homer and Ovid, which are not as good as those of Aesop. That is not the way they are made to study Moses and his works, David and his psalms, the wr ings of the Prophets and the Apostles, and particularly the life, teachings, and mysteries of Jesus Christ. But they are taught to study with great care the works of Numa, or Aeneas, or Vergil, or Plutarch, who pad their accounts with children's tales. That is why we see our children grow up without knowing who the Prophets and Apostles are, yet knowing well who the Greek and Roman poets and orators are. Quintus Curtius and Suetonius almost silence the authors of the four Gospels, and Seneca makes St. Paul drop from people's hands, so to speak, or at least drives him from their hearts. In a word, the writers of comedy are better liked than the Apostles; as a matter of fact, they are amusing folk who tell many jokes, and some of them dirty. Those base writers and their likes: the Ovids and Horaces and all those lascivious ancient poets and cup drainers from whom they have taken their name, do not cease (to use the words of the Prophets) to debase the youth. They corrupt their early years and soil their innocence from infancy and the cradle, at least that innocence which the cradle has given them and which is preserved at the hands of their parents until they fall into the hands of those wicked stepfathers and teachers who destroy their modesty.

Is it any wonder if children lack chastity and if they know filthy things which they should not know even as grownups? Is it any wonder that they do not forget lessons learned so early and over such a long period? And that, following the bad examples they read of, they give similar examples by imitating them? Who can doubt that so much pagan study makes them pagans too? And at least weakens greatly the strength of piety in them, since such study deprives them of the time to study and know the piety of the faith?

In fact, how ignorant in this matter is the youth of this age which learns the catechism by heart but does not understand it at all? How could the youth understand it, for no one explains it? Or, if it is explained, this is done incidentally, once a week, superficially, and for a very short time. The youth could explain much better an obscure passage of Plautus and an obscure verse of Persius or Horace than a passage of St. Paul or a verse of David, since it has received far more instruction in the pagan authors than in the sacred ones. We should not be surprised either if it is secularized and carries out almost every kind of secular action, in church by creating confusion, in private houses by pilfering, in streets by fighting, in secret places by gambling or doing worse things, in public ones by showing its insolence and indiscretion....[6]

But if, in places where the youth is instructed in faith, piety, and virtue, there is so little knowledge and practice of them, what must the youth be like in places where it is left to its own coarseness, to its own blindness as well as to its own corrupt nature and its evil inclinations? Hence it is deplorable to see how ignorant it is in the shops, in private houses, and in all places where there is almost no instruction.

For two or three years it is put to a trade which it learns fairly fast and fairly well but it is not put to the occupation of being Christian, which it does not learn in ten years or even in a lifetime. Should we then be surprised that it grows in vice as it grows in years? That it knows nothing but how to swear, lie, strike, and be immoral, since it has learned only how to sin? Without having eaten of the fruit of knowledge, it knows evil and often it even does evil things without knowing it. Oh, what sins of ignorance! But they are nevertheless not free of malevolence, which is all the greater because it is brutal and, because it is coarse, it is nonetheless stubborn and malign in the one who harbors it.

But, passing from public places to private ones, let us see whether in families and in private homes there is more modesty and restraint. Certainly the rich appear too richly furnished to give us examples of modesty and humility. Azure and bright gold shine in their dwellings where paintings vie with statues for their choice value.

Would anyone say indeed that Christians who so hate idolatry and idols in churches would have them in their houses? That they would have, not only human figures which represent real people and either relatives or friends, but also false divinities? If they do not adore the models or the prototypes, at least they adore, so to speak, their craftsmanship and their value. It is still idolatry, either of beauty or of value, and the craftsman and his work turn their admirers into some kind of worshippers.

In this matter of paintings I should be ashamed to reveal that, among Christians, there are too many of them which are bare and which expose nakedness which nature counsels us to cover up and which a brazen art displays to eyes which are most eager to see them. This is done under the pretext that it is merely portraying in all kinds of colors things which are done in mere black and white in the Bible and that it is but painting what is written, as if it simply copied them: for example, innocent Adam and Eve, Noah asleep overcome by wine as well as Lot in bed, David seeing Bathsheba and other similar persons of the same or different sex, and it makes no good use of them.

This is criminal art, which soils sacred things and souls as well as houses and their rooms, makes everything truly unclean and sows filth everywhere and for all eyes. It makes modest people shudder and immodest people sometimes ashamed, but usually shameless. Young people see these things as Amnon saw Tamar, old men see them the way the ancient old men saw Susanna, and all who look at them voluptuously sin as David did when he looked down upon Bathsheba from his balcony walk. What a mistake it is to think that because these things are written they should be painted. They are written to portray them as abomination and they are painted to make them an attraction. Gardens, bedrooms, and even beds, are full of them and perhaps of their imitators and of live and true examples quite as much as the painted ones. Art does not stop there. It engraves them, and lust which is embossed makes a far greater impression than painting on a flat surface. Relief emphasizes it and makes it more effective and true to life than when it is only in color. That is the effect of painting and sculpture, called arts of innocence, although they portray crimes and create criminals.

Nothing is more common among the rich than these subjects in marble, porphyry, and painting. Azure and gold shine in a thousand other types of ornament with which the smokiest and blackest fireplaces are adorned and even gleam. Porcelain vases line all the mantelpieces, just as vases of silver adorn sideboards, cabinets, and tables. Rich tapestries in which gold and silver threads set off silken or woolen ones, cover the walls, their ugliness, or their coldness. The poor of Jesus Christ are not as well clad, and have no thought of being as well padded, as the very floors on which Turkish rugs and fine fabrics abound.

In these abodes of pleasure, these palaces, these rooms, what do we see and hear? What is done there? Do we hear mention of God? Yes, but in curses. Do we hear His praises sung? No, but we do hear courtly airs, mundane songs, and wanton love songs. We even see some put into action, and not all of them secretly, since there are brazen women there. Dances and comedies are given. Violins play. There are delicate light repasts on fasting days and rich banquets, and everything occurs except what is sacred and respectable.

Alas, who would think that these are Christian houses and persons? Who would not think that they are secular and pagan? And pagan in the manner of Anthony and Cleopatra, of Herod and Herodias, Caligula, Sardanapalus, and other masters of luxury, lust, and dissoluteness? ....[7]

All these things are common among Christians today and even those thought to be the most Christian. The other vices are no less common, such as lying, larceny, fraud, dissimulation, envy, rancor, false report, rash judgment, and gossip; indecent narrations and songs; impatience and wrath, haughtiness, vanity, elaborate dress; the use of paint, vain attire; hypocrisy, lack of piety; in short, all the vices ever seen among the pagans.

I reserve one vice for the last because it seems the most widespread today, the most general, and the greatest, namely, the covetousness of wealth, which St. Paul calls that of the eyes, and the spirit of avarice which makes so many covetous. It is the vice of usurers, thieves, cheats, and everybody else. It is the execrable Mammon, the god of this age: self interest, profit, gold, silver, and riches, which people idolize, worship, and desire, seek and cherish exclusively, a demon which accomplishes, and is responsible for, everything today, the mainspring of action.

Now, to what extent is this Baal followed? On what a high altar this Dagon is placed and worshipped! Not by the Philistines or the Jews alone, but by Christians! And sometimes by those who, in their group, ought to be the truest worshippers of the true God and the most detached from the world! Nevertheless don't we see the priests of the sacrifice and the Levites, like those of Dagon and of Baal, become the first ones to join the cult of this Mammon, the god of riches, to desire them and acquire them with more zeal and eagerness and hold on to them with more greed and anxiety than the common people?

But what am I saying: Everybody is in love with this god and I think that people have been right in our day to paint a demon, loaded with sacks of gold and silver and all sewed up and covered over with fine coins, attached to the end of a pike or of a very high stake, like a target, a fine bull's-eye surrounded by musketeers, archers, stone throwers, slingers, on all sides and of all sexes, ages, and conditions, firing at it to bring it down and carry it off, with this deserved inscription or device:

"Everyone is shooting at this devilish money."

Because that is the aim of the common mania and the goal which those of low and high degree try to reach.

That is why official appointments, whether ecclesiastical or political, are venal or else solicited, either openly or secretly. For how rare is it that they come to those who do not seek them? And how seldom they are ever given gratuitously to pure merit, to genuine capacity, to ingenuity, to wisdom, and least of all to virtue?

How many wrongs, and great wrongs, are caused by these solicitations and intrigues? How many occur in the Christian states and churches? Sometimes violent and rash men, sometimes ignorant and ineffectual ones, are promoted for important posts in church and state. Wicked men push their way in and almost drive out good men, as the Barbarians would drive out burgers captured with their city. Through such quests for position the gate is thrown open to vice, since it is opened to intrigue and sometimes favor, and to the favor of women just as quickly as to that of men by whose aid it is less disgraceful to rise....[8]

But there would be no end if I had to enumerate the sins of the world here, and even of the Christian world. I shall have to be satisfied in a summary way by calling it a general criminal and a universal sinner, since St. James rightly calls the language itself a whole university of evils.

Enough said about the sins in this guilty world which begets so many other evils, and in this body of the guilty Christian world which has so many criminal members. What must we conclude from this then, if not that it is in great need of being reformed and having its woes cured? But it is utterly incapable of doing this by itself and when left to its own counsel.

The reason for this is that it has scarcely any desire to and is very careful not to thwart its passions and mortify its appetites. It is too well pleased with its practices to get rid of them, too pleased with its carnal composure to disturb it. The Christian world is a sick man who enjoys his illness and who does not want anyone to interfere with it. His lethargy is agreeable and, furthermore, even if he really wanted to get well, he is not in a condition to do it without help; but "this thirty-eight year old paralytic needs a man" (Jn. 5:2ff) and indeed a number of men to agitate him and throw him into the sacred bath.

But, someone will say, doesn't he have the Bible, the sacraments, the ministry and so many other good means and excellent remedies? That is true. But supposing that he does not know how to use them, but even misuses them. And supposing all that turns out badly and leaves him asleep, hardened, and callous in the state he is in and in the way in which he takes it? Doesn't he need something else which will awaken him, prickle him, soften him, or break him down, and which will make him once more open his mouth and eyes, or rather his heart?

Let us just take a close look at the matter and we shall see that neither the reading nor the hearing of the Word, as it is practiced for the most part, without attention, consecration, zeal and grace, nor the celebration of holy days carried out half in the Jewish style and half in the pagan, as one sees it in many places; nor even the celebration of the Lord's Supper and much less the baptismal rite celebrated with water without the Spirit on the part of the witnesses and the sponsors, nor, finally, any formal acts of religion: prayers, fasting, preaching, carried out literally and according to custom, succeed in rousing the world from its lethargy and drowsiness, and still less in curing it of the woes in which it is kept by dull practice and the letter which kills.

This is a new kind of "work carried out" or "*opus operatum*," as they say, introduced among us little by little, as if it had been accepted long ago, and in more criminal ways by others than ourselves. It is a poultice to cover the wound but not to cure it. It is the body's cloak or the body itself whose spirit has been lost. It is a rainbow, a fair appearance, a fine effect, but where is the essential and the solid element?

On the contrary, who does not see that the minister speaks well at a baptism, but that almost no one listens or derives any instruction from the ceremony? Promises of many things are given and required, but who keeps them or understands clearly what he promises? Who remembers to teach it afterward or to learn it? Who remembers correctly, whether father or child, that he was either godfather or baptized? Much less do people carry out the obligations they contract and the vows they make at baptisms.

People promise on such occasions to renounce the self and the world, and to mortify their appetites and instruct the baptized to do so. However, do parents and godparents teach this renunciation to the baptized by example and word? And do the baptized put them in practice when they don't even know the theory behind them? The same baptized persons all promise themselves, or through others who are all present, to live like Christians and like persons devoted to Jesus Christ. And yet do they cease to live as wordlings or pagans for that? And do not the rest live according to their education and examples, and do we see any who, as they all solemnly promise, shed their old self and its actions and put on a new one?

People do celebrate Holy Communion, but do they always do it devoutly? People do not fail to double their commitments at the right time and to set days for this, four or six times a year, in some places even more often; and at the prearranged time the bread, the wine, and their containers are ready, the tables covered with very clean and white linen, and people assembled in a crowd to take Communion. But with whom? With God whom they have offended, are offending, and have no firm and true intention to stop offending? With Jesus Christ whom they have outraged, are outraging, and whom they proceed to outrage again in His mystery, doing injury to the sacrament of His body and of His blood? With the church which they have scandalized, are scandalizing, and are in a fair way to continue to scandalize, by a wicked life and a relapse into every kind of sin?

All that is condemned in sermons, pastoral letters, and catechisms, it is true. But who is punished because he has been condemned? Who is any better for having heard the pronouncement? Who profits today from the written and spoken word? As a matter of fact, almost nobody. That is why people talk when it is read and either sleep or amuse themselves when it is spoken. They speak louder than God in the churches, and often noise silences Him and the mouth of man drowns out His voice.

Often, too, everything that is read and uttered there lacks feeling. And, not to claim innocence ourselves by accusing others, we may sometimes preach negligently, as they say, pray from habit, exhort without vigor, correct without zeal, instruct without affection, and do what has to be done more because we should than because we wish to; in short, merely to discharge an obligation rather than out of zeal and with the purpose of doing our duty well.

It is also not just, we are told, that we should efface our own names from the list of sinners and write in those of others. Consequently, if we are haughty and vain, greedy and stingy, proud, harsh, imperious, envious, angry, and vindictive; cheats, liars, scandalmongers; it is right that we should be accused and put in the same class as we put those who are guilty of these faults and that, in our capacity of men and changeable Christian individuals who are corrupt like the rest, we should not shun a public confession, but make it in truth when the latter requires it.

As pastors ourselves and in our quality as public men, we should not reject as lies and calumnies the complaints that may be formulated against us that we perform our pastoral duties badly, either by preaching negligently or praying without fervor or zeal; failing to instruct our sheep and our lambs, that is, the adults and children in our churches, or to visit the sick and the healthy in order to console the first and to control the others; and give to all the pasture that we owe them: solid, tender, pithy, as the Scriptures, the mysteries of God, sacred study, meditation, and religious rite give it to us for distribution.

Indeed it is precisely in this respect that we must imitate the holy prophets, David, Isaiah, Daniel, and all the rest who, in their confessions, even public confession, have shared their sins with those of the people and have confessed themselves sinners before the Holy Father. In accordance with our confessions we shall all see each other as guilty members of the same body and shall all be condemned, not only for being in need of grace, but of improvement.

This is what we must all come to, and I as well, my brothers, with this whole long description of our sins. It is not, however, as long as that of others, since we aim only to confess our major sins in order to recover from them and to find a more effective remedy than the ordinary ones, or at least those commonly practiced. I see no better one than *The project for a universal reformation* and the application of the *pastorate toward this end in an extraordinary manner*; recovering its zeal, fervor, concern, vigilance, recovering its authority, severity, and sacred evangelical liberty, as I see you are doing and must do more than ever, convinced in your consciences of the universal need for reformation in all social classes, convinced of your duties and your pastoral obligations; and, finally, convinced that you can neither omit nor delay such action without retarding the glory of God, the reign of Jesus Christ, the welfare of the church, the sanctification of the world and of yourselves.

Third Heading

The Necessity of Having and Organizing a Project for a General Reformation

What we have just seen of the *universal corruption* would seem quite sufficient for organizing the great and just project of a universal reformation; nevertheless, since the necessity for organizing and having it is exceedingly important and must serve as an urgent motive for adopting it and putting it into practice, it seems to me a necessity to set forth how it is particularly essential at this time to organize, to have, and to propose it, in order that the undertaking to carry it out shall not depend upon me.

The first proof of the necessity for this is the one that we have set forth at some length under the previous heading, *Concerning the Universal Corruption*, which we have observed in all classes, sexes, ages, places, and almost all persons according to the description we have just given and the visible evidence we have. For who is there among us who, if he has the slightest, I shall not say Christian but human, compassion, upon seeing a man mortally wounded from many blows and left lying half dead on the ground in his own blood, will not rush to him, hasten to succor him, wipe him off, and carry him, or have him carried, off to a place where he can be bandaged, and, if possible, healed of his wounds? The Samaritan of the Gospel, although apparently less pious and compassionate or obliged to be, it seems, than the High Priest and the legalistic Levite, seeing a man wounded on his way by robbers, did indeed rush to him, pick him up, and take him to a lodging house where he had wine served to him and oil applied to his wounds, took out money to pay the proprietor and to take care of all his expenses and his cure; and we Christian high priests and Levites of grace, pastors, ministers, servants of Jesus Christ, and who sacrifice through Him to God His Father, are to have no pity on the Christian world and not to rush to this victim grievously wounded and dying of his wounds?

Secondly, even the ancient law obliges one, when he sees the ox or ass of his neighbor, and even of the enemy, which has fallen into a ditch or been crushed by the weight of his burden, to run to its aid, to lend a hand, and obliges others as well to help to lift it out of the ditch or the quagmire (Ex. 23:4-5; Deut. 22:1-4). And the message from the lips of Jesus himself requires that, even if it were on the very day of the Sabbath, a man should not let his sheep die in the mire or the place where it has fallen, nor his ass, nor any other animal (Mt. 11:12f.). And the shepherds of the flocks of God, or of Jesus Christ, are not to have pity on the sheep of God and of Jesus Christ, who have fallen into the mire of sin and the abyss of the world's corruption? They will not make every effort to lift out their own sheep and, as Jesus expressed it, the children and daughters of Abraham and, what is more, of God and Father Abraham himself? Surely they must have the salvation of these at heart and must have a large heart to love them and, therefore, feet to run to them and hands to get them out of the mire and even shoulders to carry them like good shepherds to the fold.

Thirdly, if, when fire takes hold of a city or burns even a single house, we must rush to it and rush, even more, for water to put it out and cut short the conflagration in order to prevent it from reducing everything to ashes and destroying both men and roofs; if, when a vessel at sea breaks open or threatens to do so, we must quickly bring it to shore and, at least, repair its hull; if even a sown field bristling with nettles needs to have them pulled up to be rid of them, how much more the field of the Christian God requires to be relieved of its briars and vices: Doesn't the ship of the church, taking in water at every seam, need to be pumped out and its hull repaired? And doesn't the house of God, the new Jerusalem, and the city of the great king Jesus need help in its vast conflagration? In a word, we have to cut off quickly the advance of gangrene in a person's body. How much more must we do this to the body of Christianity in which everything is on the way to corruption?

Fourthly, the *necessity to adopt and to organize the project for a general reformation* must be deduced from the fact that if, by this means, we do not quickly come to the aid of the Christian Church, it is going to get worse and can only get sicker and deteriorate more from day to day. We observe that, when a body begins this process, it goes on deteriorating and rots more and more. The mortal wound which is not quickly and well dressed, enlarges and becomes more infected daily. Every moment that an ulcer is not cut out it spreads until it covers the whole face. An unextinguished fire burns up the whole house and the whole neighborhood where it started. When anyone falls from a mountain or a high elevation, he tumbles to the very bottom and is killed unless stopped on the way. In short, we die of the disease which is not combated and when we are dead there is no remedy, for in order to act it must have a live body. Indeed if we give free rein to impiety and the impious, to worldliness and the worldly, to indifference and the indifferent in the matter of faith and religion, in a word, to free thinking and the libertines of this age, what else can we expect except atheism, forgetfulness of God, complete effacement of His memory and His name?

If we do not oppose profanity and those who indulge in it, insolence and insolent people in sacred places and in others, inattentiveness and inattentive people in prayers and in praising God, in the reading of, and listening to, the Word in all other holy exercises, what shall we see in the houses of worship, sermons, and even the administration of the sacraments, except inadvertency, superficiality, immodesty? And what can we expect after all but perversion and sacrilege?

If we do not hasten to cure the Christian world of the wounds, not only of its ignorance, but of its vain knowledge, its worldly prudence, its haughtiness, and its show; its avarice and its usuriousness, its illicit or its dishonest dealings; its hatreds or envies; its gluttony, its impurity, and its intemperance in every way; what else can it become except corrupt and dissolute, prostituted to every vice, a falsely Christian and a truly pagan world?

After that can we call it Christian and regard it as a world which has a right to bear the name of Christ, since it senses so little his grace and fervor? Wouldn't we have to take it rather for a New World made up quite simply of old savages ready to eat each other and commit every kind of crime? Even at that there are more innocent as well as more harmless savages in the newly discovered lands.

We shall do better to consider the Christian world as Turkish, which after all is at least more just and even more prone to fear God in its own way and to respect Him to the point of not daring to blaspheme Him. We shall have to look upon it as dead, ready to be buried, unless we throw it on a dung heap like a rotten corpse or, at least, throw it out (as the Gospel says) like salt which has lost its savor or is quite insipid (Mt. 5:13).

A sixth matter[9] which proves the necessity of having and organizing

the *Project for a General Reformation of the Christian Community* is
its need to mend its ways or to perish. In this connection we must earnestly consider that the same thing must be said of the new Israel as of
the ancient one: the Lord Jesus did not limit himself to pointing out that
its last works would be worse than its first, but added these terrible
words: if you do not repent you will perish (Lk. 13:3-5), that is, if you
do not mend and reform your ways you are lost, you are damned, and
will be condemned by God to temporal and eternal pain which your
sins deserve.

That is the way we must also talk to our new Israel, to the Christian
world which must be exhorted to a true repentance and a sincere improvement, that is to say, in a true sense, to a general reformation; but
we must tell it that, for want of such a change, it is on the way to perdi-
tion, all of which compels me to formulate precisely this great maxim
in two little words: repent or perish....[10]

In short, if Christian Europe continues in its sinful ways, there is danger that it may soon change both its appearance and its faith. That the
Gospel which came from Asia may return there and reclaim its original
estate. That it may pass over our lands and seas in order to see others
and may, like the sun, take away all light and warmth with it. The Occi-
dent might well become so dark and the North so cold that the Orient
and the South would receive more light and warmth, and we, more
darkness and ice....[11]

All of this proves the necessity for having and organizing the project
for a general reformation for fear of a general destruction, and, at the
very least, of some great exterior loss for the Christian world corresponding to its interior loss, and appropriate even to its punishment,
which it well deserves. The symptoms from which it is suffering are the
marks and the forerunners of great misfortunes. Nevertheless, if we
wish to prevent the symptoms and remedy the misfortunes by means of
a general reformation which we propose, we can avoid them all, seeing
above all that God grants the time and the means to do it, and, what is
more, indicates that he wants this very reformation, which is a great
and final obligation for us, not only to have one, but to formulate the
project for it.

Thus I am happy, to come to my seventh point, in order to explain to
you what I think, and not I alone, but even a number of you and of other upright persons who are as full of vision as of fire, and endowed with
as much capability and wisdom as with zeal and fervor.

They believe they are not mistaken, nor I either with them, in believing that at this time God thinks, as the Gospel says, thoughts of peace
for His people and that the time for showing them mercy and re-
establishing them entirely is not very far away. We shall treat these
points elsewhere; hence we have no intention to pause to deduce them
and prove them here.

I shall only express a few good reasons or conjectures, the first of which, since it is a suitable basis for the others, is founded itself upon the Scriptures just as it is derived from them. It consists in this constant promise and assurance that God gives in general, that God does not desire the death of a sinner but his repentance and his life. How much more then the repentance of the universal Christian world than that of a private individual!

It is also founded on the fact that in the Old Testament he constantly calls His own to grace and promises not to let them fall altogether or perish but offers them His hand and His arm in order to lift them up with the one and to steady them with the other; to pull them up and sustain them at the same time; and on the fact that His purpose is not to kill by punishing but to correct and then to cure in a few days and particularly on the third day to which we have come.

It is also founded on the fact that in the new alliance He promises more explicitly a place for repentance and gives the means; and Jesus Himself indicates that He calls and awaits sinners; and in the Apocalypse He gives time for all the fallen churches to rise up and to recover their zeal and good way of life which they no longer have or have at least neglected.

The second proof or reason, founded on the same Word of God and on the ordinary practice, as the Scriptures indicate, is, that when He intends, in His own good time, to manifest Himself in a rather extraordinary way to the world, and above all to His world or Israel, He prepares it for this benefit both by repentance and faith, readies it to receive His grace at the right time and to profit by His coming and His manifestation. This is the way He prepared the ancient people for His appearance on Sinai and for the gift of His law on the first and most ancient day of Pentecost, when He filled the temple of Solomon with His glory and when later He freed it from the captivity of Babylon in accordance with the preparations made for this by the holy men of God, Nehemiah and Esdras. But this appeared much more when God came in the person of Jesus Christ and of the messiah, which was preceded by periods of repentance and grace that the world might be prepared to receive the highest grace of all in Him, since He is plenitude and we derive it from him.

If there are signs that the reign of God is approaching and if we can think and say with good reason that our time is not far away from the one of that great and final good, that divine manifestation of power, virtue, grace, and judgment, as may easily be proved, do we not also have reason to hope for a fairly considerable period of conspicuous mercy which will reform us in order to prepare us for it and put us in a suitable state of mind for such an excellent good?

The third proof is the rather common maxim, but no less good because it is an ordinary one, that God comes in an extremity and arrives when we are desperate; that His custom is to rebuild when all is in ruin and that He does everything when man can do nothing. So it was that

He came in an extremity to deliver Sarah from the hands of Abimelech, and Isaac, his son, from the hands of his father. Thus He came to the aid of Jacob against his brother and his father-in-law, precisely at the moment when he was helpless. Thus he rescued Joseph from prison and all Israel from servitude; in short, the entire world of the chosen from the chains of the devil when they could have no other resource but Him and when no other hand but His could deliver them. Hence, since things are at present reduced to an extremity and since disorder has become so great that it can hardly increase any more, it is very likely that God is on the point of intervening and reducing the disorder, that for this purpose He is thinking of compressing it [the world of the chosen] within the limits of a strict reformation which will serve as a happy bondage and will not merely restrain it but put it on the right path, that is, reorder it by reforming it.

The fourth reason, or proof, is that, when the Scriptures promise new heavens, they promise a new land where justice and holiness dwell, no doubt in place of injustice and of sin which has merely hardened it. By corrupting justice, sin has worn it out and made it old, and ready, so to speak, to perish; but holiness and justice must renew and rejuvenate it. Now that cannot be done without reformation and repentance to which St. Paul attributes the virtue of a true renewal (Heb. 6).

In different passages he deduces the two phases of this renewal which consist in stripping away the old man and putting on the new one, and therefore in a complete reformation which tends to give, in accordance with its name, a new form to everything and particularly to the human heart. God created a new heart in David when the one he had grew old through sin. God gives the heart of flesh when He takes away the one of stone, if the heart is a chosen stone and fit to be softened.

The fifth proof is that at this time godly men have this project, which fact shows that God puts it into them. For, just as, when He wished to deliver His ancient people, He inspired the thought in all of its liberators as it appears in each of them from the first to the last, from Moses to Zerubbabel, and even as He does at present when His holy men want this reformation and, not only want it, but plan it, and consider in themselves the means to accomplish it; that is no mean indication that God Himself conceives it and causes them to do so.

The sixth proof, and the last, is that a number of upright people not only desire it, but stand behind it and make of it an article of special hope by waiting for it, as well as an article of their personal faith by believing in it. It is not that one should count heavily or rely on, or set store by, personal enlightenment and one's inner feelings which are not authorized by the public seal of the Word of God, but when, very far from outraging or being upset by it themselves, such convictions supplement it and yield to it, they are not to be rejected, since they are probable and even come from people as sensible as they are pious and believable because of their grace and strength as well as their wisdom and knowledge.

Now it is established that in different places a very large number of people, who are as respected and learned as they are eminent and holy, yet without any collusion and concerted purpose, agree in thinking that a great renewal is at hand and that we must prepare to see it and, even more, to advance it.

If heaven has this plan, isn't it a necessity that the earth should conform to it? That, since the former accepted it, the latter should do so, and that, as a Prophet says, the seasons should be in harmony; the wine with the wheat and the vintage with the harvest; that in the same way the hearts of men should be in harmony with the heart of God and that His ministers and His good and faithful servants who are the pastors, should prepare to work and to do what their Lord and Master makes them want and even shows them as his wish?

This is the *project that we must organize and have concerning a general reformation.* That is how, as God himself thinks about it, godly men should think, take action from this very moment, and prepare the materials for such an important structure, approximately in the same way that David and Solomon prepared those of the ancient temple, whether they have to build it themselves with their own hands, or have it built by their successors.

Fourth Heading

The Common Obligation of the Pastorate to Work for a General Reformation and the Desire for This Among the Flocks

The last point which I have just set forth for you, my brothers, at the end, under the preceding heading, brings me to the present one, which I have no intention to forget or to fail to enter upon very gladly, since it concerns the faith, our calling, and our welfare. It is the *general obligation we have to work for this general reformation* of which we are speaking, for many divine reasons which urge us on, and among human ones the dearest of all which is the desire of the flocks that the pastors should undertake this great work, and that it should be through no fault of theirs if it does not begin in order never to come to an end, although, according to their wish, it may find complete implementation.

As for the first of these two points, no one who knows at all what the pastorate and the holy ministry are is unaware in the first place that, on the one hand, it is the responsibility of the office which obliges one to serve God and the church, since it is called ministry and takes its name from its service; and that, on the other hand too, it requires that whoever occupies the office should pasture and lead a flock and keep it in good condition by means of good care.

All that obviously carries with it the obligation to retrieve all strayed sheep, to tend them when sick, and to keep them from perishing, as God Himself explains. Bringing back a people from vice to virtue, does that mean "reforming" it? Just as we agree that to bring it back from error to the truth was to reform it? Similarly, aren't its wounds well treated when it is cured of its sins which are all of a mortal kind that would finally kill it if the pastors did not cure them?

To serve God well is also to prevent the reign of the devil. It is a great service to the church to lift it out of the mire and keep it from perishing there. We serve it well when we save it from fire and water and prevent it from burning or drowning. But that is what the reformation about which we are talking should do; and consequently the pastors, the true servants and true ministers of God, of Jesus Christ, and the church should also serve it carefully in that respect.

Secondly, who does not know, if he knows the Scriptures at all, that the pastoral vocation says that we are called to preach the Faith and repentance? (Mt. 3 and 4, Acts 2:38) To pull up and to plant? To destroy and to build? (Jer. 1:10) To tell Jacob his crimes and Israel its iniquities? To make people weep as Samuel did the people of Mizpah? (1 Sam. 7:8, 9) To make the people go straight even as Eli did? To humble the mighty and raise up the lowly, to proclaim like John, Jesus Christ, and the Apostles the atonement and the approach of the reign of God? (Lk. 3:4) Now, isn't all this to attend to the reformation of the world? And, therefore, is not the pastorate, which is called to do these things, obliged to work for them, to devote itself to them in order not to abandon its vocation?

NOTES

1. A careful recent biography of de Labadie is by T.J. Saxby, *The Quest for the New Jerusalem, Jean De Labadie and the Labadists* (Dordrecht, 1987).

2. Pp. 4-33 left out. The author articulates the direction of the theme.

3. P. 44. A passage on dishonesty in business is left out.

4. A passage on immorality in fashions is left out.

5. Pp. 49-52 left out. The author discusses the ill effects of wine, gambling, etc.

6. Pp. 56 f. left out.

7. Pp. 63-65 left out. The author discusses gambling, idleness, and other vices.

8. P. 69 left out.

9. The author fails to identify a fifth point.

10. Pp. 86-88 left out. The author continues to firm up his point.

11. Pp. 89f. left out.

Pietas Hallensis

Or an Abstract

Of the Marvellous Footsteps

Of

Divine Providence

In the Building of a Very Large Orphanage
or Spacious School
For Charitable and Excellent Uses
And in the Maintaining of Many Orphans
and Other Poor People

At Glaucha Near Halle
In the Dominions of the Kingdom of Prussia

Related by

the Reverend August Hermann Francke
Professor of Divinity and Minister of Glaucha

London, 1707

EDITOR'S INTRODUCTION

In August Hermann Francke we are confronted with the ascent of Pietism to an officially recognized movement in society. The institution he founded survived the Prussian, the Nazi, and the Communist eras and, as the "Franckesche Stiftungen," is still vibrant in 2002, comprising various schools for all ages, a library and archives, and a museum for mission history. It also houses the theological faculty of Halle. Within one generation the hope for a new reformation of the church had been translated from Utopia to the geographical locale of the city of Halle within the domain of the King of Prussia, from where it spread as an "official religion" even beyond the Prussian borders. The following selections introduce us to the early beginnings of an established piety.

Between Jean de Labadie (1610-1674) and August Hermann Francke (1663-1727) lies the work of Philip Jakob Spener (1635-1705), who in 1666, the same year de Labadie moved to Middelburg, was called to Frankfurt am Main as minister and senior of the clergy. The meetings of the *collegia pietatis* in Frankfurt began in 1670, and Spener's *Pia Desideria* was published in 1675.[1] Within a decade the ferment created by Spener's reform writing had reached the nooks and crannies of the universities as well as the local parishes. By July 1686 the *collegium philobiblicum*, a group of eight young "Magister," began to meet regularly every week in Leipzig with the express purpose of studying the Scriptures from a new perspective. Exegetical courses had almost entirely disappeared from the theological curriculum at that time. The new reading of the Bible also induced a new search for serious Christian living. Spener suggested to the group that each member ought to examine himself after their meetings, alone or together with a friend, as to whether or not his life conformed to the Word of God. The effort of examining himself gave Francke considerable trouble. In this mood he traveled to Lüneburg in 1687, where he had planned to be tutored by a well-known exegete. During his sojourn there he unexpectedly underwent a conversion experience which decisively determined the course of his life.[2]

The major milestones of Francke's life can be quickly enumerated. Having matriculated as a theology student at Kiel University in 1679, he changed to the University of Leipzig in 1684. A year later he had earned his Master's degree with the right to lecture at the university. In 1690 he became pastor at Erfurt, and in 1692 in Glaucha near Halle. After 1694 he combined his ministry with a professorship at

Halle University. In 1695 he founded the orphanage which became the nucleus of the so-called Franckesche Stiftungen, a complex of educational institutions preparatory to university training. Ministry, professorship, and the management of his educational enterprises contributed to an unusually rich life until his death in 1727.

Next to his conversion experience, it probably was Francke's encounter with Spener that became most decisive in the direction of his life. At the turn of 1688-1689 he visited in Spener's home for two months. He was then twenty-five, and Spener was more than twice his age. The companionship of these two men during the next decade became crucial for the impact of Pietism as a movement. "In the history of the Protestant church both appear intimately allied, Spener as the intellectual father and mover, Francke as the organizational genius of the new movement that now—although prepared for during a number of years and already quietly effective—struck the public eye in the form of Pietism. The person who led it into the thick of life, so that it could become a church-transforming power, was largely Francke."[3]

Beginning in 1697 Francke began to publish what one might call news brochures in regard to his budding Halle enterprises which he had started two years earlier. This was, if nothing else, a sheer practical necessity. The news of what could prosper with the support of hundreds of friends and benefactors had to be spread somehow. The first bulletin had still been read and approved by Spener for publication. Before long the growth of the enterprise called for more extensive information. Thus in 1701 the first edition of the *Marvelous Footsteps of Divine Providence* appeared. A year later a sequence sought to bring the reader further up to date. Francke continued with various additions for at least another decade.

The text of the selections is from the second edition of an abstract of various brochures translated into English by one of Francke's associates in London and published in 1707. It has to be kept in mind that it is an abstract. It is in this form that English readers for more than two and a half centuries have become familiar with Francke's thought. It seemed appropriate for the Francke portion of this volume not to introduce new selections from other writings of his, but to offer an overview from the volume in which he became influential in the English-speaking world.

In Chapter I we get an impression of how the Pietist enterprise emerged in Halle, how the first buildings went up, and what difficulties Francke encountered. Chapter II offers an insight into Francke's view of the hand of providence in it all. Chapter III outlines what benefits, spiritual and otherwise, church and society will reap from the new work. In Chapter IV we get a brief account of what went on in the various institutions that had sprung up. The appendix offers a summary of the actual self-estimate of the Pietist achievement. Interestingly it pinpoints the *terminus a quo* in 1688, the year Francke set out on his longer visit with Spener. In comparing the appendix with de Labadie's program one can sense, if not directly detect, the correspondence between the intended reformation of the Reformation and the actual outcome, even though one senses that the writer is not an unbiased judge or evaluator.

It would have been tempting to add a sermon of Francke's or a selection from his more theological writing. But nothing could show more clearly what was at the center of the early Pietist inroad into church and society than these primal documents of Francke's practical efforts. Cast into an institutional machinery, Pietism soon had an effective instrument of propagation to realize its social, missionary, and ecumenical aspirations—in some respects even beyond its wildest dreams. By the time the first decade of the eighteenth century had ended, Francke was corresponding with a man like the Congregationalist Cotton Mather in America, telling him: "Providence has cast your lot in *America*, a country abounding with numerous and barbarous nations, who, living without the pales of the Christian church, stand in need as much as those in the *East* of the saving light of the Gospel. I do not doubt, but it would be very agreeable to our missionaries, if a letter from your hand did give them a full account of all such *methods* as hitherto have been made use of for converting *West-India* heathen to the Christian faith.... I should have concluded my letter here, were it not that I thought a word or two relating to our *university* might possibly give you some satisfaction. As for the whole university in general, I shall say only that many look upon it as the most *flourishing* which is in Germany at this time....[4] Ever since—anteceding John Wesley for a goodly while!—Pietism has had a foothold in America.

In glaring instances of old English usage the text has been made more contemporary. It seemed fitting, however, to retain the quaint form of the old text to the extent that it conveys the flavor of its original setting. As with the Labadie selections, italicized portions of the text have been reduced to a minimum.

Chapter I

The Rise, Occasion, and Progress of this Undertaking

(1) There is a very ancient custom in the city and neighborhood of Halle in Germany, that persons who are disposed to make charitable distributions among the poor do appoint a particular day in which they order poor people to come to their doors to receive it. I willingly [says Francke] fell in with this commendable custom as soon as I came to be settled at Glaucha as minister of that place. I also felt constrained to give them some wholesome instructions, tending to the good of their souls, being grieved at the gross ignorance of this sort of people, which is one great cause of that wicked and dissolute sort of life to which the generality of them abandon themselves.

I therefore ordered the poor people to come every Thursday to my house and told them that now, for the future, both spiritual and temporal provision was designed for them. This exercise was begun about the beginning of the year 1694.

(2) The number of the poor increasing, I was obliged to try several ways to keep up the work once begun. I caused first an alms-box to be handed about every week to well-disposed students and all such as were willing to contribute to so good a work; but this soon proved a burden to some, and I laid it quite aside and fixed a box in my parlor with these words written over it: 1 John 3:17: *But if anyone has the world's goods and sees his brother in need, yet closes his heart against him, how does God's love abide in him?* And under it 2 Cor. 9:7: *Each man must do as he has made up his mind, not reluctantly or under compulsion, for God loves a cheerful giver.* This was intended for a tacit admonition to all that came in, to open their hearts toward the poor. This box was put up in the beginning of the year 1695.

(3) About a quarter of a year after the box was set up in my house, a certain person put into it at one time the value of eighteen shillings sixpence English. When I took this into my hands I said in full assurance of faith: this is now a considerable fund, worthy to be laid out in some important undertaking; therefore I will even take this for the foundation of a charity-school. I did not confer with flesh and blood about this affair, knowing well enough that human reason foreseeing a future want is too apt to be repulsed, and by its puzzling suggestions to break even the best ordered and concerted measures. So I caused the same

day as many books to be bought as cost eight shillings, and afterwards I got a student to teach the poor children two hours a day who then readily accepted these new books. But of twenty-seven distributed among them four only came to our hands again, the rest being kept or sold by the children left with them and never came near us again. After this we obliged the children to leave their books behind when they had learned their lesson. For the charity-school I got a place fitted up in front of my study and caused a box to be fixed on one of the walls, at the top whereof I set down these words: *For defraying the charges of putting to school poor children, and providing books and other necessaries for them*; Anno MDCXCV. And at the bottom Prov. 19:17: *He that has pity upon the poor. lendeth unto the Lord: And that which he hath given, will he pay him again.*

(4) After I had been thus employed for a while about this practice, I saw that all our endeavors upon these poor vagrants, and even upon such as seemed the most hopeful, were very much frustrated, because these good impressions which perhaps during their stay in the school were stamped on their mind were obliterated again while they were away. This therefore made me resolve to single out some of the children and to venture upon their maintenance as well as their education. This was the first occasion that prepared my mind for concerted measures to set up an orphanage even before I knew of any fund whereon to raise my design. Thereupon I experienced what usually happens when in faith one has courage enough to bestow a dime upon the poor: one afterwards will be willing to part with a dollar. Thus the first foundation of our orphanage was laid, neither upon any settled fund for this purpose, nor upon any sure promise of great persons and their assistance as has been since reported by some and conjectured by others, but entirely upon the providence and fatherly blessing of our great God who is able to do exceeding abundantly above all that we can either ask or think; and this taught me not to doubt the truth and certainty of things not seen.

(5) Such of the orphans as seemed the most promising I put out to persons of known integrity and piety, to be educated by them because we had poor children brought together before we had built a house to receive them. In the meantime the Lord inclined the heart of a person of quality to lay out the sum of a thousand crowns for the use of the poor, and two other persons supplied us with four hundred crowns to encourage the design on foot, so that we now were able not only to defray the charge of maintaining the orphans, but also to purchase a house into which we moved the twelve orphans (for that many we had now gathered) from the persons hitherto entrusted with their care. A student of divinity was appointed for the management thereof who had furnished them with diet, clothes, bedding and other necessaries, provided them

with good schooling, and so proved a father to them. This was begun in the year 1696, a week before Pentecost.

(6) After the children had been a while under this management and the Lord most visibly had relieved our wants, a larger project was set on foot, namely, to bring the orphanage to a firmer and more complete settlement, especially since we saw that the number of the children increased so much that the aforesaid house proved too small for them. All this excited me more and more to attempt the building of an orphanage myself, the renting of more houses scattered up and down being attended with too many difficulties.

(7) The Lord knows we had not so much as would cover the cost of a small cottage, much less such a building as might hold about two hundred people. Neither were there wanting those who made me aware of the rough and untrodden ways we were likely to walk if I would pursue the design. Others advised to set up a house of wood to save the expensive cost of a stone building. Some would say: What is this shack for? And by such and similar arguments I was almost prevailed upon to give up. But the Lord strengthened my faith with so powerful a conviction as if he had said expressly unto me: Build it of stones, and I will pay the charge. He supported me with such a presence of mind that I immediately resolved to lay the foundation of a new building. In the year 1698, July the 5th, the place was surveyed and adjusted. They began to break ground which was finished a few days later, on the 13th of July, when the foundation of an orphanage was laid in the name of God. However, the Lord had provided so much money as enabled us to procure some timber; but as for the building itself, I was now to wait upon God and from week to week to receive at his hand what he would be graciously pleased to furnish me with for carrying it on.

(8) The building was carried out successfully and at such a rate that in the year 1699, by the 13th of July, that is, within the space of one year, they were ready to cover it with the roof, although it did not escape the obstinate censures of ill-meaning people; it was sometimes censured on account of its bigness, and sometimes on account of its beauty and magnificence. But such people I used to tell in short: I must needs know of what bigness and value the house ought to be which is necessary to complete my design. But in the meantime I assure you that when the Lord has finished this house, he will be as able and rich to provide for the poor that are to lodge therein as he was before.

Chapter II

Of the Visible and Wonderful Providence of God, Attending These Endeavors to Establish the Orphanage and Charity-Schools from Their First Rise to This Present Time

(1) By the foregoing account any one may see in what manner our orphanage was begun, namely, not with a settled fund laid up beforehand, but with a hearty dependence upon the providence of God to which our care for a future supply was faithfully committed after it had carried us safely through the trials and difficulties of one day. Any understanding man may easily gather from this that the management of this business must have been now and then attended with many extraordinary perplexities which shall now be exemplified in some instances.

(2) Before Easter 1696, I found the provision for the poor so far exhausted that I did not know where to get anything towards defraying the charges of the following week (which happened before I had been used to such trials). But God was pleased to relieve our want by an unexpected help. He inclined the heart of a person (who it was, where residing, or of what sex, the Lord knows) to pay down one thousand crowns for the relief of the poor. This sum was delivered to me in such a time when our provision was brought even to the last crumb. The Lord whose work this was be praised forever, may He reward this benefactor with his blessings a thousandfold!

(3) At another time all provision was gone when the steward declared there was a necessity of buying some cattle to furnish the table and of providing 20 or 30 bushels of flour to be laid up, besides other necessaries, such as wood, wool, etc., if he would manage our business to the best advantage. Under these pressing circumstances I found one comfort which was a presence of mind in prayer, joined with a confident dependence upon the Lord who hears the very cry of the young ravens. When prayer was over I heard someone knock at the door, and when I opened there was an acquaintance of mine holding in his hand a letter and a parcel of money wrapped up which he presented to me, and I found therein fifty crowns which went a great way for the relief of our poor.

(4) In the year 1699, about *February*, I found myself in great

straits, and indeed it was an hour of probation. All our provision being spent and the daily necessity of the poor calling for large supplies, the divine saying made a deep impression upon me: *Seek first the Kingdom of God and his righteousness, and all these things shall be yours as well.* It banished temporal cares and turned the whole bent of my soul upon a close union with God. When I was now laying out the last of the money I said in my thoughts: Lord, look upon my necessity! Then leaving my chamber to go to the college where I was to attend my public lecture, I unexpectedly found a student in my house waiting for me who presented me the sum of seventy crowns, sent by some friends to support the orphanage, from a place more than two hundred miles away. And thus the Lord carried me through these trials, so that neither my heart was disconsolate nor our want was felt outwardly.

(5) Soon after this, there was want again in every corner. The steward brought his book and desired me to defray the weekly charges. My recourse was to God through faith. The expenses were necessary, and I saw not the least provision, nor any way to procure it. This made me resolve to retire into my closet and to beg the Lord's assistance in so pressing a necessity; but I designed first to finish the task I then was about, being occupied in dictating something to my students.

(6) Having done with this and preparing now for prayer I received a letter from a merchant intimating that he was ordered to pay a thousand crowns to me for the relief of the orphanage. This put me in mind of that saying, Is. 65:24: *Before they call I will answer, while they are yet speaking I will hear.* Nevertheless I entered into my closet but instead of begging and praying as I had designed, I praised and extolled the name of the Lord, and I hope that others who perhaps may come to read this will do the like together with me.

(7) About Michaelmas 1699, I was in great want again. On a fair day I took a walk, and viewing the bright skies I found myself remarkably strengthened in faith by the gracious operations of the Spirit of God, and these and the like thoughts were suggested to my mind: How excellent a thing it is for anyone, though deprived of all outward help and having nothing to depend on but an interest in the living God, the Creator of heaven and earth, to put his trust in him alone and not to despond in extreme poverty. Now though I well knew that the very same day I needed money, yet I found myself not cast down; just as I came home, the steward addressing himself to me said, "Is there any money brought in?" For it being Saturday he was to pay the workmen employed in the building of the orphanage. I answered, "No, but I believe in God." Scarcely was the word out of my mouth when I was told a student desired to speak to me who then brought thirty crowns from a person whose name he would not disclose. Hereupon I asked the stew-

ard how much he wanted at present. He said, "Thirty crowns." I replied, "Here they are; but do you want more?" "No," he answered. And so we were supplied in that very moment we wanted some relief, and even with that very sum that was required, which rendered the providence of God more conspicuous. [5]

I cannot forbear to mention here one instance more of a particular trial that fell upon the steward when the orphanage was being built, and of the extraordinary means whereby his sinking spirits were raised above the pressing difficulties. The substance of it was the following:

When the building of the orphanage was but just begun and the workmen employed to carry off the rubbish, the steward or overseer had to grapple with an abundance of difficulties; the laborers, one wanting stones, another sand or lime—tired him very much with their importunate demands. He was not in a condition then to afford a present supply because there were neither horses of our own, nor the least appearance of getting any hired for that use, since it was just the peak of the harvest season.

This now very much discouraged him and cast him into sorrow and perplexity. When finding his thoughts overcast with deep care and concern, he got away into his closet to be for a while by himself alone and in some measure to recollect the scattered powers of his mind. He was but just retired and venting himself to God in sighs and groanings when the master-bricklayer followed him at his heels and called him back out of his privacy. He told him that stones and other necessaries were immediately to be provided, otherwise the workmen would cease from their work and yet demand their full pay. This cast him down yet lower; however, he went away with the bricklayer, though he did not know how to break through these difficulties that surrounded him. When he came to the place where the men were at work, one of the laborers happened to find a piece of coin in the rubbish that we dug up. This he offered to the steward who took it, and looking on it he found the following words impressed thereon

YHWH	In English:	May Jehovah
Conditor		The Builder
Condita		Crown this
Coronide		Building with
Coronet		a happy Conclusion!

The reading of this inscription raised his sinking faith to such a degree that with great presence and readiness of mind he went to work again, hoping now that he should live to see the building brought to perfection, though at present, while they were breaking ground, we had to encounter many difficulties. In the meantime he contrived a way to get together such necessaries as the bricklayer had reminded him of, and within a few days it happened that two horses were made over to us and later two more and finally another, to help move the building ahead.

These instances I was willing here to set down so that I might give the reader some idea both of the pressing trials and happy deliverances we hitherto have met with; though I am sufficiently convinced that narratives of this kind will seem over-simple and fanciful to the great minds of our age.

Chapter III

Of the Advantages Which May Be Expected from Such Endeavors

(1) As for the spiritual benefits which may be expected to accrue from such endeavors and which we are chiefly to regard, they may easily be sensed, considering the main scope of the whole undertaking which is not to lay up provision for the body, but to save souls and convert them to life everlasting, and to use the former as a means only for obtaining the latter.

(2) Persons of candor and unbiased judgment may, without much difficulty, penetrate to the bottom of this affair by taking an impartial survey of the whole method whereby the work is carried on. The end we aim at and the means we use for obtaining the same are all of a piece. The Word of God is instilled into the children from their youth up. Unfeigned faith in our Lord Jesus Christ is laid for a foundation and a real sense of godliness, attended with a conscientious behavior, are the most material points, to the obtaining whereof earnest endeavors are constantly directed. As near as possible such men are chosen to manage the work of inspection and education as we can safely rely upon for their candor and integrity (as well as ability) on that behalf, expecting that they will render themselves worthy examples both by their words and actions. And if it happens that we unexpectedly make a mistake in our choice, the person convicted of any misdemeanor is obliged to make room for one that is better qualified. We prevent also, as much as in us lies, the spreading of infectious examples in the orphanage to save the children the better from the danger their tenderness exposes them to; and we take it very kindly when anyone offers to assist us with good advice towards forming a sound and complete scheme of education and training children accordingly.

(3) Two hours are set apart every day wherein all manner of poor, blind, lame and impotent persons, both such as live among us and such as come from the outside as likewise exiles and such as have lost their goods by fire, war, etc., and, in a word, all sorts of distressed people, are carefully instructed in the principles of religion, admonished, comforted, and at length supplied with some bodily relief. And this, I think,

every one will allow to be a method useful for the public good.

(4) Many poor orphans for whose education no one was in the least concerned and who otherwise of necessity had been drawn away from numberless disorders and most heinous sins have been withheld from the dangerous courses which a beggar's life might have exposed them to, and thus instructed in the Word of God that in time they may become good Christians and profitable subjects, which without question must contribute to the general good of the kingdom.

(5) Many boys of good physical condition and endowments which might make them fit for great undertakings if they would not lack the education which lies buried under the rubbish of ignorance, are now discovered and their pregnant genius (which would enable them to become great instruments of mischief) is cultivated and polished for the common benefit.

(6) For what else may such foundations be more properly accounted than schools contributing to the general good of the country? Here a foundation is laid for training good workmen in all trades, good schoolmasters, nay, good preachers and counselors; who of course hereafter will think themselves the more obliged to serve everyone, because they have both an experimental knowledge of God's providence from their youth up and the benefit of a sound and solid education.

(7) By such undertakings the country will be cleared by degrees of stubborn beggars, thieves, murderers, highway men, foot pads, and the whole pack of loose and debauched people who (as we may find if we search into the true reasons of such overflowing wickedness) commonly let loose the reins to disorder and impiety because they never imbibed so much as the least tincture of a good education. An undertaking of this nature may in due time put a stop to the fierce torrent of such headstrong vices and so contribute both to the spiritual and temporal good of the whole country.

(8) By such visible instances of alms well bestowed many may be encouraged the more willingly to contribute their charitable assistance towards the support of so necessary a work, who perhaps could not be otherwise induced thereto by the most persuasive rhetoric without such real demonstrations of the benefit resulting from their charity. By such charitable foundations people will be melted down more and more into a gentle and compassionate temper of mind, and have the intractableness and stubbornness of their natural disposition mollified and softened into mutual acts of charity.

(9) It is moreover a means to wear off, at least in some measure, that stain the Christian religion has contracted in our unhappy age,

namely, that there is such a crowd of poor helpless people in the midst of these who call themselves Christians, whereas the Lord requires of his people that there should be no poor among them. Hence it is no small honor to a city or country if the poor be regularly managed and maintained.

(10) The prayers of poor fatherless children and of all such as enjoy the benefit of orphanages are the strongest wall and fortress to defend a city and land from the invasions of any adversary; while on the contrary the tears and sighs of poor distressed people, who commonly express their grievances in that manner when they lie neglected under extreme necessity, draw down the dreadful displeasure of almighty God against that unhappy nation wherein such cruelty is practiced.

(11) A great many students, being every day employed in teaching the children, are prepared for a skillful management of schools up and down in the country, and having been used to an exact method and a plain and familiar way of discoursing with people even of the lowest capacity, they may prove instrumental to effect in some measure the reformation of schools so highly necessary at this time.

(12) Finally everyone, I think, will confess that a town or country is so much the more abundantly blessed with temporal advantages by how much effectual care is taken for the maintenance of the poor. Experience itself bears witness that those governments are the most flourishing which concern themselves most in providing well for the poor.

Chapter IV

The Present State of the Orphanage, Charity-Schools, and the Several Establishments Belonging Thereto, Erected by Professor August Hermann Francke at Glaucha near Halle

November 14, 1706

I

The orphanage (the building together with the several houses belonging to it has cost about 20,000 rix-dollars) presents to your view:

1. The education of the orphans, freely maintained in the orphanage. Their number at present 122.

They are distinguished as follows:
(1) Such boys as are of good physical condition are singled out from among the rest and instructed in languages, sciences, etc. Their number at present is 60.
(2) The rest are trained in principles of true piety and taught reading, writing, arithmetic, singing, and, after school hours, dressing, spinning wool, knitting, etc. Their number is 36.
(3) The girls are confined to a particular house, and besides the pious education aforementioned are also taught reading, writing, and arithmetic, spinning, knitting, sewing, etc. The bigger ones are also employed in household management. Their number is 26.

Both boys and girls are all day long confined to the presence of a master or mistress, even at the time when they have some hours allowed for diversion, taking either a walk into the gardens or into the fields. At night there are eight masters appointed to lodge among the boys and a nurse to be with the girls.
The general inspector of the schools has also the conduct of each particular school.

2. The management of the house, which is committed to a steward

appointed for that service. It is he who buys up all manner of provision
and sees everything done in its proper season, e.g., baking, brewing,
washing, killing of cattle, etc., and takes care to have the meat well
dressed and served at the usual hours and such diet prepared for the
sick as may best suit their particular circumstances, etc.

The persons who assist him in household affairs are (1) a lad
who goes on errands, (2) a man-servant, (3) the brewer, (4) one who
sweeps the rooms, (5) a watchman, (6) one who buys up such beasts as
are fit for provision and looks after them that are to be fattened, wherein he is assisted by his wife and two maid-servants, (7) a groom of the
stable, (8) two laundresses and certain other women employed in keeping the children clean, (9) the nurse who looks after the sick, (10) the
cook with some servants belonging to the kitchen.

These household affairs are partly directed by the physician,
partly by the inspector of the schools, together with some assistants.

There is a conference scheduled once a week to consult about
the affairs of this nature.

3. The apothecary's shop, which is managed by the apothecary
himself, a bookkeeper, four laborers, two apprentices and two who look
after the fire.

4. The printing-house. For this is appointed a foreman, four workmen, four apprentices, and a servant.

It is not only furnished with the common characters of German,
Latin, Greek, but also with the characters of most of the Oriental languages, as Hebrew, Syriac, Ethiopian, Slavonic, etc.

5. The bookseller's shop, headed by the bookseller and one ap-
prentice.

Both the printing-house and the bookseller's shop are under the
direction of the bookseller.

II

Ten schools belonging to the orphanage and furnished with
masters out of the seminary for school-masters hereafter
mentioned.

One of these schools is structured according to the method of the
Royal Collegiate School, and besides languages all manner of sciences
are taught therein. In this school such children are instructed as are
picked out from the poor orphans, besides other children both out of
this city and from other places, amounting together at present to 219.

These 219 boys being put into six classes have twelve masters.

The other nine are set up for the benefit of both boys and girls who, besides being taught the true principles of religion, are instructed in reading, writing and arithmetic, and the girls are familiarized with needlework, etc.

Most of these children are taught gratis and freely furnished with books, paper, pen and ink. Their number is at present 769.

The masters of these nine schools are 33 in number.

The number of all the masters teaching in the orphanage and in these ten schools amounts at present to 62.

The number of all the children, both in the orphanage and in these schools is 988.

They who have their maintenance free (both masters and scholars), subsisting upon divine providence, are 360 in number.

These schools have also a particular inspector appointed for them who occasionally is relieved by a vice-inspector.

III

A foundation for poor widows. Eight are maintained with a chaplain to say prayer with them twice a day, and a maid-servant to attend them.

IV

A program for the poor inhabitants of Glaucha by virtue whereof they collect alms once a week throughout the whole parish.

V

A program for beggars coming from outside our institution (see Chapter III, 3).

VI

The seminary for school-masters, from where all these masters are taken that are employed in the orphanage and the other charity-schools, the number of whom amounts at present to 70.

VII

The extraordinary tables in the orphanage. These are set up for students reduced to such straits that they do not know where to find a meal for that day. If these address themselves to the inspector of the orphanage by seven o'clock in the morning they are freely entertained at dinner every day to the number of 84. They are managed by one appointed especially for that service.

To these foundations more immediately relating to the orphanage we may also in some respect refer the following establishments:

VIII

The Oriental college of divinity wherein some masters of arts and students of divinity are constantly employed about cultivating and improving Eastern languages, instructing other young scholars in the same. The number of the former amounts to 10.

At present they are chiefly taken up with revising and publishing a Hebrew Bible; the like perhaps never has been published as yet, since it is based upon an account of the critical exactness of the text, diverse ancient manuscript copies, together with the Masora, being carefully perused, compared with many parallels and furnished with other remarks useful for setting the original text in its full luster and clearness. In this work they are advanced as far as the book of Judges, which is now actually in the press.

In this college are incorporated some Greeks, having come to pursue their studies here, and both they and such of the members of this college as have not the means to maintain themselves are supplied out of the common stock that providence has hitherto provided for us.

All the persons employed in this affair are confined to one house, two in a room, and have their meals all at one table.

The inspection of this college is committed to Mr. Michaelis, the present Professor of Eastern languages.

IX

The paedagogium regium: or Royal Collegiate School.

This is set up for young gentlemen instructed at their parents' cost and besides the fundamentals of religion, are taught the Latin, Greek, Hebrew, French, etc., languages, in addition to arithmetic, geography, geometry, history, astronomy, music, botany, anatomy, penmanship, etc. During their leisure time they may exercise themselves in gymnastics, drawing, glass-painting, etc.

They are confined to the constant inspection of a master even when school-time is over, to prevent all manner of irregularities in such hours as are allotted them for recreation which might otherwise wear off the best impressions made upon them during their stay at the school. The number of these young scholars is at present 65.

They have 12 ordinary masters and 7 extraordinary....[6]

An Appendix

Containing Some of the Most Significant Aspects of the
Work of Reformation, Carried on in the Lutheran Church
in Germany Since the Year 1688. Gathered by Some Strict
Observers of the Signs of the Present Time

(1) Catechetical exercises have been set up in a great many places
and carried on in a plain and more practical method.

(2) The Holy Bible and the New Testament in particular, having
been printed in vast multitudes, have either been given away gratis to
the poorer people, or at least sold at a very low and reasonable rate.

(3) John Arndt's book of *True Christianity* and other tracts treating upon the more spiritual part of religion have by the help of several
impressions been revived and read by great numbers of people.

(4) Spiritual and biblical conferences on more practical and ascetic subjects have been set up in several universities for the greater edification and reformation of scholars.

(5) Private exercises of piety have been set up in several places
for mutual edification and met with some encouragement and approba-
tion from the magistrates.

(6) The education of youth has been more seriously considered
than formerly. Several academics and new schools have been erected in
various places and some old ones refined from inveterate corruptions
and profane customs. Religion is now more concerned with the model-
ing and governing of children than heretofore.

(7) An easier and more comprehensive way and a method more
adapted to the capacity of children have been discovered and begun to
be practiced in many schools. Many authors, stuffed with mere heathenish trash and fancies, apt to leaven and to prepossess the minds of
children with a multitude of delusions and popular mistakes, have been
excluded, and others are taken in who savor of more Christian and substantial principles.

(8) The gentry up and down the country have been provided with
good and able tutors for the education of their children. This has proved
exceedingly helpful for spreading some degree of reformation throughout the country.

(9) There are likewise some public schools furnished of late with
able and faithful teachers.

(10) By these means children have in little time made considerable progress in learning which heretofore was not to be obtained except
through a great deal of toil and labor. Likewise there have been such
who in their younger years have given most visible proof of a real and
lively sense of piety.

(11) Several good establishments have been set up for educating

young gentlewomen in a sober and virtuous life. Hereby an abundance of fashionable mistakes obstructing a sound education of daughters has been rectified and a foundation laid for a future reformation of that sex.

(12) An abundance of spiritual hymns, composed by able persons, has been added to the old ones for the promoting of piety and devotion both in church and private families.

(13) Many writings of the Fathers and other pieces of a simple nature translated into the language of the people have been published for the edification of the learned.

(14) The intrinsic beauty and brightness of the primitive church has been more unfolded, and the vast degeneracy of the apostasy of the modern churches in all parties pointed out.

(15) Church history, especially that of the first ages, which by the wresting of partial men all along had been made to speak fair for every party, is now searched into more impartially.

(16) More particularly has the history about old and new heretics been handled in a more impartial manner. Many who long since have been put upon the black list of heretics by rigid clergymen begin to look fair again, nay, even to be deemed as the brighter instances of piety and religion in their age.

(17) A great many other writings dealing with several topics of practical divinity have been published for the increase of Christian life and knowledge.

(18) The article of justification, and its coherence with true sanctification or holiness of life, has been set in a clearer light than before.

(19) Many heavenly truths which in former ages have been hid, as it were, under a bushel have been revived and put on a candlestick to give light to those that are in the house.

(20) A better and more exact translation of the Bible into the language of the people has been attempted in these years.

(21) The abominable corruptions, both in church and state, have been laid open and methods formed for opposing further inundation by them.

(22) More particularly, many false prophets and greedy intruders into ecclesiastical positions have been stripped from their sheep's clothing, and their ravenous nature has been exposed.

(23) Likewise has the emptiness of many university professors (in whom the spirit of orthodoxy seemed to be eminently lodged and who were admired heretofore as pillars of the church) been discovered and their false light less followed.

(24) The crabbed notions and airy distinctions of school-divinity, whereby the simplicity of Christian doctrine has been all along confounded and adulterated, have been turned out of some colleges, and the sweetness and native beauty of true divinity begun to be relished and admired again.

(25) The superficial and common way of philosophizing, together

with Aristotle's heathenish trash has begun to lose its credit in some schools, and a philosophy more savoring of a Christian temper and raised on more solid principles set up again. Aristotle begins to retire before the light of the Gospel.

(26) The logical, metaphysical and homiletical schools have been less frequented and more time spent on the study of the Bible and exegetical conferences of theology, to a visible improvement of divinity-scholars.

(27) Several of the uneducated and simpler sort of people have been excited to bear witness to the truth and to confound the learned in their sophistries.

(28) The usual way of preaching, too much tied up with fallacious oratory and fitted for catching the applause of men, has been discountenanced and a plainer method, derived from power and inward experience, begun to be encouraged.

(29) The practice of spiritual priesthood, a duty almost lost among Christians, has been revived in some degree in these years.

(30) The natural itch of bespattering others with the stain of heresy begins to abate, and the edge of zeal is being turned against self-will and corrupt reason, the two great springs of all errors and heresies.

(31) Old errors and heresies the ignorant clergy would still like to rake into have been left buried, and the modern and fashionable ones opposed and confuted.

(32) Funeral sermons which used to be stuffed with I know not what vain praises and flatteries begin to be rectified, and the names of happy, blessed, dear brother, etc., more sparingly and with due regard bestowed on the deceased.

(33) Some remains of popish fancies and superstitions have been purged out more fully.

(34) The liturgy of the church or the Symbolical Books, raised by some rigid men to too high a pitch of authority, have been reduced to their true boundaries.

(35) Poetry begins to be refined from heathenish dregs and fancies and to savor more of the gravity of a Christian style and temper.

(36) In some universities the life, manner and conduct of young students has been more narrowly inspected and greater care taken, by timely discipline to form them into a pious and virtuous life.

(37) Public sermons have been more ordered for a general edification. Some entire epistles of the Apostles have been handled at large in sermons, in order to give people a full insight into the main scope and the whole drift of the Apostolic writings.

(38) The same writings of the Apostles have been handled with children in a plain catechetical manner. Hereby the very children have been enabled to give an account of the whole drift and purport of each epistle and book in particular and to read the Word of God with a greater gust than usual.

(39) University degrees have begun to be conferred with greater care and regard. Nay, in some souls degrees themselves have been degraded and their usual esteem laid very low.

(40) Brotherly love among differing parties of religion begins to sprout forth, and the rigid spirit of partiality, deadening brotherly love and embraces, begins to give way.

(41) The weakness of endeavors which only tend to unite people of differing persuasions into one religious form and outward way of worship, has been more fully discovered and the impossibility thereof better looked into than in the former ages. The uniting of people into one form, without the Spirit of Christ to raise a union on, begins to be thought of as labor in vain.

(42) The brightness of the Gospel of Christ begins to shine forth in most distant countries. The voice of the turtledove is heard in foreign parts.

(43) The distinction between the essential and accessory points of religion has been revived, and the former more emphasized in preaching by some than the latter.

(44) Likewise has the distinction between honest morality and true spiritual Christianity been set up again. The idol of heathenish morality has been turned out of some churches, and the pure Spirit of Christ as the only restoring principle of fallen nature permitted to come in again for rightly framing a Christian's life and conversation.

(45) The great points of the Christian religion, that is, of a living faith in Christ, likewise of regeneration, mortification, contrition, resignation, self-denial, imitation of Christ, and others of that nature, too slightly handled thereto, have begun to appear again and to be known among Christians.

(46) A great number of students of divinity who discarded religion too much and let loose the reins to disorder and impiety have been truly converted to God, and hereby a step made towards taking from the devil the usual armor wherein he trusts, i.e., the corruption of the clergy.

(47) Hence the number of people who by sinister means, unlawful practices and other underhand dealings and trickings get into church positions has begun to decrease.

(48) Several courts of princes and counts have been scented with the sweet savor of the Gospel of Christ, and hereby the spirit of vanity, too visibly influencing the courts of princes, has been checked and discouraged.

(49) Even some priests have been constrained to the obedience of faith.

(50) Several officers and soldiers, most of whom are apt to plead an exemption from the strict rules of Christian discipline, have begun to repair to St. John and to say: "Master, what shall we do?"

(51) Likewise has the Lord been pleased to ordain a praise unto

himself out of the mouth of babes and sucklings.[7]

(52) The powers of the Spirit have begun to appear in some in a manner more extraordinary and unusual.

(53) The number of prayer-books and communion-books, wherein too many people place the whole substance of their religion, has begun to abate, and people are taught more to mind their experience within them than the book without them. Some have laid aside the crutches, for fear of losing the use of their own limbs by walking too constantly upon them.

(54) The spirit of prayer has been revived in a more eminent degree. Many young people have united in prayers and thanksgivings, the like being but little practiced formerly.

(55) The dying-hours of some have been very edifying to the survivors. Many noble instances of a happy and comfortable death, and this even among children, have happened in these years.

(56) Many unlawful trades condemned by the Christian religion, but connived at by the superiors, have been left off by some people out of a principle of religion. And they themselves have chosen a more honest way of getting their livelihood.

(57) Stage-plays and other public nurseries of vice have begun to be opposed in the pulpit.

(58) Many stolen goods have been returned to the right owner.

(59) Some marriages have been transacted in a manner more becoming Christians. Jesus and his disciples have been called in to assist at some marriages.

(60) A spirit of piety is also stirring among servants. Some few families may be seen where the master and the whole household truly fear the Lord.

(61) In courts, both ecclesiastical and political (where Christ and his disciples too often are condemned), now and then a Nicodemus or a Joseph of Arimathea will start up in a manner unforeseen and speak a word in Christ's favor, nay, and even offer to take him down from the cross.

(62) Some violent persecutors and opposers of the work of reformation have been overtaken by divine vengeance and made an example to others.

(63) People have been generally more inspired with a generous and enlarged care for the poor and indigent. There is a widespread movement toward erecting hospitals and other good foundations for a regular maintenance of the poor.

(64) More particularly, care has been taken in some public foundations not only to make provision for the body, but to see bodily gifts and charities improved to their true and genuine end, namely, the conversion and salvation of souls.

(65) Many bad and inveterate customs with other licentious practices, authorized in a manner by a long and sinful connivance of the

magistracy, have been exposed by those wishing a reformation and checked by the rules of the holy Gospel.

(66) Several books of other nations, treating upon practical divinity, have been translated for an encouragement of our own nation.

(67) Many so-called laymen have, by publishing books on practical subjects of divinity, highly promoted the interest of religion.

(68) Several books done by pious gentlewomen and by other unlearned persons have found a favorable acceptance, and being entirely derived from inward experience of the work of grace, without any addition of human art and learning, have proved highly serviceable for influencing others with a spiritual taste of the riches of the Gospel.

(69) The apostolic and primitive Christian way of choosing ministers has been drawn [from Scripture] more impartially and published for a test of the modern clergy.

(70) The duty of clergymen and of spiritual fathers, set out in several branches and drawn up from primitive Christian writers, has been published for an encouragement of the modern clergy.

(71) Several university professors and other public teachers, sincerely intent upon the work of reformation, have chosen some fellow-laborers to help them.

(72) Many false enthusiasts and pretenders to sublime and uncommon operations of the Spirit have been detected, and some of them reduced to moderation and soundness of mind.

(73) The weakness, insufficiency and sottishness of human reason in matters of religion have been examined more carefully and she herself begun to be degraded from her dictatorship in spiritual affairs.

(74) More public-spirited men have been raised than formerly. Universal love has begun to enlarge some souls dammed up all along by the narrow precincts of private interest and party. Some beautiful blossoms of impartial love and enlarged benignity do begin to put forth.

(75) Some generous spirits begin to be more zealous, to propagate the interest of the Church universal rather than their own hereditary form and usual way of worship.

(76) Some have laid out vast sums to have the Scripture translated into and printed in foreign languages (e.g., Bohemian, contemporary Greek, etc.) for the universal benefit of whole nations.

(77) Some regiments of soldiers have been furnished with pious chaplains, and hereby care has been taken of carrying some degree of religion into war.

(78) A useful correspondence for promoting a mutual reformation in diverse nations has been started.

(79) Several great minds of the age have bowed to the Gospel and have become fools for Christ's sake.

(80) Some princes and persons of quality have been moved to great and generous acts of charity. Other people interested in the common good have been stirred up to support the missionaries in Malabar

with large and unexpected contributions.

(81) The Sacrament of the Lord's Supper has been rescued in some churches from the abominable profanation of the wicked, too promiscuously admitted by careless priests and clergymen, and has been confined to those only who after a strict search into their life and principles have been thought worthy partakers thereof.

(82) Some few politicians and great statesmen have been converted to God, and are now diligently employing their talents for the promoting of the glory of God and the benefit of others.

(83) The spirit of contention and bitterness, of strife and envy, of pride and passion, of sect and partiality, having all along covered itself with the fair and specious name of orthodoxy, of sound doctrine, of primitive church and worship, and with other fond and swelling titles, and judging all such as were not of its peculiar mode and form, begins to be stripped from its vain and shining attire and to be exposed in its own black and odious colors.

(84) The unhappy names of distinction between Lutheranism, Calvinism, and other human parties begin to lose their credit with some, and Christ begins to be more witnessed in preaching as the great and only restorer of fallen nature.

NOTES

1. Since a recent edition of this work is available, we need not bring selections in this volume.

2. Cf. Frederick Herzog, "August Hermann Francke: Francke's Conversion," *Mid-Stream*, 8:3 (Spring, 1969), 41-49.

3. Gustav Kramer, *August Hermann Francke: Ein Lebensbild* (Halle, 1880), 43.

4. Quoted from *Pietas Hallensis*.

5. In twenty-one more points (8-28) Francke adduces similar testimonies of the visible and wonderful providence of God making his work prosper.

6. The chapter concludes with a brief account of the costs for room and board.

7. See the *Account of the Children in Silesia*, printed in English in the year 1708, and another entitled *Early Piety Recommended in the Life and Death of Christlove Liveright von-Exeter*, printed in the year 1709. [Explanatory note of the original English edition].

FRIEDRICH CHRISTOPH OETINGER

Genealogy

Of the

Well-Grounded Thoughts of a Theologian

REUTLINGEN, 1818 - STUTTGART, 1859

EDITOR'S INTRODUCTION

Turning to Oetinger means entering that stage of Pietism when it becomes a "ripe fruit." We see its positive and negative aspects and can weigh its pros and cons through the eyes of one of its keenest observers and participants. In Oetinger's description of the development of his thought we can also touch, as it were, the whole history once more. Soon there appears the daughter of Johann Jakob Schütz, one of Spener's associates in Frankfurt, and later one of the early Pietist separatists who was in contact with the de Labadie group. There is August Hermann Francke himself whom Oetinger gets to know as a student. And there is Nikolaus Ludwig Graf von Zinzendorf whom Oetinger taught Greek and Hebrew. Interspersed among these people and around them appear the high and mighty, the poor and lowly, the scholars and the quacks, the esoteric and the simple folk, the knowing and the ignorant, the sober and the romantic.

But what of Oetinger himself becoming interested in talking to the spirits, or of his wonderment about the realities of the heavenly realm? What of his alchemistic studies and his speculations about the second coming of Christ? Do not these concerns lower him into a despised category of an eighteenth-century parson not to be taken too seriously? It is surprising however to note how many of these same concerns trouble many people also in today's world.

His end-time speculations do relate seriously to Oetinger's effort at making Pietism practical in the real world. Johann Albrecht Bengel, Oetinger's predecessor, in his path-breaking scriptural studies, had made a fervent prediction that 1846, less than a century away, would be the year of Christ's second advent. Oetinger shared in that end-time expectation with its accompanying social utopian associations, including a hope that private property would be abolished, class differences eliminated, and the state dissolved.

Scholars differ in interpreting Oetinger's views. Ernst Benz emphasized Oetinger's utopian/chiliastic support of freedom and made much of Oetinger's support of his Pietist lawyer friend, Johann Jakob Moser, called by some the "father of German national jurisprudence."[1] Moser's effort to better Swabian politics through reforms (including mercantilism) lost the support of his absolutist Duke Karl Eugen after Württemberg politics turned toward military affairs in the Seven Year's War. Moser suffered a brutal five-year imprisonment before being pardoned and allowed to return to politics! How much Oetinger continued to support Moser is disputed. Hartmut Lehmann insists that Oetinger like

Bengel and other Pietists always remained loyal to a reigning sovereign, seeking only to safeguard freedom in matters of faith.[2] Oetinger clearly wanted pietistic faithfulness to be responsible while avoiding fatal entangling alliances with politics.

Our selections up to a point are largely meant as introductions to Oetinger's work. Much of what Pietism is all about can be seen in the achievement of this one man. Conversely, his achievement illumines the antecedent history at its best. It ought to be added immediately, however, that Oetinger represents a brand of Pietism, not Pietism as a whole. In him we encounter piety as it found expression in Württemberg Protestantism. More so than Pietism of the Halle type or the Zinzendorf blend, Württemberg Pietism presented a well-balanced outlook. There was neither much pressure for conversion or good works, as in Halle, nor great zeal for community apart from the church, as in Herrnhut. That conversion was not ruled out, we can learn from Oetinger's own life. And that Christian community apart from the church was always within the ken of Württemberg Pietism, we can learn from him. Even so, at its center this Pietism retained integrity in its church orientation in terms of the great tradition. There was also no fierce attack upon art or "pagan" scholarship. In fact, Oetinger sought by every means available—art, philosophy, alchemistic studies, contacts with people of other faith persuasions, etc.—to broaden his horizon of experience: "I have thoroughly studied mathematics, philosophy, and everything that belongs to the knowledge of our present age." (pp. 161ff.). There was in principle nothing stuffy about his Pietism. It sought to celebrate life and to see life as the principal focus of all thought.

Somehow in Oetinger one senses what was best of Protestantism as mediated to the great German poets and philosophers that followed Pietism. It was in this form that Kant, Hegel, Schelling, and even Goethe got to know Protestant Christianity. Oetinger's thoughts on "wisdom in the street" and on the "sensus communis" that reaches far beyond the church; his deep interest in science, his emphasis on experience in the construction of theology and faith, and his vision of "bodiliness" (corporeality) as "the end of God's ways" anticipated many present-day spiritual and theological currents.

Oetinger's brand of Pietism became influential in philosophy because it struggled with philosophy itself. "I will let the Leibnizian philosophy pass after I have chopped off its head and put the idea of life in its stead."[3] Oetinger believed that Leibniz's philosophy remained too much in the sphere of the abstract-formalistic.[4] Life for him remains open to sensibility, but to reason it is largely impenetrable. The possibility of holding together nature and spirit was central to Oetinger. So God in Godself unites indissolubly the eternal powers. The wheel becomes the great symbol of the divine. All of life is rotation or revolution like the wheel. Not in the abstract, however. Only in regard to bodiliness. The body is not merely appearance. It belongs to the very nature of the real: "Corporeality is the end of God's ways."[5]

Schelling continued along this line. All of European philosophy since Descartes seemed to have proceeded as though nature did not exist. The real, however, is significant as the *body* of the ideal, which means that nature is the body of the spirit. In the interpenetration of the ideal and the real the real nature of the world is to be found, Oetinger insisted.

It is obviously impossible to pack even the most significant data of Oetinger's influence on philosophy into a brief introduction to the text. One may turn to the Introduction to the volume as a whole, where Oetinger's significance is discussed more fully, or consult pertinent literature.[6] At this point we can only underscore the need to take a look at the vast impact of Oetinger's life and work.

The present work is often referred to as Oetinger's autobiography. Oetinger himself did not use the term. His purpose was not to bring autobiographical data per se, but to show how his ideas developed, that is, how his mind grew. Therefore the title, "*Genealogy of the Well-Grounded Thoughts of a Theologian*," most adequately conveys the purpose of the work.

There is good reason, however, why Oetinger's work has been referred to as autobiography. For it was Pietism that introduced in Germany the genre of autobiographies. It took just so much interest in the personal experiences of faith, that is, the penchant for self-observation in regard to one's religious growth, in order to make the life of the individual the subject matter of literary self-revelations. In this respect, Oetinger's work is very much a reflection of what was already taking place, and what was still to come with even greater forcefulness in secular as well as religious literature.

The most adequately scholarly source for Oetinger's writing is Karl Chr. Eberh. Ehmann, *Friedrich Christoph Oetingers Leben und Briefe als urkundlicher Commentar zu dessen Schriften* (Stuttgart, 1859. Ehmann hereinafter), on which the present translation is based. The text has also been compared with the most recent edition of Oetinger's work by J. Roessle, *Selbstbiographie* (Metzingen, 1961). The other editions have been consulted as well (the earliest appearing in Reutlingen in 1818), especially the Julius Hamberger edition (Stuttgart, 1845. Hamberger hereinafter), which was the first to bring Oetinger's work as a separate volume under the title of *Autobiography*. The two earlier editions, the 1818 one included, had appeared in collections.

An original manuscript of the work, written by Oetinger himself either in 1762 or 1764, is unavailable. It appears that several handwritten copies of the original text had been passed from hand to hand by the time the first edition of the text appeared in 1818. Ehmann knew of four copies, of which he was able to use three for the compilation of his text. In comparing the various editions that appeared before 1859 with the Ehmann text, it becomes clear that Ehmann was able to collect the original materials in the most coherent way imaginable. Since Oetinger did not edit his own work, a certain mystique will continue to surround it, especially also since his way of expressing himself reflects the somewhat clumsy use of the German of the eighteenth century under the influence of Latin and French as prevalent in German scholarship and culture of that day.

For the footnotes we have been able to draw upon Roessle, who was the first to present an annotated text. The Roessle notes have been partly condensed so as to offer American readers brevity as well as clarity, and partly added unto so as to make the text more readily accessible to further research. While a goodly number of yet additional notes could have been introduced, we decided to stay within limits so as not to overburden the text. The present notes should make the message of the text sufficiently clear.

Since the text itself contains ample data for chronological orientation, suffice it to say that Friedrich Christoph Oetinger was born May 6, 1702, and died February 10, 1782, spending most of his life as a clergyman and prelate in Württemberg, Germany.

FRIEDRICH CHRISTOPH OETINGER'S GENEALOGY OF THE WELL-GROUNDED THOUGHTS OF A THEOLOGIAN

Based on:

(1) the voice of wisdom in the street, that is, philosophy,
(2) the meaning and spirit of Holy Scripture, and
(3) events decreed by divine providence.

I

God forms all thoughts by special means.

Every thought of things divine that lasts and which originates on the basis of these three means is a revelation of God. There is no supernatural effect of God's activity which does not also include a natural one (Ps. 18:7-16). But there are many natural effects which do not include anything supernatural. This is my presupposition.

If the thoughts of a theologian are not formed at the same time by these three means, if only one of the three informs them, a faulty, deficient, and even insincere knowledge results, unfit to be taught, overdoing things here and neglecting them there, reaching too high one time and too low another, demanding of others either the impossible, or superfluous, or incomprehensible things which one does not do oneself and by which one contradicts oneself in one's own acts.

II

The means by which God teaches men.

Whatever God does he does mediately as well as immediately. We do not comprehend the immediate. It transcends all reason, occurring sometimes in a general way, touching many men at the same time, and sometimes in an act of gracious governance of the individual. The mediate, however, is comprehensible; it is evident in conscience and bears certain marks of the divine presence. If somebody wants to be instructed by the immediate only, he resembles Eliphaz who depended on nothing but voices of angels (Job 4:13). If somebody wants to be instructed by the voice of wisdom in the street only, he resembles Bildad. And if somebody wants to be instructed by Scripture alone, disregarding events decreed by divine providence and the voice of wisdom in the street, he resembles Zophar. These three would arrive at a sectarian and purely imitative knowledge. Elihu teaches us to combine everything and God approves of him in his very words.

God teaches men what they already know. He forms everyone's heart. But that does not happen only directly, but through everything by which God, from within and from without, influences men. Everything has to serve him, everything is his instrument; fire, hail, and storms execute his word (Ps. 18:8-16). After the fall God influences everyone from within through his spirit, like the eternal strength within all creatures, or like the warmth that pervades all beings. From within he effects a hidden longing for himself, a hidden restlessness if one misses his promptings; anxiety if one wills contrary to his will or against the order which he established after the fall or if one hurts one's soul through vices. He causes fear, longing, desire, trust; in brief, the expansion or contraction of the heart of which so much is written in the Psalms.

Seneca and Cicero express it just as well as the proverbs of Solomon because it is a universal act of God and because he effects knowledge of himself (Rom. 1:19-21) in everyone in the same way: "A holy spirit indwells within us, one who marks our good and bad deeds, and is our guardian. As we treat this spirit, so are we treated by it." (Seneca)[7] "Law is not a product of human thought, nor is it any enactment of peoples, but something eternal which rules the whole universe by its wisdom in command and prohibition." (Cicero).[8]

Externally God works through history, through reward and punishment, either related to or apart from, man's virtues and vices but usually related to them. He acts on us through special opportunities which we either miss or use, through good instruction and advice, through examples, through public disputations, whereby the truth is carefully examined and taught at the universities, in short, through a thousand things, just as in the teaching of the structure of the human body thousands of blood vessels and mutually supportive functions are described. In natural science they take the place represented in the moral realm by Proverbs and Ecclesiastes. Here the innumerable internal and external effects of wisdom are described as well as the witness of the eternal word to Christ. If someone disregards these, he probably will say: "I stick to Paul, to Peter, or Apollos, or to Christ." But all this will show a sectarian zeal which will bring forth quarrel, restlessness, agony and pain in the heart because he despises the witness of wisdom to Christ and yields to his own arrogance. Thus he cannot become certain of Jesus' spirit in his word because the spirit of Jesus teaches by means of external aids.

The Cerinthians,[9] in contrast to St. John, have preferred a direct Quaker-like knowledge of God to the water and blood of Jesus and his spirit. This caused much confounding error. It is not surprising that true integrity is hard to find today, since the church exists in dispersion. It is difficult to discover this integrity if one does not most honestly use everything that helps to make patience perfect. Have salt in yourselves for peace, or you will be salted with another fire (cf. Mk. 9:49f.). We need this especially if we want to discern nature and grace.

(1) Wisdom in the street, the *sensus communis*, teaches us everything which belongs to primal wisdom. Therefore the general emphasis on logic, metaphysics and mathematics at the universities is a tool of the ever-present wisdom, even though the proper application of these is often lacking among the students. And an Eliphas is easily tempted to despise this wisdom, because he does not consider that spirit and grace use nature as a tool, as the whole New Testament shows.

If Jesus Christ would walk on earth today he would speak completely differently from a present-day Eliphas, Bildad and Zophar with their pious opinions based on secondhand information. He would want to have his words understood according to the Proverbs of Solomon. All who assume that they can get along without a high regard for these words will be ruined, because they separate what belongs together: Scripture and the power of God.

(2) The meaning of Holy Scripture makes truth whole. Without it nothing certain can be determined in divine matters. However, since the mere letter kills and confuses—a fact which all sects use in their defense—the Spirit and the power which drive us to act according to the complete likeness and relationship of all parts to the whole have to be added. For it is the Spirit who gives life. Below every letter of Scripture lies the Spirit. Even if I write something under the influence of the good Spirit, the reader might miss the meaning on account of a shortsighted, wrong interpretation of some words. However, if someone grasps everything as a whole with singlemindedness of heart, he will not miss the Spirit.

The Galatians missed the Spirit as soon as they were overcome by fear of the persecution of Christians and were tempted by a desire for the prerogative of the Jews. The Corinthians missed the Spirit as soon as they thought of Peter and his sectarian apostle (2 Cor. 11:4) higher than of Paul, as soon as they were irritated by Paul's alleged carelessness, weak voice, small stature, his purported acting in a worldly fashion (2 Cor. 10:2f.), persecution and other unimportant matters. Paul pointed to the most important matter, to gold, silver, precious stones which should be built upon Christ in the Spirit. He pointed to the perfection of understanding which wisdom teaches through the order of things (1 Cor. 14:20). He referred them to God's providential ordinances by which they could see that Paul was not inferior to Peter. And Paul convinced them by means of a logical argument, so that they who had initially received the Spirit would not lose it by drawing wrong conclusions.

A single-minded heart which does not have much confidence in itself, but puts the smallest thing to a personal test, does not permit a decision to arise merely on grounds of trust in prayer or the fervor of good
will or the loss of intensity in searching and knocking. Where it cannot
put a matter to a test, it suspends all judgment and waits until developments offer more facts for a certain conclusion.

There is an immediate power of Christ in the heart: there is a peace
that passes all understanding. These two are very important. But one is
easily led astray if one does not join the mediate to the immediate. The
immediate is often like a current of the love of God. Ruysbroek[10] says
in a beautiful way one should resist through the illumination of reason
(see the article on "Grace" in my *Biblisches und emblematisches
Wörterbuch*).[11] I myself can bear testimony to this lofty matter. During
my travels I have had occasion to observe this not merely in passing,
but in close contact.

Likewise one is misled, however, if one overrates the mediate over
the immediate and despises, or looks down upon, all prophecy. Thus
there is danger on all sides that those who want to protect themselves
on grounds of Scripture alone (Jer. 8:8,9) are misled by the critical understanding of the letter. They do not permit themselves to be drawn to
the certainty of the understanding and to be sanctified in truth, either by
the voice of wisdom in nature to which the Holy Scripture points so often, or by divinely decreed events.

It is necessary today to write about the letter and the spirit in a spiritual way. Sincere souls grasp it already. For their benefit it would not
be necessary to write about it, but others still need it.

III

The events decreed by divine providence

also greatly aid the certainty of the understanding. They are so far-
reaching that one cannot describe them in a few words. All historical
events come from God's hand. Jesus rules all events. Therefore one
should have a seeing eye and a hearing ear. Otherwise one fails a thousand times by trusting the critical approach. The Holy Spirit does not
only work through direct influences and contacts, but he clothes himself
in innumerable natural and supernatural processes.

Detailed Narrative of a Theologian Who Used These Three Means From Childhood On, Though Not Without Interruption.

I have been asked to put in writing how my thoughts in theology became well-grounded and how they developed historically one from the
other, by means of these three indirectly combined aids through which

God's spirit works sometimes naturally, sometimes supernaturally, or even in both ways simultaneously. I will do it, although it will be difficult to describe the development.

Early Childhood[12]

Those who took care of me in my tender childhood when I was a small baby tell me that I was called the naïve Friederlein. In Schorndorf a very intelligent young girl by the name of Agnes Wölfing brought me up. I still remember her seriousness from the time I was in her arms. They say my face did not show much expression, that I was capable of staring for a long time into one corner, and that I was of a quiet nature, even though I evidenced considerable urge for activity. So they gave me this name.

Perhaps it does not amount to much to mention such things. But since God forms the heart of man—according to the witness of all Psalms and all testimonies of Holy Scripture—by means of diverse outward occasions and occurrences as well as through inward secret traits, it serves to show how well-grounded thoughts, and not merely mirrored, imaginary ideas, are being produced and formed (of which I have written in the booklet called *Etwas Ganzes vom Evangelium*).[13]

First Years of Schooling

When I returned from Schorndorf to my birthplace[14] I had the brother of my mother, M. Wölfing, as a teacher. He was a feeble man with bad eyesight, who therefore was not very apt in teaching, but he was Godfearing. He made me learn many songs by heart. At one time, between the sixth and seventh year of my life, I lay down to sleep beside him as I was used to. Before falling asleep I had to recite by rote a whole rosary of songs. Finally I got a little impatient and thought: if I only knew what I am praying! I came to the song: "Lift yourself up to God, you distressed soul." Knowing nothing of distress I felt a strong urge to understand what it would be like to lift oneself up to God. I struggled inwardly before God, and behold, I felt myself being lifted up to God. I prayed my song to the end. There was no word in it that did not leave a distinct light in my soul. I have not experienced anything more joyful in my life. In the time following, this had the effect that when a heavy thunderstorm appeared with thunderclaps and lightning, which made my father hide behind the bedcurtain, I confidently thought: I know how to pray to God. It remained like this for a goodly while. The experience influenced my whole life, since I regarded it as a model: everything I learned I would have to understand the same way. That caused me afterwards to look down upon the poor ideas of my teacher. What I heard did not satisfy me, because it did not measure up to the indescribable reality of those first thoughts.

During the night I also had quite vivid dreams of the prisons of the damned after death. I saw an old dignified matron opening the cells with a key, so that I looked deeply into the dungeons of the various wretched souls and heard their cries. This was the most terrible of the impressions of that time, just as the experience with the song was the most agreeable. Both had much influence on the later formation of my thoughts.

Meanwhile these impressions faded under the harsh treatment of my father, my houseteacher and my preceptor Kocher, who was a true Orbilius[15] with beating, hitting, and senseless punishments occasioned by two or three words I did not know by heart. This made my life so miserable that I finally learned to curse and impatiently cried out in the words I had read in Hübner:[16]

> Nature, thou hast otherwise
> created many a monster.
> Oh, why hast thou not turned me
> into one also!

Thus I had to spend my life until I was in my fourteenth year, and the anger and the rage made me turn so spiteful that I cursed like a sailor from Hamburg. And this resulted in a life cut off from God and in many sins of youth, but never without much restraint and protection.

Something happened about the time I reached my fourteenth year. At the time my father had made me copy all the sermons of the Reverend[17] Hochstetter and of the assistant pastors Bilfinger and Gütler, and I had to pray on my knees with my father, especially on Sundays. One Sunday my mother, a noble and intelligent soul, but inexperienced in the inner life, ordered me to read in the Bible, as she wanted to take a walk. She said, "I command you not to get up from the chair until you have read several chapters from the Bible." I thought: indeed, you can well command; you take a walk, and I am supposed to read! But I reconsidered and said to myself: because I have to, I want to! I found the prophet Isaiah and skimmed through the pages here and there. Since I knew I had turned bad and had neglected the promptings of God in my childhood, I sensed all my evil very deeply. But I had a secret longing to return to God, especially because I was terribly afraid of thunderstorms since that time. My eyes fell upon the passage Is. 54:11-14. I read with eager desire, I sighed and said to myself: how beautifully this reads! If these good things should pertain to me, it would be worthwhile to become converted. Now I continued to read in the chapters with new yearning and found, especially in the last chapter, that God was not talking to me, but to Jerusalem and the people of Israel. The flow of ideas appeared to me inconceivably beautiful. They remained constantly on my mind. But [later] I forgot them again because of the harsh chastisements of my preceptor and my house-teacher. Nevertheless, this experience became the basis for my booklet *Etwas Ganzes vom*

Evangelium which appeared in 1739.

I felt hostile towards my house-teacher and my preceptor so much that I could have taken my revenge on them with poison. I made the decision that if my preceptor would again, because of several words, use the switch on my—pardon me—posterior, I would rather let my arm and leg be torn out or else run away and go by boat via Holland to America. These grim intentions suppressed my delight in the dramatic style of Holy Scripture which I had observed already. I looked at the portrait of my oldest deceased brother with tears and sighs and thought: oh, if only a human being, a brother, were alive with whom I could share my plight! My house-teacher made me so indignant that I— without having learned it from him—put my laments into verse. Thus I learned to write German verse out of anger. Frequently during that time I also wrote odes quite suitable to various special occasions. The anger made me eloquent even if I did not make verses, because I sat down and wrote my father a Latin speech against my preceptor threatening that if he would not take me out of the school of this tyrant I would do something which the parents would not expect me to do. My father noticed that I was serious about this and took me out of school.

Now I read all the books which I found, especially historical works. I begged for money everywhere, just in order to be able to buy new books. I bought all the so-called "States of Europe, Asia, Africa, and America." At the same time I also read many books on travel, concerned myself intimately with the history of nature pertaining to all areas of the world, to plants, animals, and other rarities which filled me with a unique joy. I grew fond of the idea of becoming a lawyer and government official, and this all the more since I had an ambitious mother who told me a thousand things about what a charming statesman, poet, orator, handreader and physiognomist the chancellor and privy councilor Mascowsky[18] of Darmstadt had been whom she had known from her youth as the prefect's daughter in Tübingen and who always had exchanged beautiful letters with her. Meanwhile I devoured Gessner's *Natural History*[19] with greatest enthusiasm.

One night I was still reading in this book at one and two o'clock when all of a sudden I heard an outcry that mother was about to die. She was overcome (in the year 1715) by a sudden hemorrhage, and she was lying on the bed like dead. I saw it with horror, went immediately again upstairs to my room, threw myself before God on my face and asked for her life in full confidence. My mother told me afterwards that she heard me, more than all the others, crying and praying. After it seemed, however, that she had become lifeless I defied God and said: "Are you not a cruel God? I believed so strongly that I had prayed her back to life, and now she is dying anyway!" But she improved through the *essentia dulcis*,[20] and I was comforted knowing that God had answered my prayer.

All these providential events prepared me for my future thoughts about God in physics and theology.

In the Monastery School of Blaubeuren (1717-1720)[21]

After mother had recovered she took a trip to Blaubeuren to see Professor Weissensee[22] of the monastery school who later was Prelate[23] in Denkendorf. After she had come back she told me beautiful things of the politeness, eloquence, and grace of his speech and said, "This is the man you have to go to when you enter the monastery school." Soon afterwards it happened that I was accepted by His Most Gracious Highness[24] at the monastery school of Blaubeuren. Among the twenty-five students who took the first examination I finished second-best. That was in the year 1717, when I had already entered my fifteenth year.

When I was in Blaubeuren I had Weissensee as a teacher and Johann Wendel Bilfinger[25] as prelate. Weissensee was not only at home in natural history, but was also a deep mystical theologian, the most outstanding poet in Württemberg, the most wonderful orator, and the most accurate surveyor. I spent three years at Blaubeuren. Weissensee imparted to me completely new ideas about mysticism, prayer, and about Telemach's education by Mentor from the well-known book by Fénelon.[26] He interpreted this French writer beautifully for us. When Duke Eberhard Ludwig[27] came to Blaubeuren I immediately wrote a French poem for him.

Soon after this, Professor August Hermann Francke[28] came to Blaubeuren. He changed Weissensee's mystical and Arnoldian ideas[29] and gave beautiful, impressive speeches for the seminarians which moved me very deeply. We also copied his sermons in Ulm, and Francke afterwards always sent me his regards from Halle.

The wife of prelate Bilfinger was an extremely intelligent lady. She gave me much good advice and told me many things about her son's abilities, his research and habits, and she predicted a high position for him which he indeed later attained. This man, Georg Bernard Bilfinger,[30] was at that time with Wolff[31] in Halle, returned afterwards to Blaubeuren, became associate professor of philosophy at Tübingen and later professor of physics in Petersburg. After returning home he was professor of theology at Tübingen and finally became privy councilor and minister of state who ruled over the whole land of Württemberg.

When I returned home occasionally, I learned that there was a chemist, Dr. Kirchmajer, in Adelberg. I had an urgent desire to see him, because I thought chemistry would penetrate to the essence of things more effectively than other disciplines. But I never got there.

I came again to Blaubeuren. Weissensee had the commendable habit of asking every seminarian after the public evening prayer how he had spent his day, which characteristics of God had come near his heart and which of his thoughts and resolutions tended towards the good. He asked me often, and I answered according to my experiences. But one time I did not know what to say. He asked: "What have you read today?" Answer: "Boileau-Despréaux!"[32] "What did you find there?" Answer: "That being ashamed of the good is the root of all misery." [*La honte du bien c'est là de tous nos maux le fatal fondement.*] It pleased him very much. And he said this was just as good as the application of a Bible verse. Another time he asked again. Then I said that already before coming into the monastery I had read in Isaiah upon behest of my mother and had found that the sayings there were aimed at whole peoples and not at individual persons. And I wondered how I could know that they also pertained to me. He answered me, that what was said to all was also said to me. But I was silent and thought to myself: I knew that already. For a long time I did not get a sufficient answer to this question from anyone until God himself showed it to me through the providential events of my life. For it happened two years later that I became involved in a conversation with the Inspired[33] in my hometown of Göppingen where they often met, because Friedrich Rock[34] was born in the Göppingen district. There the insufficient answer which Weissensee had given me was complemented in a way which gave me, logically as well as spiritually, sufficient certainty.

In the Monastery School of Bebenhausen (1720-1722)

From Blaubeuren I came to Bebenhausen into the higher monastery school. My prelate was then the old Dr. Johann Andreas Hochstetter[35] whose son followed him later in this position. My preceptors were Weissmann and Canz,[36] who later became the famous professor in Tübingen. From Bebenhausen I always went to Tübingen and visited associate professor Bilfinger who advised me how I should study everything in logical order and stay with the basic principles of every subject for a long time. Upon his suggestion I also read the logic of Crousaz[37] seriously.

I was a good-looking young man, very lively and quick, and famous for my diligence in study. People therefore tempted me now and then to study law; this way they would like to have me as son-in-law and help me to become a very important person in the world. Especially the privy councilor and director Osiander[38] to whom my mother was related had strongly prodded her. She kept bothering me with the idea that I should give up theology, for which my father had destined me, to study law according to Director Osiander's advice. Therefore I read the books of Thomasius.[39] I imagined the study of theology to be difficult, especially because of the administration of Holy Communion which already in my boyhood filled me with horror. And I eagerly pursued the thought of becoming a statesman. However, since my father, who already from my birth had destined me for theology, threatened me with a kind of curse if I should act against his decree I became very anxious on account of this matter. I wrote whole pages filled with considerations, for and against, read Fenelon's *Véritable Politique* and could not come to a decision.

Herr Weissmann and Prelate Hochstetter noticed my quandary and treated me with great sympathy. Herr Weissmann said: "Why do you waste time instead of studying law? You should follow your heart's desire. You fit better into the world than into the clergy. You have the talent to become a statesman. I cannot picture you as a devout man." Then I said to myself: "But sir, how little do you know what my innermost thoughts are like! My bent toward godliness is much stronger than meets the eye!"

Prelate Hochstetter often reminded me to make a decision and not to get hung up on uncertainty. But I could not come to a conclusion. Finally Prelate Hochstetter, a very straightforward and sincere gentleman, ordered me to come to his room for this very reason and commanded me, as it were, to make up my mind. I said I had as many reasons for as against the matter, and therefore could not do it. So he said: "Then go to Tübingen to your cousin Elias Cammerer[40] (whose wife was the sister of my mother), and what he tells you to do you should do!" I went there and he said: "Go and leave the monastery; you are not made for the cloth." But I answered: "Sir, you don't know how I feel. I fear God in secret." This is exactly what I told the prelate. Then he decided: "Go to your room, fall down on your knees before God and pray for a clear decision!" I made a dart for my room, fell down on my knees and wanted to pray, but I could not, because I had as much interest in the world as in God. I had the same experience as Augustine who also was torn between two options when he wanted to become converted to God.

Meanwhile I started thinking: what will it amount to later if you wear the most stylish clothes, if you are in command and reach the top of the ladder? It is still better to serve God. *Deo servire libertas*—to serve God is freedom! Then I called upon God to empty my soul of all worldly intentions, and this happened immediately. I was now completely determined to stay with theology, and I told this immediately to my prelate.

From this hour on I was a different person. I no longer wore elegant clothes. I gave up my social life. I talked little and read in God's word and no longer in Cicero and other secular writers.

The seminarians saw my transformation and were surprised. Through a little window in my room they often saw me pray and came to me with the wish to have me pray with them. I did so, in a simple way.

I got so tired of studying for worldly purposes that I thought I wanted to study theology right away and leave philosophy alone. Thus I began reading Hoffmann's *Synopsis*[41] and wrote an abstract of it on a long piece of paper which I could wrap around my finger and roll up and down. I still have this roll.

I read Goodwin's[42] books, made abstracts from them on such rolls and all of a sudden wanted to understand the basis of theological truths as clearly as I once had understood the song "Lift yourself up to your God...." But I could not find clarity there. I especially worried about how I could be sprinkled with Christ's blood. I wanted to believe it if indeed someone sprinkled me. I wanted to know how Jesus had come with water, blood, and spirit and how this was to be understood. But I could not grasp it in any way, neither through prayer, nor through research. Nothing satisfied me.

This fearsome searching wore me out completely. I lost weight, and a swelling developed at my neck which could not be cured and which was supposed to be cauterized. Therefore, I had to go home, and there the sins of my youth, the curses against my preceptors and other sins came back to me. Then I experienced the psalms of repentance and felt what David felt.

The Encounter with the Inspired[43]

According to my decision of complete world-denial, I took to the road again from Bebenhausen to meet with the Inspired. At that time, a person by the name of Kessler, a rector from Memmingen, was present. He told me how many people had been moved by the words of the Inspired and had been influenced to make a new decision. This caused me to consider the matter very carefully, and I thought: these people suffer chains, prison and beatings on account of their witness; our pastors and conference superintendents never suffer anything. These people look much more like the apostles than the pastors. Thus I was challenged to examine the matter exactly and to find out according to God's truth whether they were God's servants or were deceived by their own mind. I acquired their books about inspiration[44] and read them all. I compared this with the calling and words of all the prophets, but found that the Inspired, while taking over many characteristic phrases from the prophets, did not match their style and their power to witness to the issues of the kingdom. Their moral views seemed all right to me, but altogether too popularized. In the prophets, however, I saw a sacred stage on which the highest and lowest things were joined in such a scene that I could not by far compare the words of the Inspired with it.

At the time of my conversion I had decided on never trusting even my most serious objections to a certain matter, but on always being concerned about the possibility of being deceived by my preference for my own opinions. Therefore I wanted beforehand to bring such objections to God in prayer and afterwards examine them again. Thus I searched in Holy Scripture for the characteristic marks of the prophetic spirit and tried to find out whether there are lower and higher grades of prophecy and whether the lower ones could include mistakes, since St. Paul says: "Do not despise prophesying; but test everything!" (I Thess.

5:20f) On the other hand, I was afraid I might judge too favorably and through the reading of these books and the association with these people might get caught up in fanaticism. This caused me to look for an antidote against fanaticism, and that, according to Bilfinger's advice, was supposed to be the logic of Crousaz. So I read it, comparing it with the literature of the Inspired and paying attention to the way in which Scriptural references were used, in order to find out whether this was done more logically by Crousaz than by the Inspired. I found this indeed to be the case; but I thought nevertheless: that still does not give you the right to consider these people false servants of God.

I spent three quarters of a year in this manner and wrote down the reasons for and against the cause of the Inspired. But I could not bring myself to condemn those who said of themselves that God was talking with mocking lips through them to the people, and that the world would need no other messengers from now on. Finally I went to my upper room, threw myself down and said: "My Jesus, if you would be walking on earth with your disciples today I would be able to test you in three or four days. But these people I cannot test. You have said: 'If I had not come and spoken to them, they would not have sin; but now they have no excuse for their sin.' (Jn. 15:22) But Lord, I said, I am permitted to use this excuse: I do not like to condemn someone. You have many kinds of servants. But since I can neither condemn nor accept them, I have nothing to do with them." This way I really became free of them, according to logical thought as well as to the inner sense of truth. But God put me through this trial, so I would have a model by which to judge Count Zinzendorf later on with whom I was to come in contact in 1729.

The insufficient answer which Weissensee formerly had given me was supplemented by these studies in a way that was logically as well as spiritually sufficient to make me certain. This happened in the following way. The question arose in me as to how I knew that I, too, would be among the perfect followers of Christ, like his disciples, if he would now live on earth. Then the following well-grounded thoughts clearly entered my heart: in my fourteenth year I read with great desire in Isaiah, chapter 54: "Oh Jerusalem, all your sons shall be taught by the Lord." (cf. Is. 54:13a) Already at that time I saw that this was said, first, about the end of time and, second, about a certain situation and a whole people. Therefore I could not apply it to myself, because my first principle— that there should be clear thoughts for something to be certain—was from the beginning before me. Therefore I mistrusted my self-love so much; therefore I considered my unexamined judgments my greatest tempters; therefore I viewed logic as a gift of God if it were used beside other aids. Logically I concluded as follows: in John 6:45 Jesus interpreted those words, which the prophet related to the end of time and to an entire people, in terms of the Jews who were standing around him. If Jesus applied it to such a time which was much earlier than the end of time of which Isaiah spoke, then I properly conclude that I can apply it to my time. Thus the verse from Isaiah 54 certainly concerns also me, and therefore I certainly would have been in his time among his disciples, just like Peter, James and John. I was all the more certain and definitely assured in this matter, because all previous answers given me had been so insufficient.

After this time, I went through another trying experience with the Inspired whom I have described already. But after frankly uttering here and there that I had separated myself from them, they later sent a delegation to Tübingen and threatened me with God's judgment. However, what I answered them made them leave quickly.

Years in the Tübinger Stift and the University (1722-1727, 1729)

After I had spent two years in Bebenhausen, I was promoted to the Stipendium[45] in Tübingen. Here I listened to Georg Bernhard Bilfinger[46] more than to any other professor, because he was familiar to me from Blaubeuren since his mother had praised him so highly. He, too, had a mercurial,[47] although already steadied, disposition and a prodigious power of the imagination, so that he sometimes, in thinking intensely about a matter, dropped off his chair unconscious. But he counteracted his liveliness with the rules of wisdom, with logic and mathematics and other learned exercises for which he still as a *repetent*[48] in the Stift practiced with hands, feet, eyes, mouth and ears. His lectures were edifying, erudite sermons about God, the world, and the soul of man, in which he constantly used the philosophy of the godly Malebranche[49] for comparison. I therefore frequently read Malebranche's *Entretriens sur la Métaphysique,* his *Meditations chrétiennes, the Traité de la nature et de la grace,* his letters and the *Recherches de la verité.* Although I had renounced philosophy, I had to be well versed in it for the sake of my chosen profession if I wanted to retain second place among my classmates.

For some time Bilfinger had a great influence on the development of my thoughts. But what he shaped had to be unshaped again later on. And God gave my thoughts a completely different form. However, of all I had learned I kept what was good.

Bilfinger, at that time only associate professor, was in the eyes of the other professors, and especially of chancellor Pfaff,[50] an insignificant man and was hated somewhat because of the innovations he had introduced. I knew that I as his most ardent follower would get my share of this. But because I believed that he taught more clearly than all the others, I disregarded such considerations and adhered mostly to him, in spite of the others. I was his faithful *fidus Achates,*[51] and he called me his most beloved friend.

Bilfinger gave lectures in logic, metaphysics, mathematics, algebra,

and other academic subjects. I took his course in logic which afterwards appeared in print, edited by Pastor Vellnagel. I also attended his
class on the metaphysical concepts of Rudrauff[52] which he explained so
clearly that through him they took on their true meaning. Most impor-
tantly he offered a lecture on the fundamentals of Leibniz's *Principia
philosophiae monadologicae*[53] which was attended also by my class-
mate Krafft, later professor of mathematics,[54] Herrn Beyschlag, now
senior pastor in Halle, Herrn Repetent Griesinger, now superintendent
in Calw, and Herrn Repetent Fischer, now court chaplain in Stuttgart,
Here I became completely immersed in Leibniz's monadology. Quite
confidently I applied to it the verse (Heb. 11:3) that out of invisible
things the visible ones were made. I thought matter was only an ordered
manifestation of aggregate primal units of which many millions existed
in every object which I touched. I thought that a simple object could
not have a moving force in itself, and so the soul could not have it either. The idea of the soul's influence on the body I thought to be mis-
leading. Since the soul could not influence the body, and vice versa,
God must have previously synchronized body and soul as to their
movements and thoughts like two clocks beside each other. But afterward God, through his Word, made me suffer much pain in my innermost being until I gave up this basic thought pattern and allowed it to
be shaped in a different way, that is, according to the fundamental
thoughts of the prophets and apostles. This will become clear from the
following.

I lived with my brother Wilhelm Ludwig, a very lively and hand-
some boy who had the same mercurial disposition as I. According to
my strict demand he had completely learned by heart the *Officia Cicer-
onis*, with all the especially indicated phrases. I intended to make a professor out of him and to steady his mercurial disposition through mathematics. I went with him to a private seminar of Bilfinger's on algebra,
applied mathematics, mechanics, optics, architecture, etc. Afterwards
he took notes, without my help, of Bilfinger's metaphysical lecture on
the *Dilucidationes*. He had received a good basic training in logic and
metaphysics, and in his fourteenth year he defended with much approval in the *Collegio illustri*[55] a scientific paper on the mirror of Archi-
medes while Herr Johann Friedrich Reuss,[56] at that time still Magister,[57] served as critic. My brother's instruction demanded great effort
and practice of me, because I had to study everything with him repeat-
edly. Afterwards, on account of his marriage to Miss Pfeil, he became
the son-in-law of Professor Mauchert. But he died young as a doctor of
medicine in Tuttlingen after he had been appointed professor of anatomy, for which he already received the official approval of the Duke.

Herr Beyschlag of Schwäbisch-Hall was my best friend. I often discussed with him Bilfinger's and Malebranche's philosophy. We frequently prayed over it and thus studied this philosophy with greatest
devotion and reverence before God.

About the same time we read various booklets of the legal councilor Fende[58] which he had published as secretary of the famous legal scholar Schütz.[59] In these he promoted Schütz's ideas and coated his Arianism from the *Cabbala denudata*[60] with expressions from the New Testament. This caused our souls much trepidation and led us to make a special study of all Bible passages pertaining to the Godhead or the shape of God in Christ.

Being thus concerned about Arianism I developed my own Christology with the help of Malebranche, and in order not to become an Arian I assumed according to Malebranche that inherent in the eternal Word there had been a primordial model of mankind in which all men were embedded as in a matrix and through human procreation had been brought to light one after the other. Their shape had been there before and had entered them through begetting and birth. I pondered these thoughts for a long time until I finally was freed of them by God's special providence.

Reuss at that time was the most learned Magister at the University. Besides Johann Albrecht Bengel's *Gnomon*[61] he studied algebra under Bilfinger. He especially spent much time on the dynamic-algebraic class on the theories of motion, and he often said that if he had not attended this lecture he would have learned algebra without this application only symbolically or mechanically.

My brother Wilhelm Ludwig also attended this lecture, and so did Krafft, Griesinger and Maier of Kirchheim who previously had been a cooper and afterwards Magister and who became the best scholar in algebra, so that Bilfinger considered himself nothing compared to him. Later on as professor in Petersburg Maier declared algebra of little value for true physics.

With Reuss I was together already as a candidate of theology and later as Magister. I shared my living quarters with him. He taught higher geometry or kinetics to his brother, the later court physician, who was then fourteen years old. He was devoted, with body and soul, to mathematics, and like Tschirnhausen dreamt only of mathematical propositions and problems. Bilfinger, as I often heard, would have liked to have but a few students of this kind, for he knew none of such depth in thinking, none of such patience in developing basic principles and none of such integrity in pursuing everything that belonged to the totality of a particular subject.

Reuss, in contrast to me, had a cheerful disposition which was revealed in his beautiful blue eyes. I, however, was so strongly engaged in theological thinking that I at the time was unable to give that much consideration to mathematics. Bilfinger often wondered about me and said I must be melancholic, otherwise I would become stronger in mathematics. Of course, he did not know that God had guided me in my innermost being so strongly towards the only and highest object, God's glory, that I could not rid myself from it. He also did not know my preparation from childhood on. Therefore he considered me melancholic, just as Professor Canz in Bebenhausen had done who was never able to see through me and therefore accused me of melancholia.

Friedrich Christoph Steinhofer[62] also joined our philosophical circle. I walked about pregnant with Malebranche's system of the primordial structure in the Godhead. Steinhofer contradicted me as a student of Canz who could not, with his sharply honed metaphysics, grasp this primordial structure.

I was restless and therefore read in the New Testament day and night. However, I could not find anything but the seven spirits of God who are represented as something special before God's throne and as burning torches (Rev. 1:4; 4:5), and the "form of God" in Philippians 2:6. This caused me to think that if no such primordial model (Proverbs 8) had existed the world would not have been worth having been created.

Encounter with Jakob Böhme's Writings

In God's providence it so happened that for my constitutional I often walked to the powder mill in Tübingen. Here I met with the powder miller, Johann Kaspar Obenberger, the most utopian dreamer.[63] He had dug a deep hole in the ground in order to have a safe place when Babylon would be brought to ruin according to his calculations. He related his dreams to me. I laughed at him, but with modesty. He said: "You [theological] candidates are people under constraint. You are not permitted to study in accord with the freedom which is in Christ. You have to study whatever you are compelled to." I thought: it is almost true; but we do have some freedom. He said: "You are forbidden to read in the most excellent book next to the Bible!" I said: "What do you mean?" He invited me into his living room, showed me Jakob Böhme[64] and said: "There is the right theology!" I read in this book for the first time and felt uneasy about the suggestive words Sal, Sulphur, and Mercurius[65] which Jakob Böhme used to describe by way of analogy the powers of the seven spirits of God and the threefold life. I laughed at this and went on my way. However, I found something reasonable in these most fantastic expressions, and I thought one should correct the terminology of this layman with the help of Malebranche and Leibuiz. So I asked him to lend me the book and I read it this time eliminating all prejudice. Here I found the refutation of my imagined primordial scheme. I was startled and said to myself: you have considered Jakob Böhme a fantastic dreamer; but now you realize you yourself constructed a fanciful scheme out of Malebranche.

Böhme refuted the Schwenckfeldian sectarians[66] Stiefl and Meth. Their system corresponded to what I had taken over from Malebranche, that is, that everything, from the greatest to the smallest, had been prefigured in the primordial plan. Böhme says that this would mean all worms had also been inherent in it, which is absurd. Finally I realized that Jakob Böhme's dark words had to be judged by his clear ones. He has spoken so clearly and genuinely of the eternal Word that my Malebranchean system of the preexistence of all men, prefigured in infinite smallness, dissolved in confrontation with the authentic doctrine of the divine character of the Word. Thus Arianism and the theory of Malebranche collapsed for me simultaneously.

The eternal Word, according to Jakob Böhme, is not a being in which every form is resting as in a matrix and is motionless as *in speculis monadicis* [monadic reflections], as I had imagined it and as all Arians have to conceive it. The eternal Word instead is *actus purissimus* of the Godhead inasmuch as it presents itself in its own being or as, in eternal manifestation of itself, it is always working against itself. This means talking in accordance with our doctrine of God as *actu purissimo* (namely, that he is the eternal One, containing the creative force, its action and its effect). Those who, on account of several words, arrogantly and shortsightedly pass over such heavenly things, as I did in the beginning, do not by far have the patience which God has taught me already during my study of the Inspired and later even more. They persist in their stubbornness and do not test a matter according to the rules of wisdom in the Proverbs of Solomon; they do not consider all aspects of an issue and do not pass the right judgment according to the Book of Job. Therefore they build on Christ with wood, hey and stubble (1 Cor. 3:12).

Elias Cammerer, the senior professor of medicine, was married to the sister of my mother. He was one of the most learned, most wise, and most experienced men who have ever been in Tübingen. He had also experienced the central theological vision[67] as Johann Jakob Moser[68] had described it in his *Beiträge zum Bau des Reiches Gottes*. He thus knew in every matter how to judge the best way, through the logical knowledge which is gained from the outside as well as through the spiritual knowledge born from within. Rarely a man stands out in a century in whom so many gifts are concentrated. There are still beholders with one perspective, but no persons with Janus-like perspectives. This man kept studying mystical theology more than anything else and worked with the rarest books of Therese of Bordeau (Therese of Jesus), Margarethe Alacoque, [Abbé] Brion, Pére Maure and others.[69] With him I discussed everything and listened to what he said. The many conversations I have had with him cannot be described. He knew how to coordinate Wolff's philosophy, with the exception of the monads, and the mystical view, especially in regard to the theory that God, according to the present dispensation, does everything in accord with the order of nature and grace and does not overstep his laws. Thus Cammerer did not dispute Leibniz's *causes finales et efficientes*, although he ridiculed the theory of the prestabilized harmony and other extravagant sophistries.

Jeremias Friedrich Reuss was the most beloved among the former students of the great Johann Albrecht Bengel. Therefore he served as his correspondent in academic matters. Bengel always wrote him about his apocalyptic discoveries or gifts of grace, and I got to read it also, and this from the time on when he wrote *Inveni numerum bestiae Domino dante* (With the help of the Lord I have found the number of the animal). All this I discussed with Elias Cammerer. As a physician he did not care very much for text criticism, because he thought one would limit oneself too much to details and would lose the feeling for the whole. But I did not let Cammerer dissuade me from admiring Bengel highly, because I knew that our thoughts about the meaning of the Scriptures have to be shaped and developed in a very accurate way and not only *secundum religionem medici*). When I had told Bengel about Cammerer's *sentiment du coeur ouvert* (his heart's frank feelings)—as the latter wished me to—he was often very sad and said it would not hurt him by far as much if people of the world would underrate him. But if πνευματικοι, men filled with spirit and life, made him appear suspect, that would cut him to the quick. However, I said to Herr Bengel: "These various judgments befall us in order to teach us patience."

Philosophical Studies

While my studies were continuing in this manner, I finally became Magister in 1725, after having defended the thesis *de principio rationis sufficientis* under Christian Hagmajer,[70] the most exacting professor of metaphysics, who declared Wolff's argument for this principle as insufficient. After I had become Magister I took the course of Professor Hoffmann, a theologian, on the synoptic Gospels. His book on this topic I had already completely absorbed in Bebenhausen. A still existing roll of paper which can be wrapped around a finger gives proof of this. Hagmajer afterwards became a professor of theology, too. I learned many good things from his lecture in which he interpreted the epistles. Weissmann, the excellent church historian, came to Tübingen after Hoffmann had left, and I profited from him also.

Besides all these studies I worked on mathematics for another whole year in order to get more practice in logical argument. Reuss gave lectures in mathematics which I gladly took advantage of. But a little later he left the university to become a private tutor for General von Gräveniz in Stuttgart. So I assumed his position as correspondent of Herr Bengel,[71] and from time to time I took a trip to see him, at least biannually, often every three months, sometimes even more frequently, so that once he indicated I came too often. I witnessed the origination of Bengel's apocalyptic system in all its parts. It was a joy to see the ways in which God gradually purified, clarified, and fortified the increasing knowledge of this instrument of wisdom.

However, as for myself, I felt that everything I had learned was insufficient. Wolff's philosophy had taken such deep roots in me that I was very troubled I might inject a wrong nexus into the Holy Scriptures, since the devil today would no longer work with obvious falsehoods as during the first centuries, but with "truths" he would form in the soul through a wrong nexus of ideas. Therefore I thought if I would harbor Wolff's basic ideas within me without sanctification of the spirit and without being very certain of them on grounds of Holy Scripture I would without doubt inject a wrong nexus into Holy Scripture and thus misguide myself and others.

With Reuss I spent very much time in order to discuss Wolff's philosophy. In theology he did not know his way around as yet. I saw that Reuss, according to the certainty of mathematical knowledge, also wanted to work through theology which from the very beginning appeared to me impractical. By now he also considers it impossible. I noticed, too, that Reuss wanted to base everything on Wolff's definitions. At one time he could not help remarking: if he only knew theology as much as the first definition in geometry, the resulting definitions would carry certainty in themselves. However, later on God changed his thinking as well as mine completely and showed him that these principles are not certain enough to build on. I induced him to read Jakob Böhme. He made excerpts and said finally that this seemed the only possible system of thought. But now as chancellor he says something else.

This affair with Reuss later on caused me to be still more careful concerning philosophical ideas. I always looked for their counterweight in Holy Scripture, since St. Paul reproaches all teachers who do not know what they are saying in definite terms or what they are certain of in their argument or in the concatenation of their definitions (cf. Tim. 1:6f.).

I realized that the evidence of the Spirit and of the power of God could not be set over against the exact logical argument, but that Apollos gave reasonable proofs (cf. Acts 18:24-28), and that St. Paul wanted to unite his Colossians by guiding them into all the riches of assured understanding (cf. Col. 2:2), not through inexplicable utterances, but through conclusions sanctified by the Spirit. Thus I did not doubt, however far the philosophers may push their concepts, that the holy men of God must have had just such ultimate concepts, only not in the same elaborate form, but as to their correspondence with reality a hundred times better. Consequently it was my daily and nightly effort to find such ultimate concepts which would either confirm or overturn those of Wolff. That was hard work for me, but I saw that it had to be done, because otherwise I could not have served the will of God in a perfect way among the present generation.

In Wolff's philosophy I found that the composite, just like numbers, consists of units. But I thought this to be an arithmetical fraud.

Certainly there were no such abstract units in nature like the units in numbers! So the idea became very suspect to me. But which basis the apostles and prophets had instead of these units I could not fathom.

In Wolff's philosophy I also found that no monad or unit could of itself have a moving force, and that therefore the soul could not influence the body. I saw that Malebranche, too, had built his whole system on this sentence which had also induced him to establish the entire system of *causarum occasionalium*. Thus he stated already before Leibniz the three following possibilities: This influence either happens through the effect of the soul on the body, or through God's touching the powers of the soul, or through predetermination of the movements of body and soul. Since I noticed that it was not necessary for the apostles to decide on these principles, I asked myself especially whether the apostles presupposed such moving forces as Leibniz did.

At one time I went to Professor Canz and urged him to clarify whether he dared to be certain that Jesus Christ and the apostles had the same basic concepts as he and whether he would find them to be the same after his death, just as he so presumptuously claimed in his teaching. He said, yes. But I replied, no, he would not find them the same. I also insisted that this was an important issue, even more important than one would think. It would be worth the effort to apply all diligence to arrive at a real certainty in this exceptional matter. In short, I rejected Canz's application of Leibniz's philosophy to theology. Weissmann, too, fought it with all his strength. The idea that the world is eternal and the best of all worlds should not be taken seriously, since it is based on artificial and not on true conclusions.

As to the moving forces, the person who wants to know whether the apostles had the same basic concepts as the philosophers has to be clear about what he says: he has to have distinct concepts of the moving forces, and these in turn must be reducible to their distinct characteristics. One moving force originates in others that work together, that is, a moving force is a composite. But it is as impossible philosophically to grasp the simple individual forces of which the composite ones consist as it is to grasp the ultimate simple movements of which the composite movements consist. One can imagine a geometrical analogy: on the diagonal lines of a square or a parallelogram draw again a parallelogram and again draw a diagonal line and keep doing that as long as you can. Thus you get a picture of countless composite lines, since every diagonal line appears as composed of the side lines. Out of these finally result crooked or circular lines as sides of a curvilinear parallelogram. But what does this amount to? Whether it be light or darkness, it is useless to determine the inherent right or wrong movements. It is certain that God's revelation through the eternal Word cannot be conceived of without composite movements of the seven spirits of God. Also no circular movements can be conceived of without the centripetal force and the resisting centrifugal force. It is only through the counteraction of these two forces that a circular movement appears as becomes evident from a sling that is swung around. Finally, there are no moving forces that do not resist each other. Everything above and below is involved in action and counteraction. But a simple [not composite] being—which is actually inconceivable—cannot have a manifold direction, but only a simple one. Thus, it cannot involve an action and counteraction. What is the use, then, of pressing so far the analysis of matters which *reveal* themselves? It makes sense only in algebra, but nowhere else. The apostles let God take care of all that, and so the philosophers should come to an agreement among themselves where useful knowledge has its limitations. They should exclude all concepts of a simple thing and of the—actually impossible—moving force within it and disregard them completely like the apostles. Everything is a composite: God's revelation, too, is not without the composite movements of the eternal Word. It is sufficient that Wisdom says:

> When he established the heavens (through incomprehensibly many movements which God alone knows), I was there, when he drew a circle on the face of the deep, I also was there, and worked together with him as the archetype, playing before God everything I now also create, form, and make (cf. Prov. 8:27ff.).[72]

Likewise the whole first chapter of Ezekiel tells of many composite circular movements. What use is it to reduce them to their simpler movements? It is better to take over from the Savior the basic terms of light and darkness which he uses in full accord with the prophets and apostles, and to respect the limits of Holy Scripture. "If then the light in you is darkness, how great is the darkness!" (Mt. 6:23) What more is necessary? God tells us in the book of Job enough of the original darkness. David says, "The darkness is not dark to thee." (Ps. 139:12) These basic concepts are the counterweight to those of Leibniz and Malebranche. "For it is the God who said, 'Let light shine out of darkness,' who has shone in our hearts." (2 Cor. 4:6) That is sufficient for us. In this way, the apostles understood themselves while Leibniz himself with his monads did not know what he was saying, even though he reasoned it out ingeniously with his *principio rationis sufficientis*. Such concepts count for less than nothing. Satan is playing a game in luring the scholars through vanity, so that they think they have more subtle definitions than the Scriptures. This is the devil's trick: with matters of such little weight he burdens the world as with many hundredweights and twists the straight use of reason (Prov. 8:8,9). I know how these things have made a fool of me and upset me, even though they are nothing but a pretentious puppet play of the wordmongers of our time. Muschenbroek[73] opposed Wolff's physic with Newton's scientific experiments on all counts.[74] But since he could not get ahead in his academic position without the Wolffian chatter he finally followed the fashion and took over the idea of the monads, too. That, too, is vanity!

I am writing this, so everyone can see how long nowadays one is driven back and forth until one arrives at the basic concepts of the apostles, even though they are actually easily to be understood. My *Inquisitio in sensum communem*[75] says enough about this. It is therefore not necessary to write more about it.

Of course, wisdom does her work among all these efforts of the scholars, even though it involves much vanity. But stupidity is much more active in them. In the end, however, they must contribute to bringing forth all of God's wonders. "Nothing is covered up that will not be revealed" (Lk. 12:2). But it is necessary, as for every century, also especially for our time in which the dragon will talk like the lamb, to recognize the motives of the spirit of darkness. Therefore I have thoroughly studied mathematics, philosophy, and everything that belongs to the knowledge of our present age. "We have received not the spirit of the world, but the Spirit which is from God, that we might understand the gifts bestowed on us by God" (1 Cor. 2:12).

Patristic and Rabbinic Studies (1725-1727)

In the following years I tried thoroughly to explore theology in this manner: I read the church fathers over and over again with respect to the basic concepts of the apostles. The first was the *Shepherd of Hermas*. In reading this book I learned to understand why Irenaeus thought so highly of it that he quoted it with the words, *Scriptura dicit* (Scripture says). In Hermas, who without doubt is the one mentioned in Romans 16:14, I have observed with surprise how he presents the great mysteries of salvation in such economy of language and uses a style which is similar to the "wise fables" (σεσοφισμένοις μύθοισς), and through which he presents the glory of God sometimes concealed, sometimes openly, and very differently from how it is done today. Similar to Solomon's Proverbs he often presents moral truths in a forceful and beautiful way. I took down many notes in reading this book, especially in regard to the fact that the basic ideas of the primitive church were articulated very differently from the way they are expressed today. I read also the letters of Ignatius and Polycarp with surprise. Their style differs a little from that of the apostles, but the basic concepts are the same. I have read with astonishment the *Recognitions* of Clement, that is, the description of the life of Peter, together with all his speeches and conversations, and I am still reading them. How one imagines Peter to be lacking in logic and reason if one does not read this book! Strange things are mentioned in it. However, all the church fathers learned from it. I have studied the Platonic philosopher Justin Martyr in every possible regard in order to discover how much he had retained of his philosophical ideas and how much he had abandoned. I have read Irenaeus in the most thorough way in order to understand the doctrine of the Cerinthians and thereby the epistles of John, and to know why the Cerinthians were opposed to the spirit, water, and blood of Jesus. Like the Wolffians, they considered matter, and thus also the body of Christ, a mere appearance and not real flesh. Here I learned how philosophy spoils the basic principles and what people are like who are "depraved in mind" (1 Tim. 6:5).

Afterwards I studied Clement of Alexandria, the teacher of Origen, and Origen himself with great attention. How far-reaching was the learnedness of the church fathers as compared with that of later theologians! Then I read Athenagoras who delivered such a wonderful speech before the emperor Antonius, the philosopher, and Theophilus of Antioch. What parrhesia he showed before an emperor! Eusebius and Sozomen should necessarily be read by every student of theology, since otherwise one does not know the original documents of church history. Therefore I did it with all diligence. I especially liked the system of Eusebius. On account of the mystic theology of the fathers I always keep Macarius in mind and read him from time to time. I also studied the other church fathers, like Cyprian, Tertullian, and Basilius. But since I found that they contain already too much polemics, I did not put so much effort into reading them. However, Augustine and Jerome I studied often, since they opposed each other and—the latter being a critic and the former an orator—they constantly fought each other without necessity. Augustine was a great theologian, and Jerome a great exegete. Augustine's book *De spiritu et litera* I have taken to heart with special seriousness in all its aspects. I have found that he treated this subject exhaustingly for his time and that one today, for clarifying the matter, need not do anything but present his teaching and relate it to the present issues. Augustine has very beautiful concepts. He knew what he was talking about. Few theologians work out their principles as thoroughly as he does. Plato is shining brightly out of the pages of Augustine. But whatever is pagan or exaggerated in Plato he did not take over. Malebranche has copied whole pages from Augustine in order to illumine his philosophy and to show how wisdom in the street speaks to men. Augustine is such a perfect theologian because he allowed three things to work on him and to give his thought the right shape [Gestalt]: first, letter and spirit; second, wisdom in the street, or philosophy; and, third, events decreed by divine providence. From this perspective I read Augustine with much edification.

I copied down excerpts from all these church fathers on special sheets according to their basic ideas and read through them with the intention of comparing the principal sources of their style with the present-day way of speaking as well as with that of all prophets and apostles, and of Jesus Christ. Without this the reading of the church fathers is almost useless. He who boasts that he has read the church fathers, but does not remember their basic ideas as compared with Scripture is not familiar with them. Of course, one can read the church fathers like devotional books. But that does not contribute much to understanding the wisdom of Jesus Christ.

Now I want to describe the second aid which I used in order to study theology from scratch: the rabbinic authors and the philosophy which they extracted from the Bible. If I compare the style of Ecclesiastes with the style of Proverbs then it seems that I notice something of the rabbinic atmosphere. But there is also much to be learned from Ecclesiastes, even though the way of writing is not as concentrated as in Proverbs. The Proverbs aim at memorizing, Ecclesiastes at edification and doctrine. This requires a different style.

In order to familiarize myself with the oldest way of thinking which is so different from the German I read the rabbinic writers over and over again, partly with my rector Bernhard, partly by myself. Because of my intense desire to grasp the old Jewish way of thinking I hindered my own progress. Besides, one stays behind in this subject, if one does not become familiar with it already as a youth. I read the following: Joseph Albo Sepher Ikarim, R. Saaida Sepher Amnah, R. Abarbanel Maschmiah Jeschuah. Michlal Jophi I read constantly besides the regular reading of Holy Scripture. I liked especially R. Bechai. But I found that the rabbinic authors no longer write genuinely according to the way of Rabbi Schimeon ben Jochai in the book of Sohar.[76] Therefore I looked for an opportunity to read the cabalistic sources firsthand. But because it is difficult I postponed it until I would have occasion to be with more learned and experienced Jews.

The First Journey

In Tübingen I had freed myself from all seminars and lectures and had moved into the house of the Expeditionsrat Härlin. Here I taught my three brothers Wilhelm Ludwig, Johann Christoph and Ferdinand Christoph. But all four of us caught the fever and had to go home.[77]

Here I have to interject that in 1728 I often met with Dr. Kayser,[78] a very learned man who had accompanied our prince Friedrich Ludwig, son of Duke Eberhard Ludwig, as instructor on his travels and had practiced medicine in Stuttgart. At that time I was extremely worried that I would not act consistently if I would stay with theology. And I had firmly decided to associate with Dr. Kayser and to give up theology to practice medicine. Dr. Kayser, like myself, was a great admirer of Jakob Böhme. He was a strict separatist and harshly criticized Madame de Guyon[79] and Böhme, the latter especially because on his deathbed he had permitted a pastor to visit him and had answered his questions affirmatively. I said, one need not hold this against Jakob Böhme. We got involved in a discussion of the whole system of Jakob Böhme. He published many booklets about this in which he centered everything in separatism. He wanted to convince me that what Böhme had written about Baptism and the Lord's Supper in his booklet was erroneous; Böhme had drawn the wrong conclusions. But I said: No, for it follows logically from his whole system. Thus we were at odds with one another, and I left to start my first journey.

After the long-lasting sickness was over I asked my father for money, so I could travel. He gave me little. But my desire to travel made me leave anyway. I intended to visit Jena. An awakening, as in the time of the apostles, was supposed to have arisen there, according to what my friend Reuss had written me. I passed through Frankfurt am Main and went to the Councilor Fende with whom I had exchanged letters about his Arian booklet earlier. I had hardly arrived there when from the room upstairs the wealthy Miss Schütz came down to me.[80] She carried the *Cabbala Denudata* by Baron von Rosenroth under her arm and presented it to me. She also offered me money and through Fende indicated it would be good if I would stay in Frankfurt for study. With all her wealth and furniture she had an aversion against marriage. She loved contemplation and in conversation revealed solid knowledge, since in her youth her father (Johann Jakob Schütz), the famous law scholar, had taught her in a number of academic disciplines and in Holy Scripture. When once I appeared too grateful for her favors she turned cool and punished me, as it were, for my overly affected politeness which seemed out of place in view of her serious character. I was not looking for anything and was content with the *Cabbala Denudata*, because this book is very hard to get.

Councilor Fende introduced me to the most learned cabalist, the Jew Cappel Hecht. He grew very fond of me, because of the unusal questions from Jewish philosophy which I asked him, for example, what the meaning of "wide vision" and "small vision" in God was. I came to him just at the time of the Feast of Tabernacles. He demonstrated from chronological considerations and from the Talmud, on the basis of the rarest documents, that Plato had been a student of Jeremiah and had taken over his basic ideas. I thanked God for this providential experience.

In studying Plato I had already wondered for some time from where he could have derived his description of the city of God which merely corresponded to that found in Revelation. I had not been able to understand how he could write so vividly of the "Word from the beginning" and of the three highest Sephirot[81] or three shapes of the Godhead. I also did not know from where he derived the concept of the eternal ideas or original images of the creatures in God, since he writes that physics should be based on experiments, but theology on utterances of God. I was wondering, too, why he so often appealed to the central vision since he said: "I recognize that I am part of the higher world and have reached eternal life with an incomprehensible light. But since through weariness I sank from the contemplation of that pure knowledge to the level of mere imagination, the light left me."

When he told me of such beautiful historical documents about Plato I was struck with awe and fixed my gaze at his mouth and eyes. His little daughter sat at the side and similarly gazed at my mouth and eyes. When I now started looking at her also somewhat directly, he reprimanded me, asking whether I did not know what Job had said: "I have made a covenant with my eyes; how then could I look upon a virgin?" (Job 31:1) I apologized by saying I had regarded her spirit and not her flesh. But it was of no use, I had to be in the wrong. I accepted it. I was often reminded of it, and even though it was inappropriate at the time, it still taught me a good lesson.

I loved him more and more and asked him how I would have to go about trying to understand the Cabalists. He said I should save myself the trouble, I would not succeed anyway. I should concern myself with the text of Holy Scripture. As to the Cabala, we Christians had a book that spoke much more clearly of the Cabala than the book Sohar. I asked: "Which one?" He answered: "Jakob Böhme!" and showed me immediately where his language agrees with that of the Cabala. Then I was still more surprised and concluded he must be a Christian. He finally showed me the Syrian New Testament in which he always read and said, he agreed that "Messiah" had come, but could not convert to the Christians, since they had such strange doctrines. Our doctrine of the Trinity was presented too unreasonably. In his opinion, there was no separation of persons in God, the Messiah was not to be considered the second person. Evidence of this was for him the Messiah king who in the book Sohar was thought of as higher than Olam azilut (the emanated world), but in the manner of cabalistic thinking he was always present as king Messiah and not as second person. Everything would have to be expressed in a completely different way in order to satisfy the conscience.

Finally, I asked him about the corollary character of St. Paul's thinking. He said it would be impossible for us to get inside this or any other subtlety of St. Paul's language in the manner of a true Israelite. St. Paul had spoken and written as an instrument filled with the Holy Spirit. We would never spend enough time on these things to grasp their force from the inside.

Finally I left Frankfurt. Miss Schütz presented me with many gifts. And Fende gave me the advice neither to go forward nor backward too quickly.

On my trip in the stagecoach I met Herr von Marsay,[82] a Huguenot refugee who afterwards wrote many booklets under the title *Zeugnis eines Kindes* and who also had the audacity to assign living quarters on the planets to the most excellent souls like Bourignon,[83] Guyon, Böhme and others for their life after death and to pass off these notions for inspirations. Above all he praised Madame de Guyon. But I said that Madame de Guyon had not been crucified for us. One should not cling to human beings in such a way. With this I angered him greatly. We were not able to agree and parted at the stage.

Once I interrupted my journey, and on a tour to Berleburg I met Herr von Marsay again in Schwarzenau. There he was a watchmaker.

In Berleburg I heard some singing. I walked toward the town, and in a large assembly-hall I found a big meeting in progress. The Count of Berleburg[84] motioned me to come closer. I approached him and found Johann Conrad Dippel[85] and Adam Struensee,[86] who later became chief superintendent, in a vehement dispute over the verse, "The blood of Jesus his Son cleanses us from all sin." (1 Jn. 1:7). I was perplexed over these two men; they were almost without breath over their quarrel. I thought to myself: little truth can come out of this! Later I often talked with Dippel, especially at the table of the Count of Wittgenstein. But I did not think very highly of him. I was more fond of Canz though, the brother of the Tübingen theologian.

I left Berleburg again and hiked to Schwarzenau. Again I met Marsay. But he was still harping on the old aversion to Madame de Guyon. This Marsay later regained his estates and moved from Schwarzenau to Wolfenbüttel. There he learned to understand the ways of God more fully, went to church, partook again of the Lord's Supper, and declared that he had been in error and that it was difficult to convert a separatist.

Meanwhile also Dr. Kayser became uncertain of his separatism because of Marsay's change of mind, and no longer stressed it so much, but let everyone go his own way. However, he did not want to recant publicly, as also Marsay did not retract his booklets, but indicated his change only in his manner of life.[87] Dr. Kayser was in his eighties. At the end of his life he became fearful over having shown so little love for all of mankind. He trembled with fear. He gladly let the pastors visit him and said: "They are my comforters!" He received the Lord's Supper from Herr Spittler in Stuttgart and thus retracted what he had criticized in Böhme.

I arrived in Jena and went to August Gottlieb Spangenberg,[88] who was a *Magister legens* [instructor]. I visited their newly established schools [of the group that had experienced the awakening] and was surprised what a close communion these people had among themselves in order to magnify Christ in their souls. One time I came into a meeting where fifty or sixty of them, of all departments of the university and also of the nobility, fell down on their faces and prayed. Afterwards they gave speeches and invited me to speak, too. Thus I explained that, with the endorsement of my Consistory, I had started traveling in order to discuss a certain matter with others and to find out whether they were also concerned about it. I said that according to the true biblical understanding everything depended upon the basic ideas which Jesus and the apostles had had, just as much as the philosophers who attribute their concepts of the soul to the monads and those of the bodies to the moving forces. The philosophers base everything on the *principium contradictionis* and *rationis sufficientis*. I believe, however, that also St. Paul supported his ideas with the *principium contradictionis* when he says: "But if it is by grace, it is no longer on the basis of works; otherwise grace would no longer be grace." (Rom. 11:6). However, St. Paul used this *principium contradictionis: quicquid est. est.* or, *impossibile est idem simul esse, et non esse* not only in a way which regards nature apart from the Spirit, but in connection with the power of God in Christ. Consequently it means acting wisely if we use the true basic concepts of the apostles and Jesus in the same way. We do not need other philosophical principles, but only those which Jesus spoke of. The evangelist St. John started his Gospel with the words, "In the beginning was the Word . . . ," and this Word, I said, is life and the light of men; the light had shone in the darkness, and the darkness had not overcome it. These are the basic concepts of the apostles; everything has to be grounded in them. If someone instead introduces monads he carries an alien doctrine into the Gospel. But if one understands everything that relates to Jesus Christ in connection with these basic concepts he is tending in the right direction.

These and other observations I injected into my speech. But their way of thinking was not geared to my ideas. Only in Spangenberg I noticed that he thought strictly according to Scriptural concepts, since he said publicly that the drinking of the fruit of the vine was to be understood in its direct meaning.

I for one am certain that St. John wrote the first ten chapters of his Gospel in view of the three basic concepts: (1) Word, (2) life, and (3) light. Through the Word, Christ was before John (1:15); through the Word he changed water into wine (2:1-11); through the Word he said: "We bear witness to what we have seen" (c.f. 3:1 1); through the Word he said to the Samaritan woman: "I who speak to you am he" (4:26); through the Word the angel troubled the water (5:4); through the Word Jesus said: "Take up your pallet, and walk" (5:11); through the Word he said: "My Father is working still, and I am working" (5 : 17), etc. The sixth and seventh chapters speak of life, as is manifest from all verses. The eighth, ninth, and tenth chapters refer to the light. Whoever does not see this blinds himself.

From Jena I traveled (in 1729) to Halle in Saxonia. I inquired there about the institutions of the orphanage. Baumgarten at the time was a very devout and serious man who directed the institutions together with Professor Francke. I accepted a teaching assignment there. After some time I gave it up and kept in close contact with Professor Pauli, a Reformed, since he preached in such an unbiased way of universal grace.

After I had gathered enough information about the situation at Halle University, I planned to teach there as a *Magister legens*. I presented my dissertation which I had debated with Professor Hagmajer in

Tübingen whereupon councilor Gundling and chancellor Ludwig immediately authorized me to lecture publicly. Ludwig asked me whether I knew an example of someone learning logic while he was still wet behind the ears, that is, under forty. I answered that no one learns logic from rules, but by practice. The Frenchman says: "Les affaires sont l'homme." It would be possible to work out logical arguments here or there, I admitted. But forty would still be too early to learn logic in such a way that one would act logically in all circumstances. He was very satisfied with this answer and talked very kindly with me. I acquainted him with my plan to teach *philosophiam sacram et applicatam* as it relates to Holy Scripture, and said that this would have to be derived mainly from Proverbs.

I kept thinking about this, but since the students in Saxonia are used to getting everything dictated in their classes, and since Baumgarten then already had a large following, I could at that time not succeed with my plans.[89]

Meanwhile I started studying with a cabalist, a Jew in Halle, in the book Ez chajim. I bought the manuscript for a high price and concentrated all my thoughts on the holy philosophy of the cabalists.

After half a year [in Halle] I decided to travel to Count Zinzendorf[90] in Herrnhut in order to find out whether I could there get a better response to my "sacred philosophy." When I arrived in Herrnhut (in May 1730) I attended a meeting, and after the speaker had finished I said: "Oh, you good people, I hear everywhere that you are not grounded in Holy Scripture, but in the hymns of the Count." They defended themselves and said that this was not the case. Nevertheless, after I had introduced myself to the Count they encouraged me kindly to stay with them.

A Swiss law student by the name of Wolleb had also visited the Count. He was a most subtle philosopher who in the manner of Hobbes had all his ideas in counting order at his fingertips and outwardly carried himself with appropriate seriousness. But he did not take any part in the community. He, like myself, was persuaded to stay. What I appreciated in the Count was the way he let everyone keep his concepts and was content if a person's life was consistent in itself.

In Herrnhut I wrote *Halatophili Irenai aufmunternde Gründe zur Lesung Jakob Böhmes*, "demonstrating how much Jakob Böhme's writings contribute to a vivid knowledge, defending them against ungrounded objections on the basis of a thoroughly studied similarity between Scripture and nature, and offering explanations through many notes."[91] This booklet, printed in 1731, "was hastily written with many interruptions. It contains my thoughts of the necessity and praise of knowledge and of how the books of Jakob Böhme and others, especially those of Thomas Bromley,[92] could be useful for this purpose. I should have presented my ideas in a more succinct order, should have avoided the long-windedness and thus made the content more agreeable. But since I got involved in this against all my intentions when I was asked to write a preface for the first small book of Herr Tschesch,[93] and since I did not have the necessary time for it, it was published in the present form. I am not seeking anything but God's honor through the perfect knowledge of Jesus and his glory and transfiguration, and I try to show that one should not have such low esteem of the Holy Spirit, but should believe that knowledge through him affords a greater joy and comfort for the soul than all knowledge of nature which derives from reason.... It should further be noted that precautionary qualifications for the reading of Jakob Böhme have been omitted in this book because of deletions by the printer, without which, however, the book is of little value, in my opinion, since on account of Jakob Böhme already countless illusionists and image-makers have appeared on the scene. But though this book has given men like Spener,[94] Anton, and others a lot of trouble one does not have to throw out the child with the bath. As I see it, God disclosed to Jakob Böhme in a supernatural way the potential of the natural forces, but because of incomprehensible terminology Böhme made himself suspect. He did not sufficiently distinguish his conclusions from his data and did not have the proper esteem of his gift which St. Paul did have who said: 'Whether [he was] in the body or out of the body I do not know....' (2 Cor. 12:2) His books thus call for countless reservations which in turn would make it possible to encourage philosophers to read Jakob Böhme, especially in connection with Newton's philosophy which would compel one to abstract the imagery from his writings without impairing the truth."

The count privately tried to interpret to me all his opinions. But time and again I said that I would not accept one word of their language, but would love their fellowship. When they wanted to use me for a mission in France I excused myself by stating that I could not decide this on my own, since I was under obligations to the Duke of Württemberg. The Count immediately wrote the Duke. But I was quickly called home.[95]

An Instructor in the Tübinger Stift (1731-1733)

Because of my obligations as alumnus of the Stift,[96] I had to assume the tasks of a *Magister legens* or *Repetent* [instructor] in Tübingen. As it was the custom, in Tübingen I had to instruct those who were *Magister* in debating the theological loci and to tutor the theological candidates in various philosophical and theological subjects. Moreover, the obligation included occasional preaching in the city church and administration of the Lord's Supper. The latter I tried to avoid in every way possible, since I was unable to prepare the communicants beforehand.[97]

In all this, I made a tremendous effort to gather all my strength in

God and especially—according to Plato's advice—to go to sleep with a collected mind, so that no power of the imagination or evil desire might overtake me in my sleep. I practiced this more than anything else, and I can truthfully say that I slept as protected and guarded as though the shield of God covered me in a special way.

Meanwhile Bilfinger had returned from Petersburg and had become professor of theology. He turned over to me the task of instructing the candidates in applied mathematics. This disturbed the purity of my sleep, and since I was longing to attain it again, I sometimes blamed my philosophical studies, at other times the noise in the Stift, or still other things. My inexperience in the ways of the inner life made me imagine that my studies kept me from inner purity and chasteness of heart. Therefore I was eager to start traveling again, especially since I had received my inheritance from my deceased father (who had died January 27, 1733) and to devote myself completely to the *philosophia sacra*, and this all the more, since shortly before I had written the book *Evangelische Ordnung der Wiedergeburt*.[98] With these sacred intentions I left Tübingen once more.[99]

The Second Journey (1733-1737)

Meanwhile Count Zinzendorf came and asked for a *responsum theologicum*.[100] Bilfinger was willing [to grant it]. When he asked me whether the Count was a sincere man I said his main interest was the matter of communion with Jesus, that much I knew, but no one could sufficiently anticipate his secondary human objectives. Weissmann foresaw plenty of them. But Bilfinger as Dean obliged the Count. Since he passed himself off as a candidate of theology, he was even permitted to preach.[101]

Zinzendorf promised me every assistance in my sacred intentions, and I left Tübingen in his company. Later on I traveled alone after I had told him I would certainly come. I passed through Erfurt and nearby (in Ruderstädt) made the acquaintance of a farmer who was supposed to have the *cognitio centralis*.[102] His name was Markus Völker, an unusual man with tremendous physical strength, so that he could lift a wagon with one hand. He was of tall stature and had an unusually lovely and serious face. His grandfather had been an Austrian count and colonel, but without real estate. During the war a Turk had hewed off the upper part of his skull, without wounding the outer membrane of the brain itself, however. Since he could no longer be a soldier, he bought a farm with the money he had managed to save, married a country girl and begot children, among them the father of Markus Völker, who himself in turn had twelve children in all. They acquired wealth through mining and became quite knowledgeable in this field. Markus, the youngest child, had been neglected after the early death of his father. He learned neither writing nor reading and had to work as a stable-boy. During that time already he experienced in the fields the inner vision in which, like Joseph, he saw the fate of his siblings, though not in a dream in his sleep, but in waking. I have written in detail about the *cognitio centralis* in my translation of Therese of Bordeaux's[103] book, even though some consider it an empty phrase. Becker is of the opinion that Christ's temptations only appeared to be such. The Wolffians will not dislike the idea. But I conclude from the text that the devil showed Christ all the kingdoms of the world εν στιγμή [in a moment of time] (Lk. 4:5), and that Jesus permitted the devil to make him see these kingdoms through his magic εν στιγμή, that is, centrally, from within. Whether Jesus made use of this central vision at other occasions I do not know. It could be the case when he says, "The Son can do nothing of his own accord, but only what he sees the Father doing." (1 John 5:19) Consequently this word is not an empty phrase, as the short-sighted scholars of this Pelagian time pretend.

I was told that Markus Völker had the same characteristics which I had read about in Ruysbroek's interpretation of the tabernacle and with which this illumined and extraordinary man had sketched his own portrait. Ruysbroek says the following:[104]

> Among the twenty birds which by God's command were to be considered unclean by the Jews the eagle was the first. He is king among the birds. He flies the highest, he looks into the sun, and all birds fear him. Likewise also the holy men in heaven as well as on earth resemble the eagle, but only in some respects. The life of those who resemble him in all things is unclean. Here the reader should note what nature, and grace beyond nature, can do, which I now want to explain in a few words. If someone in his contemplation can completely free his mind of all pictures and similes and can lift it into the quiet void he is by nature a king over other men; for he soars as high as nature permits, and he builds himself a nest and finds rest in his single-minded being. He also directs the keenness of his mind towards the simple truth which always is evident in his own being as well as in that of others. Because his vision is single-minded and without much comparative reasoning, he looks at truth itself with unmovable and unimpaired intensity of vision. This delights his nature so much that he despises all comparative reasoning, differentiation and rational reflections which might hinder his pure vision or might fill it with images, and he considers all this as alien, impure, ignoble, and trivial. The eagle also prevails over the dragon because the devil might not tempt men in this pictureless void. But as noble and pure as such a man is in his turning inward, as awkward, clumsy, and unclean is he in his turning outward to the external world. He easily considers those who do not measure up to him as inferior and far from perfection. But he deceives himself. For he wants to see and not believe, have and not hope, own and not love. And although he soars high like the eagle, he will not be

lifted above himself. For no one transcends himself through the light of nature. Only love and grace lift him above himself into God. Such a man embraces and loves all reasonable works which correspond to faith and primal truth and regards them as wonderful fruits which grace him. Even though he has advanced so far as to know the One who is from the beginning, he still abides by the order of the congregation. In his words and his example he shows such great grace and loveliness that all his enemies are forced to retreat. So much about the eagle who is forbidden us according to his nature, but above all other birds offered us [as a model] according to grace.

This is the picture drawn by the enlightened and humble Ruysbroek. With it in mind, I tested Markus Völker and considered it worthwhile to stay with him for a goodly while and to examine his central visions which he recounted to me. There was much nature in him, but also much grace, an unusual humility and modest politeness; and profound insight was hidden under the outward appearance of a clumsy farmer. But he also had many faults which followed from his deficiencies in logical reflection. This proves to me how easily a person who tastes the inner peace is tempted to despise the restraint of step-by-step logical thought. Tuschiah (essential wisdom) he had in large measure. He understood the highest order of the birth of all things. But he did not make any effort to transcend himself by way of [logical] distinctions, so as to place his central visions before himself as in a mirror and to express them in words, one by one, in reasonable order. There are those who are strong ἐν λόγῳ γνώσεως according to the Spirit (1 Cor. 12:8), or have the Binah, which is the understanding according to the Word of God, based on the experience and characterized by mature discernment. They despise those who, like Markus Völker, have the λόγον σοφίας through the spirit, or the Chochma, which is the central wisdom, and regard them as fanatics. Whereas these again despise the reasonable step-by-step way of thinking, although this is almost more necessary for the piecemeal perception (of our present age) than the perfect central vision which is void of images. Arndt[105] would have become unfit for his modest daily tasks had he seen prematurely what he beheld at the end of his life.

I often said to Markus Völker that he was wrong in wanting to have everything from God, that he did not preserve what he had received, and that he despised reason. But he was incapable of keeping in mind what he had understood for a few moments, so deeply was he immersed in the central vision of the Spirit. He did not even care reasonably to save the money he had earned as a carter. Technical reason and the reason of central wisdom are hard to join.

Once I addressed him in the following way: "Dear Markus, all loss and damage and all disorder in your house is caused by the lack of reasonable thinking. You delight so much in tasting the sweetness of the central vision that you neglect alertness, preservation, and distinction in outward things, that you receive much grace in vain, and on account of failing in reflection do not use your faults to your advantage. You fear to lose your central gift if you join it with logical differentiation. It is true that the free flow of the Spirit recedes during the time of concentrated thinking. But you must take time for the latter as well as the former. You want to visualize the time you observe on the face of the clock with the inner eye. You want to receive the spoon, which God once and for all gave you for eating, again and again as a gift. This is folly and loftiest reason in one. The devil does not tempt you inwardly, but he confuses you inwardly through external means." Markus realized all this. But he was not able to correct himself greatly.

He read much in the Holy Scriptures and taught himself reading and writing. He was able to put together the whole harmony of the Evangelists; he even visualized it in contemplation. But he had too much Tuschiah, the essential wisdom, and too little of Daat and Tebhunah, the reflective logic that belongs to reason.

There would be much more to say of this matter, but I will leave it at that. Socrates and Plato also had the central vision of nature. But they had just as much differentiating reason and the willingness to express their concerns in writing, so they could afterwards review them again. For the sake of such people Plato traveled very far.

Finally I traveled again to Herrnhut to Count Zinzendorf. But I did not accomplish my purpose there, although I spent much time with him on the Scriptures.[106] I taught him Greek and Hebrew and explained Solomon's Proverbs. Why did I not succeed? The Count had a plan to subject half the world to Christ, and he was much too intent upon this to allow Holy Scripture to direct him in moderate understanding away from his image-making. Since I described this in the conversation about Job[107] and in the discussion between Zinzendorf and Dippel,[108] I do not want to elaborate on it here. I did not make much progress with my plan to discover the basic unity of Holy Scripture ever more succinctly and to connect them with each other. But I became quite competent as a spiritual counselor instead.

In Herrnhut the well-known Jonas Korte was my very dear friend. He wanted me to become his traveling-companion on a trip to Jerusalem, as can be found in his account of the trip on page four of the introduction.[109] First I wanted to accept. But when I afterwards left the decision up to Bengel he advised against it, so I missed the otherwise fine opportunity for free travel. When I spent my first year in Hirsau, Korte came back from Venice and wrote the account of his trip in my home.

After much heartache I left [Herrnhut] and went to Leipzig, since I had my brother (Ferdinand Christoph), a young student of medicine, now professor of medicine (in Tübingen), with me. There I went to Dr. Wipacher, another extraordinary man. He treated his patients in the old fashion, and he, too, had central visions, but they were quite different from those of Markus Völker. My brother attended philosophical and medical classes in Leipzig, after he had already learned much in Herrnhut under the Danish court physician Grothausen, a very learned anatomist.

In Leipzig I wrote the book about God's condescension.[110] From there I undertook a journey to Berlin, and on the way back I came to Klosterbergen and met Abbot Steinmetz.[111] At the time, I was still very uncertain as to whether or not I should accept an appointment in the service of the church.

Again I went to Halle, and now studied medicine myself under Dr. Junker and lectured on the *philosophia sacra* in Holy Scripture, especially on the Proverbs of Solomon and Job. Afterwards I visited Markus Völker once more, traveled from there to Holland, passing through Nijmegen and Leiden, talked there with S'Gravesande, Mark, and others, and then arrived in Amsterdam where I got to know the sectarians.[112] But I did not stay long.

Having arrived again at Frankfurt I went to Dr. Kämpf[113] in Hesse-Homburg because of my interest in medical practice. He was a unique man, too. He had written his own biography, an edifying book to read. At first he had been steward and private tutor for a young man in Strasbourg. Later he went to Colmar and opened a private school in which he taught mathematics, logic, rhetoric, Latin, Greek, and other subjects. He used a certain method by which he first tried to get an idea of the student's talents from his physiognomy and his speech and then predicted to teach the one logic within six to eight weeks, the other one mathematics and geometry within a certain time, and again another one metaphysics. The tuition which was rather high had to be deposited with a court of arbitration, and if the students in the presence of the arbiters proved their learning he collected his money. But if they had not learned anything they did not have to pay.

Like the old privy councilor Sturm in Blaubeuren, father of the well-known Miss Beate Sturm,[114] Kämpf had an appropriate method for almost any kind of personality. Herr Sturm taught himself an oriental language within a month, whether Persian, Abyssinian, Coptic, or Arabic. But for this purpose he had to continue uninterruptedly from hour to hour. He could not take two months of this, but only one; the following month he had to rest and think of nothing. Almost in the same vein Dr. Kämpf calculated for every kind of personality what it would take to learn a certain field of knowledge in such a way that at a definite day and hour success would be certain. This way he earned over two thousand Taler annually and certainly achieved his purpose. All this proves the great genius of the man and shows how exact, intelligent, and universal a man he was.

His disposition was jovial. He had bright blue eyes. The stature of this type is of medium height, the face is oval and of rosy complexion, the forehead beautiful, the hair above the forehead long and a little brownish-black, the voice penetrating, the eyes are sometimes blue and sometimes black, the eyebrows are high, the nose is slightly curved, the mouth is big, the upper lip is rounded, the shoulders are broad, the hands and feet are big. In behavior this type is very balanced and ironical, in speech always articulate, discreet and reserved, in his actions loving, determined, friendly towards children, profound in serious matters, just, clean, compassionate, knowing how to keep his anger within bounds, to hide his greed, and in all things to create harmony.

Dr. Kämpf was all this and more. In Strasbourg he learned anatomy and watched the ill-fated cures of the medics. He had much contact with the chancellor and privy councilor Mascowsky[115] in Darmstadt. From him he learned chiromancy and physiognomy according to proper principles. He found out that one could accurately predict how a merely natural human being would conduct himself and how he would fare. But for a person who allows himself to be motivated by divine impulses one could not predict anything on the basis of natural indications, since the naturally given is changed considerably under the influence of the divine.

Dr. Kämpf later became court chaplain and consistory councilor of a count. When he made out medical prescriptions he was always very successful in his treatments, for which reason the Duke of Zweibrücken appointed him his personal physician. For almost three quarters of a year I learned the practice of medicine from him. Every morning at eight o'clock a lot of sick people would come to see him. As we observed him we had to determine the sicknesses and then hear from him how the prescriptions had to be made out accordingly. But I also enjoyed being with him for other reasons, since he always had many case histories of all kinds in mind and liked to tell about them.

He had become the leader of the Inspired not by election, but by a kind of casting of the lot. He was a separatist, but in such a way that he tried to establish a congregation corresponding to the early Christian community. He opposed the teachings of Zinzendorf, and yet the Count loved him because he knew how to direct the fellowship with his friends in the manner of a congregation.

In Hesse-Homburg I met a Jew, a Karaite.[116] He was a sincere and honest Israelite. He had lofty thoughts about the Messiah and said, Messiah must not only be able to do miracles, but also to give a new heart. Since he was a Karaite he recognized neither Talmud, nor Sohar,[117] neither tradition, nor Cabala, but he wanted to form his language only on the basis of Holy Scripture. His speech was as pure and distinct as I had never heard it before. His spiritual conversations could be remembered easily, because they corresponded to the *sensus communis*. I concluded from this that Jesus' disciples could easily remember the forceful discourses of their Lord, since I myself could remember the conversations of the Karaite so distinctly and easily; they even emerged in my mind without my thinking about them. For this reason I loved the

Jew very much, and he loved me too. He promised to visit me some time.[118]

Dr. Kämpf suggested that I stay with him and give up theology for medicine. But I was still undecided what to do. I knew I would have to overcome many doubts if I were to take a position in the church. I was able to come to grips with them theoretically, but I was afraid they would bother me more once I got into the practical work.

Kämpf's reasons why I should separate myself from the Lutheran Church as a Babel I countered not only with my book about the condescension of God,[119] but also with Bengel's *Jus publicum divinum* based on the book of Revelation.[120] My experiences with the Inspired during my younger years did not permit me to give in to his entreaties. Instead, I confronted him with the principles of Bengel's system so clearly that he said to me at one time: "Stop talking! You want completely to change my entire direction." He admitted that Bengel's reasons were in conflict with the concepts which he had already formed for himself. Thus I left him alone, and we remained in peace with each other.

Returning Home (1737)

Finally,[121] after having become acquainted with medical practice, I wanted to return home, since among all the communities away from home I had not discovered a well-founded unity. I found nowhere someone basing his certainty on the principal ideas of the apostles and prophets. But everyone insisted only on the guidance of God according to that interpretation of Scripture which he made to fit his point of view. I let that pass as their personal opinion, but it could not satisfy me. I needed three pillars on which my edifice could rest: (1) The basic wisdom I found in human society and in nature. (2) The meaning and spirit of Holy Scripture, and (3) God's ways with me on these grounds.[122] I have often been tempted to avoid these claims upon myself. Sometimes I tended too much toward the basic wisdom of nature—I had already planned to visit Wolff in Marburg,[123] since I had talked to him there, but Psalm 8 kept me from going there—and sometimes I was close to going among the Jews together with Herr Schulze[124] in order to discover the meaning of Holy Scripture. Then again I almost gave in to the temptation to avoid the preaching ministry by becoming a professor for which I would have been able to find ways and means.

At this point I thought of the important advice the learned Herr Wachter in Leipzig had given me. I had been eager to speak to this man, among others. This is the scholar whom Professor Canz held in such high esteem that he said whenever he only heard his name mentioned he took off his hat. He wanted to stay single and take on only an independent profession. Thus he became an epigrammist for King August of Poland and later a distinguished member of the Deutsche Gesellschaft with a pension. I went to visit him. His study was in great disorder. There were books lying around everywhere, and there was hardly room left for a chair. He asked me why I did not want to accept an office at home. I replied: "Because that would force me to do things against the truth." "Oh," he said, "just take a lesson from me! I wanted to live the same way. Now I am old and can no longer change anything. But you can. I also see that you are of good courage and have a cheerful heart. What a great pity if you were to follow in my footsteps! I warn you! Take on a decent job, otherwise you will regret it, the way I do." Afterwards he discussed with me Spinoza's system. He was of the opinion that one could interpret it in a more acceptable way than was usually thought. But it would be better to take the generally accepted roads and to serve God in some useful capacity instead of remaining in individual separation. I took this to heart and remembered it often, especially at this time.

I said to my God: "What shall I do? I do not know what is the best. Guide me! I consider the offense of Christ greater wealth than all the treasures of Egypt. I know I will regret that I made this decision. Abbot Steinmetz also advised me not to remain a lone wolf.[125] Whom should I follow? If I begin the suffering of a profession that goes against my grain I will regret it. But, oh God, in Jesus Christ, do not then listen to my whimpering and sighing, but according to your wisdom lead me into glory."

Pastor in Hirsau and Literary Studies (1738-1743)

In this frame of mind I traveled home and got to Stuttgart.[126] On account of my book[127] on God's condescension and because of other misgivings the consistory would have liked to see me leave home a third time. Therefore I presented myself with the comment that, in any event, I had also studied medicine. If the gentlemen considered me questionable they should themselves determine me for medicine. However, they did not make a clear decision. So I went, according to my position [in the church of Württemberg] to Tübingen as a Repetent,[128] and finally, in 1738, I accepted the small parish in Hirsau (near Calw) instead of becoming associate pastor in Göppingen, since I was loath to begin with too extensive responsibilities. Already before that time, through my book on God's condescension, I had come to a somewhat clearer decision in my deliberations as to whether or not to marry and to accept a [church] position. In my traveling I had found little unity among sincere Christians and the scholars, and I came to the conclusion that I would have more freedom to search for truth in a small pastorate than in working together with others. Thus I married[129] in my thirty-sixth year and fathered children. But I also took time to search for truth in an all the more radical way.

I saw that Count Zinzendorf had turned Holy Scriptures into a collection of aphorisms [*Spruchkästlein*] and had not read them according to their textual connection. He had also not made a point of speaking convincingly to the needs of the present time, but had simply followed his intentions of quick and easy acceptance and success among the "souls." Therefore he thought one should completely give up the Halle method of reasoning in accord with the sentiment of the time [which is understood as follows]: neither in a too modern, nor a too old-fashioned way, not too quickly denying the practical errors which had been introduced, and striving to maintain a balance with the church fathers, on the one hand, and with modern scholarship, on the other. Zinzendorf saw the wisdom of this position, but his jealousy of the Halle circle kept him from using the proper moderation. So he chose a stance which was the extreme opposite [of that at Halle]: as person of high rank he opposed all religious constitutions by means of a new one and yet he wanted to unite them all. He tried to simplify the doctrine of the Trinity. He rejected the law. He also did not want the textual connection within the Scriptures, since he thought that also the apostles had not considered it, as one ought to see from quotations of Old Testament passages in the New Testament. He proposed two basic guidelines: (1) that we have become sinners and (2) that we have to feel the blood of Christ on us. He presented all this without any connection with the highpriestly office [of Christ]. I, for one, learned this much: even though the apostles might not have stood in need of tying themselves to the logical connection of scriptural passages (because, at that time, through the effects of the Holy Spirit, people had a much more direct understanding of the basic ideas), we are nevertheless in need of it, since the Holy Spirit no longer works as immediately as in the time of the apostles, and since the essential wisdom should no longer be kept concealed, but brought out into the open.

Thus I outlined a booklet after the pattern of the preaching in Isaiah,[130] published it, and dedicated it to the Count just when he came to Hirsau.[131] He pretended he wanted to change his approach completely and prefer the basic ideas of the Scriptures to his deliberate private ideas. He almost deceived me. But I noticed soon that he had remained the same old Count. Therefore I wrote the article about the law and the Gospel against him and his followers.[132] But I gave them considerable credit as to their grasp of community on the basis of the Gospel. Afterwards I read the books of Hopper on jurisprudence and spent a whole year on them in order better to be equipped to present the doctrine in my profession and in fellowship with others. I also read Hippocrates in order to become familiar with the very oldest and the very simplest ideas about man which also Zinzendorf was searching for, but not deeply enough. In opposition to the Moravians I also wrote hymns. But this aroused various distractions in me which hindered my development, since I wanted too quickly to grow inwardly, disregarding the dispensation of the present time which calls for special moderation and, according to Spener's approach, for a slow rational discernment in order finally to come to an immediate understanding. For the same reason, Bengel's *Gnomon* is written in this vein.

In Hirsau, too, I studied the book of Proverbs intensively. I distributed verses of a chapter on slips of paper, put them in little boxes, and let the children draw them. In short, I guided them in various ways and realized how necessary the Proverbs are for the present dispensation, since the primordial wisdom cannot be kept in concealment in the present state of the church, but has to be brought out into the open. In the time of the apostles this was not so necessary, although I read something like it in the *Shepherd of Hermas*. The reason was the following: the new model of the extraordinary effects of the Holy Spirit made it easily possible to reach a perfect understanding of the basic ideas of order (1 Cor. 11). But now, after so many sects have developed, the understanding has to be deepened by logic and metaphysics. This does not have to be done in Latin, but in German and in popular terms, however in keeping with the work of the Spirit. Johann Arndt,[133] too, was not ashamed to borrow the following ideas from Valentin Weigel[134] for use in his passage on prayer: (1) God knows better than we everything we need before we ask it. (2) God entices everyone to pray. (3) God is no respecter of persons, but equally offers his gifts freely to all. (4) It would be just as great a sin to pray on account of one's own piety as to abstain from prayer because of the sins one has committed. (5) for prayer one does not have to run after God to definite places. (6) One should not pray to God only at certain moments, and (7) the Lord's prayer comprises all principal doctrines.

During the time of the Apostolic Church it was not necessary to present all these basic ideas in a popular form, but now it is. This is why also mysticism finally developed into a scholasticism, since at the present time there is a great need for the logical and metaphysical universal truths in regard to which the mystics may have gone too far. These truths are nowhere presented in Holy Scripture except in Proverbs and in Job. Today Proverbs contributes a lot to the understanding of Jesus. If someone does not see this, he does not understand what St. Paul says: "In thinking be mature [perfect]." (1 Cor. 14:20).

It would be great if at the universities the logical and metaphysical truths would initially be taught in such a popular vein as any farmer already knows them. The secret of Socrates' deftness in communicating with persons was completely based on this. But we are much too clumsy to comprehend Socrates' effort to be a midwife of thought. It is necessary always to combine the teachings of Holy Scripture with logic and metaphysics. It has to be done, however, on a twofold basis: (1) Holy Scripture itself, and (2) wisdom in the streets.

This wisdom in the streets invites every man to study two things well: to know *God* and *himself.*

God is of himself and is not in need of anything. The creature is not of itself and is always in need of God. Therefore David says: "When thou takest away their breath, they die and return to their dust. When thou sendest forth thy Spirit, they are created." (Ps. 104:29, 30).

Oh, thou eternal God, thou art an invisible and unknown master workman, but thou dost reveal thyself in thy creature, so that one may recognize in it thy eternal power and divinity. Oh, how should I know thee? Draw me to thyself and to Christ as thou dost do it to all creatures, in drawing them to thee and to their salvation!

Through the creatures we ascend to God as on a ladder and learn that God is in heaven, and we on earth, and the abyss is under the earth. The starry sky is visible, the real heaven is invisible. The sky is light, but not like God, because God is pure light. Everything created is not without darkness. Since the abyss has the least light, it is the dwelling place of darkness, and the devil belongs into the abyss, since he has lost his light.

Oh God, light is the garment that thou dost wear. Heaven and all the heavens of heaven do not comprehend thee [cf. 1 Kings 8:27], but thou comprehendest them all. Guide thou my heart out of this dark world into thy light, since Jesus did not talk more about anything than that thou art light. Let me walk before thee, that is, in thy light, and not do the works of darkness.

The stars are in the sky and do not fall down. God has attached them to the nothing or to this inner power which one does not see ([cf.] Job 26:7). Many times daily one has to enter this inner power, this invisible world, and try to imagine that one is more in it than in one's own home or more than in the evil world. Out of this inner power which again contains innumerable powers arise all cooperations and effects, *complicationes* and *explicationes*, of the creatures.

While God is all and since his powers are indissoluble, he is perfectly good. But the powers of the creatures are dissolved by sin and thus do not exist in the goodness and truth of the divine coordination. Sin dwells within the wrong judgment. It is a wrong conatus of the powers of the soul, occurring without change of place and yet doing great damage to body and soul. It is sweet, and easily committed, but the restoration is difficult, since it is spiritual.

These and similar universal truths, as they may be found in Job and in Proverbs, contain the basic concepts and are very much needed today, because of the above-mentioned imperfections of the church. But Count Zinzendorf jumps right into things with both feet and says only: Jesus Christ! In his fantasies he does not want to hear of the eternal Word, since he does not want to admit of any other basic concepts besides his community. But without the *sensus communis* we will all become popes and rulers over men's conscience, tyrants and soul-catchers, that is, haters of man's freedom.—This is what I studied in Hirsau.

I often had the opportunity to go from Hirsau to Calw, since it was a walk of only a little more than fifteen minutes. It was there that I met a very unique person, Mr. Schill, headmaster of a school. He always communed with God, was very spiritually minded and listened to the workings of the Spirit.

Dr. Weissmann, who later became professor of theology in Tübingen, had been associate pastor in Calw before that time. Nearby is the mineral spring of Dainach [Teinach]. Many learned people went there, especially also prelate Oechslin.[135] He was supposed to become consistory councilor. But he did not want to, since Dr. Johann Heding-er[136] had called the consistory a dragon-stool.[137] Schill was in close contact with both of these men, Dr. Weissmann and Prelate Oechslin.

Weissmann read a lot in the books of Jane Leade,[138] of Jakob Böhme and of the Philadelphia Society. Formerly there was also a pastor Sey-bold there, who also studied the writings of Leade and Böhme and wanted to persuade Schill to do the same. But Schill continued on the spirit's inward road and did not read Jakob Böhme. He advanced so far in his inner sensorium that the deceased, especially the Separatists who had left the church as, for example, Schmoller,[139] the step-brother of Dr. Hedinger, appeared to him. Schmoller told him that as a punishment for his separating himself from the church he had to sit in the vestry for a long time after his death. Schill did not see the spirits, but he heard them speak very clearly with their former voices. The Separatists confessed [to him] that their lot in the world beyond was not the best. There was also a superintendent Zahn at the place. He came to Schill and brought him all kinds of detailed news about the personal fate of some of the blessed souls in heaven. Since these communications were without exception particular cases arbitrarily chosen, it was not surprising that Schill did not want to accept Jakob Böhme's ideas of the universal ground or the basic wisdom of things, since he was afraid he might mix them up with his special experiences.

Schill loved me very much. I chose him as godfather for my children. He often visited me and told me of marvels in the world beyond.

Zinzendorf also came to Hirsau at that time. Schill did not like it that I talked to him and got involved with him. He said, the Word of God dare not be twisted according to the intentions of the Count. In the world beyond, it would be manifest how much one needs the clear understanding of the divine Word. The Count left again, however, and traveled to Tübingen where he preached publicly, even though Dr. Weissmann did not like it.

My association with Schill continued. He told me that many thousands of spirits took the sentiments which they felt on earth along into the world beyond and did not give them up so soon. I found it terrifying to hear that a person on arrival in the other world was very much in danger of being drawn into the factions of a thousand opinions that he had carried along. If someone would not take along the pure meaning of the divine Word as a gift received, he would easily be confused also in the other world. There would be a greater confusion of opinions over there than here. The many factions would entice the newcomers and would want to draw them into their fellowship. They would be in the same position as the foolish virgins, having confidence and good hope and yet being basically uncertain. I thought of the *Esprit fort* of the late Herr von Muralt, in his letters about the English and the French,[140] and noticed that [Schill's reports] largely agreed with the accounts of the *Esprit fort.*

Meanwhile Oechslin, the venerable prelate, died. His views were very different from those of the others, and he had preached in public that one should pray for the dead. Schill had often presented to him the reasons for the doctrine of the restoration of all things, but the verse, "They will go away into eternal punishment, but the righteous into eternal life" (Mt. 25:46) and still other critical ideas kept him from accepting anything of Schill's. So he persisted in his opinion and in his critical stubbornness under the pretext that a person should stay with God's Word. This seems to be right, and there is also good reason for the exegetical rule that the same word within one and the same saying should not be interpreted in a twofold way. But this rule contradicts a higher rule, that one should never assume a meaning which stands in contradiction to clear interpretation and to the obvious conditions of the matter at hand. In terms of the gist of the matter, eternal pain cannot last as eternally as eternal life, and 1 Cor. 15 and Ephesians 1 seem to contradict the endlessness of punishments.

Thus Oechslin persisted in his critical stubbornness under the pretext of having to cling to the Word of God. He died. Not long after his death Oechslin came to Schill. Schill had just wanted to go out of the door of the living room, which he afterwards pointed out to me with his finger. Then he heard Oechslin's voice: "Stand still, brother!" So he remained standing in the door, and the conversation lasted long. Oechslin reported that after death he had come into a darkness in which he did not know how he felt. Fear and anxiety overcame him, since he carried with him his conviction of the infinity of the punishment. He reproached Schill harshly for not having changed his opinion with strongest entreaties. Schill answered, he had often refuted him. But Oechslin said he should have shaken and jolted him and should not have yielded until he had been convinced of the opposite. In this desperation he had sat there for quite some time, but finally God had answered his prayer and had granted him light, so that he had recognized his error and had said: "Oh, you theologians, how blind you are in the narrow confines of your claims!"

It can be concluded from all this what must have happened to Lukas Osiander who wrote a book against Johann Arndt[141] for certain doctrinal reasons and who accused him of heresy along the lines of Weigel, Tauler, and Ruysbroek. One can also conclude what superintendent

Burk must have felt when he entered eternity, in critical certainty of the letter of Scripture as a faithful and very committed laborer in the Lord. Here we will add a letter about this matter.[142] If I at that time would not have heard the reports of Schill already for almost six years, I would not have accepted Emanuel Swedenborg's[143] *visa* and *audita* [visions and voices] so easily. But I have simply examined them and have not, because of his erroneous tenets, rejected also that which agreed with Schill s reports. It is true, one does not need the reports of the dead. But one should also not reject what trustworthy persons communicate with sincerity.

No one has written as thoroughly about the *non éternité* (of the torments of hell) as Petitpierre[144] in his book which was published in 1761 (n.p.) under the title *Mes reflexions, ouvrage relatif aux defensions.* The apology of Petitpierre, pastor at the church in La Chaux de fonds, of June 4, 1760, is added to it. To stubborn scholars, God uncovers much through thorough, incontestable proofs. But they persist in their favorite opinions and do not hate their souls which harbor nothing but errors. It would do them good to read Ruysbroek. And yet the Lord knows how and whom he should show forbearance in regard to professional errors. I will not pass judgment in this matter, since there are many who never transcend their professional errors during this life. God has his reasons for this.

I remained in Hirsau for six years. During the first year of my ministry there Herr Korte[145] visited me and reproached me that I had not traveled together with him. He told me his entire experience, stayed until he had described his trip, and then left for Altona.

Since Probst Bengel lived in Herbrechtingen, I looked for an appointment nearby and accepted a pastorate in Schnaitheim near Heidenheim. From there I often visited Bengel, the man of God, and he also came to me.

In Schnaitheim (1743-1746) and Walddorf (1746-1752)

In Schnaitheim I worked on several small books, especially the *Historisch-katechetischen Vorrat*,[146] and I finally got to the point in my theology of having no doubts in what I believed.

From Schnaitheim I traveled to Ulm for a serious hydrocele operation which almost took my life, so great was the loss of blood. But God sustained me, and I am grateful to him for the many humbling experiences through which he taught me so much. I had actually planned to undergo the operation in Stuttgart and therefore had looked for an appointment nearby. Although meanwhile the operation had already been performed in Ulm, I nevertheless accepted the charge in Walddorf.

After I no longer had any doubts concerning theology, I found myself compelled to work at chemical experiments for the sake of emblematic theology[147] when I had already bought the books of all alchemistic authors from Hermes to Sendivogius (Philaletha).[148] I read them over and over again without finding a basic coherence. After God had shown me the two main subjects, I finally discovered the principle from which to understand the *via humida* [humid way] as well as the *via sicca* [dry way], so that I could safely experiment afterwards.

The philosophy of the adepts[149] contributes unusually to the understanding of the physics of Holy Scripture, and this in turn to the understanding of Holy Scripture itself. Therefore I used all the patience which this subject matter requires. The book *Fabri anatomia totius universi* is of great importance for interpreting Rev. 14:7. But God who already during the times of Johann Arndt opened the door to the true physics will continue to interpret this verse through his instruments, countering the absurd naturalism of the idealists.

The intention of making gold results in the impossibility of ever finding the true physics in terms of this verse [Rev. 14:7]. There are also many adepts who are content to know the pharmaceutical art and do not ascend beyond it. They profit no one but themselves. But I am basing my chemistry on the emblematic theology and leave the outcome to God. If someone takes a comprehensive look at what I am destined to do, he will find that I work in everything with a divine calling without letting my ministry suffer, since if someone works at it the right way he will not find it greatly expensive. It takes a greater effort to understand the adepts than one would think. It is not so hard to work at it if one is independent. But it is difficult and almost impossible if one has a job. Nevertheless, I sometimes experiment in sacred philosophy and physics whenever I find the time.

The verses of Johann Arndt show that he has understood the art better than Jakob Böhme. But it is impossible to learn the technique through the central vision. Raimundus Lullus[150] had the central vision. But without a teacher he did not know how to practice the art. Arndt, however, was introduced to it through the testament of an adept, who wrote the following verses:

> *Corpus Apollineo vivum dissolvimus igne,*
> *Spiritus ut fiat, quod fuit ante lapis.*
> *Hujus et e mediis trahimus penetralibus aurum,*
> *Aegra quod a matris sordibus aera lavat.*
> *Semine natali postquam sejunximus ossa,*
> *Haec consanguinea deinde lavamus aqua.*
> *Nascitur ex illis, varios induta colores,*
> *Ales, et in coelum candida facta volat*
> *Tum nos igne novo dejungimus illius alas,*
> *Lacte coloratas imbuimusque suo.*
> *Atque, quod est reliquum, cum sanguine pascimus illium,*
> *Mulciberis rabiem donec adulta ferat.*
> *Hinc morsi volucrem Sophiae ter maximus Hermes*
> *Dixit, et in toto non habet orbe patrem.*[151]

If one understands the meaning of *corpus vivum* [living body] and *ignis Apollineus* [Apollonian fire] one understands the basic principle.

I received the following letter from an unknown place. The writer[152] who did not give his name is a playwright. Since he is completely wrongheaded in theatrically degrading alchemy as ridiculous *nonens* (nothing) and a vain effort, his style is not surprising. He writes as follows:

"Sir:

"Among the many things which human beings eagerly seek, but which profit nothing, there is also the attempt to discover the philosopher's stone or the making of gold.

"Suppose this art would be discovered some day (to change simple metals into gold), what could be gained except that gold would lose its value? Since the value attributed to gold is arbitrary and based solely on the rare occurrence of this metal, the price cannot but go down as soon as it is available in great amounts and everywhere. If all copper mines would be changed into gold mines, and the gold mines in turn into copper mines one would not gain anything by this change, except the possibility of trading a pound of copper for a hundred pounds of common gold. And that is the way it is with all things whose value is based only on rarity and not on some inner natural value. Iron and steel are much more useful. Therefore the Americans valued them much more highly than gold, since they saw that handy tools and all kinds of guns could be manufactured from them. Imagine someone would discover the art of sowing genuine pearls in such a way that out of one pearl would sprout a hundred others as out of a seed: what would result except that pearls would gradually lose their value and that one could finally trade a genuine pearl for a bean? It would even be possible to buy the genuine pearls by the bushel, as one does peas today, and for a still lower price, since with peas one can at least satisfy hunger. If an alchemist would have really discovered the art, he could boast of no other success except that he managed to invent something very nice and yet of no greater usefulness as if grey stones would have been changed into white ones, or a yellow color would be given to something that was grey before.

"There are certain things which always carry their natural usefulness. The stone cuts, the wood burns and warms, certain plants heal, and the water quenches fire or thirst. Thus we would be greatly indebted to the person who could change lead into steel, a thorny bush into a fruitbearing tree, and the salty sea into fresh water. The value of other things, however, consists only in their rarity and in the agreement which people have made with each other as to how much they should be worth. Certain cards are of great importance in card playing, and this is based solely on the will of the players. As soon as they agree that they want to choose different cards, the previous ones are worthless. It is the same way with the changing of certain metals. As soon as they become frequent and common, they lose their value, and at the same time the previous agreement on their price is null and void.

"Thus the work which makes so many distinguished men rack their brains and on which many spent almost all their possessions, is not only completely useless, but the invention would even in case of success be very harmful for the human race, since it would cause an indescribable misery and confusion among people. Many would lose their prosperity in a moment, if the money which they have either gained through their toil and sweat, or have received in exchange for other expensive commodities, would turn into nothing in their hands. In such a case one would either have to manage to get along with exchange of commodities, or find another way of estimating [the value of] things. But both would result in unspeakable difficulties. However, we can find consolation in the fact that this invention will hardly ever become reality. Most of the stories in circulation about the philosopher's stone are either made up, or there was some fraud involved in the experiment, as I have shown in the play about the Arabic powder. But wherever the matter really took place it was so expensive that it was not worth the trouble and the money spent on it could not be regained. Most of the people who pretended to be makers of gold died in poverty. When once an alchemist dedicated a book to Pope Leo X in which he pretended to have discovered the art of making gold in hopes of receiving a reward, the pope sent him only an empty bag and told him that, since he mastered the art of making gold, he did not need anything but an empty bag to keep it in.

"Sincerely yours ...."

There is nothing to comment on in this letter except that this gentleman does not know the [alchemistic] authors. He did not read Augurellus who wrote to the pope in beautiful Latin verse, and probably did not even know his name. Although it is not known whether Augurellus himself experimented or not, he in any case is praised and recommended by Irenaus Philaletha as a writer who gives an excellent survey. That is sufficient. The arguments of Holberg are, of course, well suited for the theatre. It is easy to make ignorant people laugh. But the wise pay no attention. They act according to well-founded reasons.

Other ignorant people think that this demonic shadow-boxing puts a person under a magic spell in a rather vulgar way. These people I answer as follows: a wise man does not easily get angry. When the Pharisees reviled Jesus, claiming that the devil dwelt in him he replied: "The devil is not in me." [Cf. Jn. 8:48f.]. That was enough. Those who are slaves of sin, anger, and lust will cause the Holy Spirit to punish them. People who do not even notice that the Holy Spirit cannot help them on without inner, gradually merging exercises in wisdom, one can only commend to God with pity until they get sober and stop slandering what they do not understand. *Temeritas est. praecurrere perceptioni judicium.* (It is rash to judge a matter before one understands it.)

In Walddorf I wrote the *Inquisitio in sensum communem*[153] in Latin. It contains all the basic concepts of Scripture, and the purpose of the book is expressed in the final words: "(1) Search for the most useful and the most simple in the learning of the present time, like Socrates. (2) Try to appropriate those concepts of physics and ethics which are closest to the terms of Holy Scripture, so that the words which you coin from the fundamentals resemble the style of Holy Scripture. The witness of Jesus is the spirit of prophecy. Learn to feel, think, speak, teach and live according to this resemblance. Save all the rest for the unwrapping of the other world, since time is wrapped-up eternity, and eternity is unwrapped time. In these things try to find the right balance. Then you are wise."

I also wrote in Walddorf *Die Wahrheit des sensus communis in den Sprüchen und Prediger Salomo.*[154] Included in it is the translation of the English book by the Count of Shaftesbury (Anthony Ashley Cooper),[155] so that one could see how the Count with his naturalistic philosophy interpreted the *sensus communis.*

I can recognize various rays of truth also in the naturalists. I am not so narrow-minded that I immediately reject everything whereof I have many reservations. I am mindful of the word of Jesus which made me suspend my judgment a thousand times: "Do not forbid him; for he that is not against you is for you." (Lk. 9:50) "By your words you will be justified and by your words you will be condemned." (Mt. 12:37)

In addition to my research in science, I also wrote (in Walddorf) a Latin theology at the behest of my consistory-president, Baron von Zech, which I based on Newton's philosophy as Canz based his on Leibniz's.

This work, *Theologia ex idea vitae deducta*, is still in manuscript form,[156] as are also the commentaries on Romans and the Hebrews.[157] But I had an abstract of the *Theologia* printed under the title *Sylloge Theologiae ex idea vitae deductae.*[158] This is an improved digest of the propositions I wrote thirty years earlier, without being sufficiently mature, in the book *Evangelische Ordnung der Wiedergeburt.*[159] Professor Canz started an argument with me. I have answered him in the *Inquisitio* and in the end of the *Sylloge* (pp. 62ff).

I have to add something here before I conclude my report about Walddorf. In the congregation I found much edification, and many students from Tübingen came out to see me. The Count of Castelli[160] also came and asked me to find a student for him who was strong in mathematics and experienced in astronomy. I had a Magister by the name of Johann Ludwig Fricker[161] come from Tübingen. The Count found him quite suitable and took him along to the artful craftsman Nesstfell in

Wiesentheid in Franconia in order to help him complete the celestial machine. Nesstfell was a carpenter who observed the sky by day and by night with tubes and telescopes and learned to understand the movements of the sky without a teacher. News about him reached the Roman emperor.[162] So he summoned him. And Nesstfell promised to build a machine, which can still be seen in Vienna and Würzburg. Fricker knew more about calculus than Nesstfell. He had to rebuild half of the machine and had to set it up according to Bengel's calculations. After completing it, Fricker had to travel to Vienna, and he waited there until it would please the emperor [to receive him]. But the waiting became too tedious. After he had left, the emperor returned and was quite indignant that they had let Fricker leave. He certainly would have employed him in his service.

Later Fricker took a position with Cornelius von der Flint as a private tutor. There was also a certain Miss Volklin. She paid Fricker the same as Cornelius. He had to instruct her in my writings and give lessons in them every day. Finally he returned and became a pastor in Dettingen (near Urach). But he died early. He surpassed me, his teacher, by far, especially in mathematics and physics. He invented the new theory of music. But it is so profound that few understand it. His theory can be found in my book about the *sensus communis*, and more [about it] in some other books of mine.

At this point I have to tell a story. A man by the name of Crevoisier from Montpellier, who lived in Rouen at the time, and who knew the art of building adding machines, came to me in order to talk with me about science. He told me of his experiences in Walddorf in 1750. His parents had been innkeepers. As a young man he had been unable to stand the commotion in the house, and had read about the ancient hermits in the old books. This had caused him to go into the desert to search for God in stillness. After climbing high mountains he had come to some highlands and then into a plain. There an old, venerable man had met him whose face looked very young, in spite of his aged appearance and who said to him: "What impudence has brought you here?" In reply Crevoisier said he had pleaded his desire to live as a hermit. Then the old man had given him instructions as to how he had to go about becoming a true hermit who lives in seclusion from the world. He had accepted this with the greatest devotion. The old man then had taken him along until he came to a very pleasant grotto with a fountain at its center on which in glistening letters could be read: Living water from the three kingdoms of nature. The old man had taken a glass full of this water and had put a metal into it which dissolved like milk, and Crevoisier had to drink of it. After this his mind had been very enlightened. And the old man had said that now he would be able to stand it for forty days without eating and drinking. That had pleased him. And he had been content. Then the old man had interpreted for him for ten days the first chapter of Genesis, for ten days the first chapter of Ezekiel, for ten days moral philosophy in contrast to the foolishness of the world as practiced by the courts, which he had seen intuitively, and for ten days the true theology of God in Jesus Christ.

I suspended judgment on this story, accepted it as the dream of a waking person and thought: it is altogether a nice fable. I do not take it for anything more than that.

I myself have not learned from any old man, but learned the same things from Holy Scripture. It is for this reason that I write books, but I do not pretend that my writing consists of anything but arguments which can be tested by sound reason, even among plain folk. If someone does not want to accept this, he can make his own choice. I know this is a time when we should not care if someone considers us foolish and insane, because Jesus own relatives considered him such.

In Weinsberg (1752-1759) and Herrenberg (1759-1765)

In 1752 I was called from Walddorf to Weinsberg as superintendent. It was there that I was severely tested by hellish lies.[163] Besides the Biblical Dictionary[164] I wrote there also my discourses about the Gospels and Epistles.[165]

The defamations of Hymenaeus,[166] the town piper, and Alexander,[167] the schoolmaster, drove me away.[168] I have been here three years undisturbed and have written during this time the three parts about the Golden Age[169] as well as about Ancient Philosophy returning in the Golden Age.[170] Otherwise I spend my time educating my four children, after six others have died. I am teaching my (older) son Halophilus Irenaus medicine and chemistry, and the little Johann Friedrich, Latin. One daughter, Benigna, had been married, and afterwards died in childbirth. The other one is still with me. I teach the people very quietly, not causing a great stir.

In Herrenberg I also wrote the conversation in the realm of the dead between Demokritus (Dipper) and Zinzendorf,[171] in order to make it plain why Count Zinzendorf has lost sight of the doctrine of the priesthood on account of his intimate bridegroom love for the Lord. Few people recognize this. But without this perspective one cannot judge the dynamics of this church.

In my *Golden Age* I asserted that all universities should make an effort to purify their principles and to strive for the best model of reflection. I know that this is not done. I am not a professor, although I could have become one already since 1732 when von Pfeil[172] was still Acting Director and the Right Reverend Propst Weissensee assisted him. However, I am a philosopher, first of all for myself, in order to trample under foot all spurious intentions which deviate from the truth; but then also for others, in order fearlessly to speak the truth which I could not express equally well at the university.

After I had proposed some ideas in the *Golden* Age as to how theology, jurisprudence, and medicine could be improved on the basis of this model—although I knew that in the *Golden* Age (the millenium) lawyers would no longer be needed—I wrote a booklet along this line of thought, on the basic wisdom for jurisprudence.[173] I dedicated it to my brother, the General Food Administrator, not only to remind him of his former studies, but also to present to his son, who was a student in Tübingen, the best way of studying law. I condensed the first four books on General Law by Hopper, minister at the court of Philipp II, son of Charles V, since no one has written as thoroughly on law as he. The professors in Tübingen were angry with me that I interfered with jurisprudence. But there is no danger. If a person studies the fundamental wisdom, which is philosophy, for his own sake he should be well acquainted with the general principles of all three faculties. For this reason I have written the *Basic Wisdom for Jurisprudence* not as a law-scholar, but as a philosopher. It is well-known how Mr. Gerstlacher, chancellery-lawyer, got ridiculed by a professor whom he had paid high compliments in his Library of Law. But others, not I, will uncover this satiric malice. God knows how to justify honest and disinterested intentions through his instruments.

Likewise, as a philosopher, I have also presented the general principles of medicine in [the] book entitled *Die Philosophie der Alten wiederkehrend in der güldenen Zeit*.[174] Similarly I am writing now Die *Theologie der Alten wiederkehrend in der güldenen Zeit*.[175]

While I am pursuing all these studies I look into Fenelon's ingenious writings. There I read the following: "Those persons who hold high offices have to fulfill so many unavoidable duties that they hardly have any time left to be with God, unless they carefully schedule the hours for it. As little as one is inclined to set aside hours of leisure, those hours which one has not spent in the service of God and neighbor are lost. Thus one has to adhere strictly to a schedule. Its exact observance seems to go too far. But without it everything turns into confusion. One is distracted, yields, loses strength, removes oneself imperceptibly from God, abandons oneself to one's inclination, and does not sense the deviation into which one falls until one is that far gone that there is no more hope to get straightened out again. Let us pray! Prayer is our only salvation. The Lord be praised who hears my prayer and has not turned his mercy from me! If a person wants to pray the right way he has to be careful to schedule all daily activities in such sequence and with such regularity that they will not be disturbed by anything." Thus Fenelon.[176]

I have often experienced, when in my inward struggle through praying, seeking, and knocking I turned my confusion into order and my restlessness into quietness, that I could let it go at that and content myself to bring it before God during my regular working. But I found out that it was a wonderful thing to approach the throne of grace also at times when I did not know how to pray, that God looks mercifully even upon our childish prayer, that he even inspires us with thoughts which surpass all rules, according to the word: "[He] is able to do far more abundantly than all that we ask or think." (Eph. 3:20).

The wisdom in the street, the spirit of Scripture, and the divine dispensations are instruments, but it is God who in Jesus sometimes works beyond all this. Thus I never want to depend on acquired grace, but come before him as a beggar who does not have anything and cannot do anything. Then my soul finds rest, and the spirit of Jesus gives the powers of grace a new form. This calms the heart and increases grace and peace.[177]

After I had had in Herrenberg[178] until 1762 a much more restful life than in Weinsberg I succumbed to a dangerous disease. I was in a critical condition. I had been invited to a brotherly synod with Chancellor Reuss, Stiftsprediger Storr, Superintendent Glöcker of Tübingen, Superintendent Becherer of Tuttlingen and Köstlin, senior pastor at Esslingen, in order to renew our old ties in Christ. I already noticed the beginnings of pleurisy, but traveled anyway, and returned home more ill than before, went to bed and became sick for half a year with phthisis which developed from the pleurisy. I was in the fangs of death; all medicine was in vain. At eleven o'clock at night the fever began. Then I could not unburden my thoughts until I took a slate into bed and began to write. I wrote the second part of the earthly and heavenly philosophy[179] before the portals of eternity in the conviction that I would die. It was supposed to be my last will and testament. Then I found rest. Finally, when no hope was left, Privy Councilor Georgii sent me Hecalios white drops through Mr. Storr, and afterwards I found out what they consist of. They made me well. The Reverend Philipp Matthäus Hahn,[180] who constructed the celestial machine and who at that time was not yet in Onstmettingen, was my assistant. He knows the whole course of my sickness. After I had gotten well, Swedenborg's book came to my attention. I translated it, made it into the first part of the earthly and heavenly philosophy and with official permission gave it to the printer in Tübingen.

As Prelate in Murrhardt (1766-1782)

Meanwhile the position of a prelate in Murrhardt[181] became available. I knew I had enemies, although I had been suggested as a prelate already ten years before. Therefore I wrote a letter in French to Serenissimus,[182] and His Highness (Karl Eugen) answered within four days with two letters.[183] Upon order of the Duke I became prelate. My book [about the earthly and heavenly philosophy] was discovered only afterwards. The consistory was very upset about it.[184]

By decree of the Duke of December 11, 1765, I became a member of the "Landschaft"[185] and resided for almost a year in Stuttgart. Finally I returned to Murrhardt. There I occupied myself with the philosophy of Scripture at my leisure. But the Consistory drove me to turn to the Privy Council by virtue of my position in the state. The Consistory prohibited my publishing anything inside or outside the country. Thereupon my son who is a general practitioner had the book *Metaphysik in Connexion mit der Chemie* printed under his name.

Meanwhile I instructed my youngest son, Johann Friedrich, in Latin, Greek, Hebrew (Arabic), and in rabbinical literature.

On November 30, 1768, Serenissimus was supposed to arrive here. But he was not able to come. His brother, Prince Friedrich Eugen,[186] came instead. On St. Andrew's day I delivered a sermon before the gentlemen of the court and afterwards paid my most humble respects to His Highness, the Prince. Meanwhile his wife, Her Royal Highness, also arrived by carriage, and I was invited to dine with her. Her Highness talked with me very kindly and still remembered all the conversations I had with her three years earlier about Princess Antonia. Since then my book [about Antonia's tableau] has become known.[187]

Secretly I wrote to Swedenborg in Stockholm. He answered, and the whole correspondence can be read in print in Klemm's *German Theology*.[188] Everyone can see that I did not appropriate anything from him, except what belongs to the philosophy of Scripture. I detest his exegetical ideas. He sent me his books about the earthly body of the planets, on marital love and finally his last one on the true Christian religion. This last one made me turn away from him completely.[189]

Meanwhile Swedenborg again had various letters sent to me of which I included one in the translation of the book about the earthly body of the planets. The translation was done under my guidance by an extraordinarily gifted fourteen-year-old boy, son of my nephew, the Kammerdirektor Dertinger. In this letter Swedenborg threatens me: "I would be sent to hell after my death, unless I accepted his teachings."[190] I read this with indifference and did not hold it against Swedenborg. I knew that a visionary is not an interpreter of Scripture, and that the mistakes which grow out of the profession of a well-intentioned scholar should not be taken as heresies.

Even so, people thought of me by now as a promoter of all Swedenborg's doctrines. Therefore I published two small books which were brought out by Messerer in Hall: (1) *Mediation of the Conflict between Swedenborg and the Consistory of Gotenburg*, and (2) *Evaluations of Emanuel Swedenborg's Important Doctrine of the Condition after Death*.[191] The Consistory was very angry with me and issued an order to the effect that all of Swedenborg's books should be collected and confiscated. Prelate Faber who had been working against me for some time, although he had been my best friend before, collaborated with the Consistory to have the Privy Council send me a letter *ex speciali resolutione*. It contained the order not to accept Swedenborg as a guest if he

should come. This letter made me feel quite uncomfortable. But I trust-
ed Serenissimus who agreed with my opinion that Holy Scriptures
should be interpreted without a secular philosophy, and who told me
that even if I had a thousand persecutors they should not harm me. Faber defended an opinion which was in contrast to that of my enlightened Duke and opposed me in a scholarly treatise about the moral sense
in which he proposed that one should base the natural law on Wolff's
philosophy and consequently judge jurisprudence and theology according to the same rules. I refuted this in the last part of my book about the
Ancient Philosophy.[192] That hurt Faber. He became a member of the
Consistory in 1767, and he tried then to restrain me. But I thought: I
serve my Lord in heaven. The Lord will "fight for you; you only have
to keep quiet." (Ex. 14:14) This is what I relied on, and I knew that
God was with me.

I felt obliged, however, to deliver a paper in defense of my stand to
the Privy Council in which I refuted the accusation of the Consistory.
This has been included in the book "Evaluations of the Important Doctrine of the Condition after Death and of Related Ideas of the Re-
nowned Emanual Swedenborg."[193] The Privy Council knew that the
Consistory had acted unjustly, and that it was against the government
contracts to confiscate a prelate's book and to declare the author a here-
tic without a trial, which the Consistory wanted to avoid because they
knew my parrhesia. I did not want to oppose the Consistory too much.
However, I considered a public disputation in Tübingen. But I shunned
the great stir it would create. Thus I contented myself with writing another book which is to be printed in Frankfurt.[194] The contents are the
following: (1) Open letter to the theologians that, according to Serenissimus, one should not interpret the Holy Scripture with the help of a
secular philosophy, but should use only the fundamental wisdom of
Holy Scripture itself. (2) That in order to grasp the high priestly office
of Christ and to understand the whole world one should try to learn
from the charismata which God bestowed in special times on a Jakob
Böhme, a Swedenborg, and a Postellus,[195] but that this should be done
with discretion and exclusion of the false doctrines, and that thus Holy
Scripture should be interpreted in its normative points. Especially Ezekiel's teachings should be used as a basis, and nothing should be accepted from Jakob Böhme and from Swedenborg which would not find
its norm in Holy Scripture. (3) Johann Salomo Semler's[196] teachings
should be rejected. Against Semler I wrote a book [to the effect] that
the apocalyptic formulas should be interpreted on grounds of the fundamental wisdom of Holy Scripture. Now there is nothing left but to let
myself be guided by God with blindfolded eyes.

Meanwhile (1770) a big fight developed in the Landschaft.[197] Chancellor Reuss, myself, Prelate Faber, and Assessor Dann,[198] member of
the Landschaft, protested against the improper practices of the special
board. The court chaplain Fischer said in his sermon that in this case Pi-

late and Herod had become friends, although they had been enemies before. I let all this pass, and the conflict in the Ladschaft was ended. I
committed everything to God and to Jesus Christ, my Lord.

Herr von Braun, vicedirector of the society of the nobility in Thurin-
gia, dedicated to me his book on the analysis of water. I sent it to Serenissimus, and as a gift in return I sent to Herr von Braun a treatise with
the title *Societas de propaganda Physica Patriarcharum*.[199] Therein I
explained the most important words of the physics of Holy Scripture on
grounds of chemistry, so that it became clear that I studied alchemy on
account of Holy Scripture and not for the purpose of [making] gold.

Meanwhile I acquired a much more thorough practice of alchemy
and penetrated deeply into the cause of the processes....[200] My son, Halophilus Irenäus, also published a book about metaphysics based on
chemistry in which I sketched Lullus' process rather distinctly. In this
book various tenets of philosophy as well as of theology and medicine
are examined. On the one hand, there are the pantheists who give themselves airs with the book on the system of beings, and even want to
drag in Newton with his concept of space,[201] as though the immaterial
space would imply a necessity without freedom. Newton on the contrary proclaims nothing but freedom and elevates the ideas of Scripture
above everything else. Christ exists in order to temper the necessity of
God with the eternal freedom.

It is well to have disputes, since the contention reveals the yearning
(Lk. 12:51ff). On the other hand, new perverters of Scripture are rising
up. In Halle, Semler brought to light the ideas of Oeder which are rather detrimental to Holy Scripture and sacred revelation. He declares that
the seven spirits of God, the throne of God, and the incense on the altar
of God are material and fanatical imaginings of Cerinth. While this follows from modern idealism, one is surprised that these slanderers of
Scripture are not afraid of eternal judgment (Heb. 6:2). Thus it is imper-
ative to counteract these false concepts with others, however materialistic they may sound. The great day of *Chemia universalis* will make
their idealistic ideas materialistic enough.

If one puts together from Holy Scripture from the beginning to the
end all the seemingly absurd passages, one notices that the entire Holy
Scripture agrees in principle: "God was manifested in the flesh" (1
Tim. 3:16) and: "For in him the whole fulness of deity dwells bodily."
(Col. 2:9) Here everything exists in one bodily confluence. If one scales
off these massive concepts from bodiliness, there is no coherence, no
nexus, no connection left in the entire Holy Scripture. Someone should
put his mind to this, and Semler would be most effectively refuted. For
either idealism is wrong, or the materialism of the Scriptures is wrong.
But the latter is not wrong. For these words, says Holy Scripture, are
trustworthy and true. [Cf. Rev. 21:5] Therefore the other is foolishness
and absurdity in the eyes of God. But all writing will profit little until
God will take away the cover that hides all peoples, and remove it from

the nations. Meanwhile everyone bears witness in his own generation.

The time has not arrived as yet that God will bring about for the nations a more purifying change of language through a new metaphysics (according to Eph. 3:9). We only cart stones and limestone, and leave it up to the reader to judge what is closer to God's intentions for the Golden Age. God governs everything. He will make our ways straight toward the sanctification of his name.... The time has come to write unusual things, for it is close to a revolution and the tempering of the children of Levi.

Now my next task is the philosophy of Scripture and a biblical dictionary opposing Teller's dictionary.[202]

Rektor Hasenkamp[203] in Duisburg sends me very important news about a person[204] who is in even closer contact with the citizens of heaven than Preceptor Schill (according to Heb. 12:22). But since I have passed my seventieth year, I do not care very much about all these things. "For here we have no lasting city, but we seek the city which is to come." (Heb. 13:14) (This means: Believers know that no one can snatch them out of Jesus' hand (Jn. 10:28), and as the firstborn of God's creatures they care little about such news. They live and die for the Lord. (Cf. Rom. 14:8) What it looks like on the planets they want to find out only in the future. Now they do battle according to the battle rules of the New Testament—and Swedenborg does not contribute much to that—for the crown of life.)

Meanwhile I see from afar that my doctrine of the philosophy of Scripture is sprouting like a shoot and like a root out of dry ground.[205] Therefore I leave it to my sons, especially the youngest one, how he will understand and accept my teaching.[206]

NOTES

1. Ernst Benz, *The Mystical Sources of German Romantic Philosophy*, tr. by Blair R. Reynolds and Eunice M. Paul (Allison Park, PA, 1983), p. 45, quoted Oetinger's three conditions for non-absolutist government after the 1836 "Golden Age" begins: "1. True happiness, in a kingdom, implies three conditions, first that the subjects, despite the variety which order implies, and despite differences in condition, know among themselves an equality similar to that which is presented to us in the division of the country of Israel.... 2. Secondly, they should possess all goods in community and not get upset about things being their own property. 3. Thirdly, they have no need for any kind of obligation one to another, for if everything were superabundant, there would be no need for government or property...." Karl E. C. Ehmann, Oetinger's *Sämtliche Schriften*, Bd. 6, 2. Abth. (Stuttgart, 1858-64), 29-30.

2. Lehmann, Hartmut, *Pietismus und Weltliche Ordnung vom 17. bis zum 20. Jahrhundert.* (Stuttgart, 1969), p. 112. Note also Mary Fulbrook's comments (in *Piety and Politics*, N.Y., 1983, pp. 147-148) about how Moser's battle for state "improvements in policy, manufacturing, trading and economic affairs" incurred suspicions from fellow Pietists also representing the Estates, which undermined the cause of their own Estates, battle for reform against the Duke! She describes Moser's "martyrdom" as being "isolated" and "idiosyncratic."

3. Ehmann, p. 588.

4. For the following see Kurt Leese, *Von Jakob Böhme zu Schelling* (Erfurt, 1927), pp. 25-64.

5. See Oetinger's *Biblisches und emblematisches Wörterbuch*, 1776 (Biblical and Emblematic Dictionary).

6. An American contribution is by Frederick O. Kile, Jr. *Die theologischen Grundlagen von Schellings Philosophie der Freiheit* (Leiden, 1965), and Harry Yeide, Jr. discusses Oetinger on pp. 109-123, in *Studies in Classical Pietism: The Flowering of the 'Ecclesiola'* (New York, 1997).

7. *Seneca Ad Lucilium Epistulae Morales* (tr. Richard M. Gummere. London, New York, 1917), letter 41.

8. Cicero, *De Re Publica, De Legibus* (Tr. Clinton Walker Keyes. London, New York, 1928), II, 4:8.

9. The followers of Cerinthos who lived around 100 A.D. Opposed to a real incarnation. See Oetinger's remarks in his chapter "Patristic and Rabbinic Studies."

10. Jan van Ruysbroek (1293- 1381), one of the great medieval mystics and author of widely read books. A German translation of his works was edited in 1701 by Gottfried Arnold. Cf. note 29.

11. Oetinger is referring to his biblical dictionary published in 1776: *Biblisches und emblematisches Wörterbuch, dem Tellerischen Wörterbuch und Anderer falschen Schrifterklärungen entgegen gesetzt*. In this book he seeks to

counter the rising rationalism with the substance of biblical truths.

12. The headings of the various parts of Oetinger's "Genealogy" are later editorial additions. We will largely follow the pattern of the Ehmann edition.

13. Published in Tübingen in 1739.

14. Oetinger was born in Göppingen, about 15 miles east of Stuttgart.

15. The first teacher of Horace (65-68 B.C.), dreaded because of his strictness.

16. Johann Hübner (1668-1731), headmaster of the Johanneum, a school in Hamburg.

17. The term Oetinger uses here, "Spezial," refers to a senior minister who is adviser and administrator for a group of pastors in a certain area.

18. Wilhelm Ludwig von Mascowsky (1675-1731), 1696 secretary to the Württemberg minister of state, 1720 chancellor of the Count of Hesse-Darmstadt.

19. Konrad von Gessner (1516-1565), great physician and scientist, died as a professor in Zürich.

20. A medicine produced in the Franckesche Anstalten at Halle and sold through the pharmacy of the orphanage. Its history and also its influence in the United States is described in Julius Friedrich Sachse, *The German Pietists of Provincial Pennsylvania* (Philadelphia, 1895), pp. 57f. "One of the members of the *collegium pietatis* in Erfurt, Burgstaller by name, who was an alchemist and chemist, on his deathbed bequeathed to Francke the recipe for compounding certain medicines, which were sold by the different clergymen in sympathy with the institution. These remedies eventually yielded an annual income of more than $20,000 and made the institution financially independent." Sachse goes on to remark that Burgstaller's chief nostrum was the *essentia dulcis*, or extract of gold. "Prior to the Revolution these remedies were sent to America in large quantities, and were disposed of to the Germans and others by the resident Lutheran clergymen. In Philadelphia the main supply was stored in one of the side porches of St. Michael's Church, corner Fifth and Appletree Alley. By many persons these remedies were supposed to have magical or supernatural properties, against which neither Satan nor disease could prevail." In another context Sachse remarks that as much as he knew the remedy was still being used in the United States in the early fifties of the nineteenth century.

21. "Monastery School," or—as later in the text—simply "monastery," was a kind of prep school for theology students. Some of the former Roman Catholic monasteries after the Reformation in Württemberg had been turned into preparatory schools for the clergy.

22. Philip Heinrich Weissensee (1673-1767), preceptor at the Protestant monastery school of Maulbronn and Blaubeuren, died as a prelate in Denkendorf.

23. The term "Props" which Oetinger here uses might be translated "provost." But since "provost" has a less ministerial image, one might best think of a "prelate" or "prior."

24. Oetinger here refers to Duke Eberhard Ludwig of Württemberg. Cf. Note 27.

25. Johann Wendel Bilfinger, the father of Georg Bernhard Bilfinger, Oetinger's teacher in Tübingen. Cf. note 30.

26 François Fénelon de Salignac de la Motte (1651-1715), royal tutor and since 1695 archbishop of Cambrai, wrote *Les aventures de Télémaque*, a "mirror of royalty" for the grandson of Louis XIV. The book was published against

his wish in Holland in 1699.

27. Eberhard Ludwig, Duke of Württemberg (1677-1733), one of the less illustrious rulers of his land. Noteworthy of his reign is the founding of the Stuttgart orphanage (1710).

28. August Hermann Francke took a trip through Württemberg in 1717-1718.

29. Oetinger is here referring to Gottfried Arnold (1666-1714) who wrote the *Unparteiische Kirchen- und Ketzerhistorie* and tended toward separatist Pietism.

30. Georg Bernhard Bilfinger (1693-1750), philosopher, mathematician and theologian, represented Leibnizian and Wolffian ideas. Professor in Tübingen. In 1737 he became regent of Württemberg as guardian of Prince Karl Eugen. The church of Württemberg owes him the famous 1743 "Reskript" which made private meetings within the church possible.

31. Christian Wolff (1679-1754), professor of philosophy at Halle from 1706-1723 when the King of Prussia banned him from his territories because of his deterministic ideas and also as a consequence of his conflict with the Pietist theologians. From 1723-1740 at Marburg University. Frederick the Great, upon his ascension to the throne, invited him back to Halle.

32. Nicolas Boileau-Despréaux (1636-1711), French poet and writer, famous for his satires.

33. The congregations of the Inspired can be traced back to the French Camisards who after the repeal of the Edict of Nantes (1685) resisted the suppression of their faith in the Cevennes mountains. Characteristic of their cult were individuals who as "instruments" uttered words in a somnambulistic condition.

34. Johann Friedrich Rock (1678-1749), born near Göppingen as the son of a pastor. A saddler by profession, he was expelled from Württemberg in 1708 because of separatist activities. Since 1728 known as leader of the Inspired.

35. Johann Andreas Hochstetter (1637-1720), prelate in Bebenhausen since 1689, under Spener's influence tried to renew the Württemberg church. Sometimes called the "father of Swabian Pietism," August Hermann Francke referred to him as the "Württembergian Spener."

36. Israel Gottlieb Canz (1690-1753), preceptor in Bebenhausen from 1721-1723, since 1734 professor in Tübingen.

37. Jean Pierre de Crousaz (1663-1748), from Lausanne, spent part of his life in Germany and in his writings opposed Leibniz's philosophy, especially the deterministic connexion between all events.

38. Johann Osiander (1657-1724), director of the Württemberg church consistory since 1708, controlled the church as well as the school system. Was instrumental in introducing confirmation in Württemberg in 1723.

39. Christian Thomasius (1655-1728), law scholar, since 1679 teacher at the University of Leipzig. One of the first professors to deliver his lectures in German. Called to Halle by the Prussian government, he became cofounder of Halle University in 1694.

40. Elias Cammerer (1673-1734), physician and professor at Tübingen, highly regarded by Oetinger for his steadfastness in the faith founded in the Word of God.

41. Gottfried Hoffman (1669-1728), professor in Tübingen and Ephorus (director) of the Tübinger Stift since 1707, wrote *Synopsis theologiae purioris*.

42. Thomas Goodwin (1600- 1679), English preacher and author of devo-

tional books.

43. The Camisards (mentioned before in note 33) were a group of French Huguenots. Together with all French Protestants, they were victims of the persecution of Protestantism in France. Although in 1704 they had achieved a victory over the French king, they were soon again subject to persecution. Initially having fled to Switzerland and England, by 1711 the English group emigrated to Holland and Germany. It was this group that Oetinger encountered.

44. Ehmann adds here in parentheses: "Probably these books were 'Erfahrungsvolle Zeugnisse' and Rock's book 'Wohl und Weh'."

45. The theological seminary called "Stipendium" or, abbreviated, simply "Stift" (from "stiften" = to donate). Founded during the time of the Reformation to provide Württemberg with preachers, councilors, and public servants imbued with the spirit of the new age. In 1547 the Duke of Württemberg transferred the holdings of the former Augustinian monastery in Tübingen to Protestant ministerial education. Ever since the "Stift" has been identified with the building that was the former Augustinian monastery.

46. Cf. note 30.

47. The term "mercurial" is an older psychological concept. Mercury was the image of movement and agility. This was transferred to the human disposition. The mercurial disposition corresponds to the sanguine temperament. Oetinger regarded himself as a mercurial individual.

48. A tutor in the Tübinger Stift.

49. Nicole Malebranche (1638-1715), French philosopher.

50. Christoph Matthäus Pfaff (1686-1760), chancellor of the University of Tübingen from 1720-1756, a rather ambiguous figure as a scholar and a human being. Upon his leaving Tübingen in 1756, Oetinger wrote in a letter to the Count of Castell: "We are rid of the rogue" (Ps. 9:17).

51. Achates, in Virgil's Aeneid the friend of Aeneas.

52. Kilian Rudrauff (1627- 1690), theologian and philosopher, at the end of his life superintendent in Marburg.

53. Oetinger's lifelong struggle with Leibuiz's philosophy is one of the most striking aspects of his career. After renouncing it he considered it his task to replace it with a philosophy corresponding to the content of Scripture, a "sacred philosophy."

54. Georg Wolfgang Krafft (1701-1754), 1744 professor of mathematics and physics in Tübingen

55. Duke Ludwig founded this school for future civil servants. Duke Friedrich I changed it into a school for princes and nobility in 1596.

56. Jeremias Friedrich Reuss (1700-1777), 1747 chief church superintendent of Schleswig and Holstein; 1756 successor of Pfaff as chancellor of the University of Tübingen. Representative of a moderate pietism.

57. The master's degree, usually with license to teach.

58. Christian Fende belonged to the separatist group of Johann Jakob Schütz in Frankfurt. Cf. note 59.

59. Johann Jakob Schütz (1640-1690), legal adviser and state councilor in Frankfurt am Main, and one of the founders of the *collegia pietatis*. Gradually he withdrew into even more private circles. Since 1676 he refrained from participating in Holy Communion and more and more also from taking part in the life of the church. Spener's attempts at mediation failed. After Spener had left Frankfurt in 1686 Schütz cut all ties with the church. Buried without participation of a pastor. In 1727 Oetinger became acquainted with his daughter.

60. The *Cabbala Denudata* (revealed Cabala) was edited by Christian Knorr von Rosenroth (1636-1689), the first volume appearing in 1677-1678, and the second in 1684, thus offering the contemporaries a more intimate knowledge of Jewish mysticism.

61 Johann Albrecht Bengel (1687-1752), 1713-1741 preceptor of the monastery school in Denkendorf, 1741-1747 prelate (Propst) in Herbrechtingen. 1743 Oetinger accepted a pastorate in Schnaitheim nearby because he wanted to be near Bengel. Since 1747 Bengel worked (as prelate of Alpirsbach and as Konsistorialrat) in Stuttgart. His most famous work is the *Gnomon Novi Testamenti* (1742). Through his moderate and mediating attitude toward the prayer meetings (Erbauungsstunden) he contributed considerably to keeping Pietism and church united in Württemberg. Became known not only for his important achievements in the field of Greek New Testament research, but also for his stimulation of a new approach to eschatological questions. Computed the second coming of Christ and the beginning of the millennium for 1836, but considered the possibility of an error in his calculations.

62. Friedrich Christoph Steinhofer (1706-1761) became known for his associations with the Moravians. In 1733 he accompanied Zinzendorf on his trip through Württemberg. In 1749 he cut his ties with the Moravians and spent the last years of his life as a pastor of the Württemberg church.

63. Ehmann (p. 35) identifies him as one Johann Kaspar Obenberger.

64. Jakob Böhme (1575-1624), German Theosophist who via Oetinger greatly influenced Schelling who in turn again influenced Paul Tillich.

65. Sal, Sulphur, and Mercurius are frequently mentioned in Jakob Böhme's writings. Sal (salt) is the property or power of nature by which a being becomes solid and palpable. From the beginning, it inheres in the acid, astringent property of eternal nature. Mercurius is the fiery life spirit, the second Gestalt of nature, which tries to free itself from the astringent property of nature that keeps it shackled. It is the cause of all movement and life. Sulphur is the third Gestalt of nature, a fiery salt to feed the fire. According to one interpretation, it is the burning anxiety in the soul which lasts until the light dawns and separates itself from the darkness.

66. Kaspar von Schwenckfeld (1489-1561), since 1518 leader in the Reformation of Silesia, because of doctrinal differences opposed by Martin Luther, spent much of his later life as a fugitive among friends and followers. Schwenckfeld did not found a church. But many followers united in churchlike groups. Persecuted throughout Germany, a majority emigrated to Pennsylvania where today there are still Schwenckfeld churches.

67. Oetinger says of the central vision: First, it cannot be deceived, since it originates in the central ground. Second, it is passive, yielding to the activity of God. Third, it is a supernatural gift which cannot be attained through any search. Fourth, it is an ineffable union with God, mediated through the death and resurrection of Jesus Christ.

68. Johann Jakob Moser (1701-1785), Württemberg lawyer, author of theological and devotional writings, besides several important works in the field of secular and ecclesiastical law; imprisoned on the Hohentwiel 1759-1764. See Reinhard Ruerup, *Johann Jakob Moser, Pietismus und Reform*, Wiesbaden, 1965, and Mack Welker, *Johann Jakob Moser and the Holy Roman Empire*, Chapel Hill, 1981. Also Yeide, pp. 125-140.

69. Therese of Bordeau (1640-1717), member of the Carmelite order. In 1734 Oetinger edited her autobiography. Marguerite-Marie Alacoque (1647-

1690), nun in the Bourgogne and an early forerunner of the heart-of-Jesus cult. Oetinger published her biography in 1735. Abbé de Brion is mentioned by Oetinger as a secretary of Therese of Bordeaux. In another book Oetinger quotes an excerpt from a writing by Père Maure.

70. Christian Hagmajer (1680-1746), 1716 professor of philosophy in Tübingen, later professor of theology. He died as abbot of Hirsau.

71. Ehmann here refers to Oetinger's letter to Bengel of April 16, 1727, in which he expresses the wish that, besides reporting academic matters to Bengel, he might also get some advice from him for his own studies (Ehmann, p. 429).

72. Ehmann refers here to Prov. 8:21, which obviously is a mistake.

73. Peter von Muschenbroek (1692-1761), 1723 professor at Utrecht University, 1740 professor of mathematics and philosophy at Leyden University.

74. Isaac Newton (1643-1727), originator of the new physics and astronomy, to whom Oetinger was indebted in his view of physics.

75. Oetinger's *Inquisitio in sensum communem et rationem* (Tübingen, 1753), was reissued in a facsimile edition by the Friedrich Frommann Verlag (Günther Holzboog), Stuttgart-Bad Cannstatt, 1964, with an introduction by Hans-Georg Gadamer.

76. The standard work of the medieval cabala.

77. From Martini 1728 (November 11) to around Georgii 1729 (around April 24) when Oetinger returned once more to Tübingen for a short time (Ehmann, p. 57).

78. General practitioner in Stuttgart and a follower of Jakob Böhme. In several books he defended his opposition to the established church, the first published in 1712. Also turned against the circles of the Inspired.

79. Jeanne Marie Bouvier de la Mothe Guyon (1648- 1717), French quietist writer. Her complete works appeared in 40 volumes (1767-1791), several also in English.

80. Cf. note 59.

81. The term is to be traced back to the Sepher Jezirah, a work of Jewish gnosticism appearing about 500 A.D. Originally the word "Sephirot" meant numbers.

82. Carl Hector Marquis St. George de Marsay (1688-1753), Huguenot since 1711 living in Schwarzenau, a village in the Grafschaft Wittgenstein. Earlier in his life defending the teachings of Madame de Guyon, he later turned toward the Lutheran church and represented a mild Pietism.

83. Antoinette Bourignon (1616-1680), Flemish quietist who attacked every form of religious organization. Large following in the Netherlands, France, and especially Scotland. Three of her works were translated into English.

84. Count Kasimir of Berleburg died in 1741.

85. Johann Conrad Dippel (1673-1734), physician and theologian. After a checkered career he settled in Berleburg in 1729. His complete works were edited in 1747 after his death. Mainly emphasizing the idea of sanctification, he also battled the prominence of the clergy in the Lutheran church. His opposition to the inspiration of Holy Scripture brought him into severe conflict with the theology of his day.

86. Adam Struensee (1708-1791), 1730 court chaplain to the countess of Sayn-Wittgenstein in Berleburg, 1759 chief superintendent in Schleswig-Holstein.

87. According to Ehmann, Oetinger here inserted the following footnote:

"Marsay published many booklets. They sold well. But no one bought Dr. Kayser's booklets. This tempted Dr. Kayser to imitate Marsay. Thus he gave up making excerpts from Jakob Böhme and instead made them from Madame de Guyon, since he thought his books would sell better this way. But they did not." (p. 62).

88. August Gottlieb Spangenberg (1704-1792), since 1732 assistant at Halle University and inspector of the orphanage. Compelled to give up his position in 1734 on account of his connections with Zinzendorf, he worked for years in the later United States laying the foundations for the still existing Moravian congregations in America. Having returned to Europe in 1762, he became known as the biographer of Zinzendorf. Author of the basic Moravian dogmatics, *Idea fidei fratrum* (1779).

89. Ehmann (p. 65) carries a note on the courses Oetinger taught at Halle University, basically in Bible and logic.

90. Nikolaus Ludwig, Graf von Zinzendorf (1700-1760) in 1733 visited Württemberg for the first time in the hope that the theological faculty of Tübingen would certify his orthodoxy. In 1734 he returned to Württemberg in order to become accepted as a ministerial candidate of the Württemberg church. While this was granted, Duke Karl Alexander denied him his wish to become prelate of St. Georgen in the Black Forest. He came to Württemberg a third time in 1739, preaching in various places. Tried to influence the Württemberg churches through his messengers who were successful in engaging a number of younger theologians for the Moravian cause, among them Oetinger, Steinhofer, and Hehl. Oetinger and Steinhofer returned to serve the Württemberg church. Matthäus Gottfried Hehl, however, joined the Moravians and died in 1787 as Moravian bishop in the United States. In regard to the relationship between Zinzendorf and Oetinger see R. Geiges, "Die Auseinandersetzung zwischen Chr. Fr. Oetinger und Zinzendorf," *Blätter für württembergische Kirchengeschichte*, 1935:3/4 and 1936:1/2.

91. The book appeared in Frankfurt and Leipzig in 1731.

92. Thomas Bromley (1629-1691), first a follower of Jakob Böhme, later developed his own doctrine of the "inner light" around 1660, and together with John Pordage and his wife and Jane Leade founded the "Philadelphian Society."

93. The work of Joh. Theod. Von Tschesch was published together with Oetinger's interpretation. See Ehmann, p. 837.

94. Oetinger here refers to Philip Jakob Spener (1635-1705), the father of Pietism.

95. The mission to France Zinzendorf had proposed was a visit to the newly persecuted Camisards in the Cevennes mountains. See Ehmann, p. 69.

96. Cf. note 45.

97. Oetinger's difficulties seem to have been caused by promises he made at Herrnhut in regard to refusal to administer the Lord's Supper. See Ehmann, p. 80.

98. An interpretation of the Protestant view of the *ordo salutis*, published in Frankfurt and Leipzig in 1735.

99. Ehmann adds: at the suggestion of Bengel; p. 98.

100. Cf. note 90.

101. Ehmann, p. 99, points out that the preaching in Tübingen took place only during his second visit, on December 19, 1734, after Zinzendorf had been accepted as a ministerial candidate of the church of Württemberg.

102. The central vision. Cf. note 67.

103. The translation was published in Frankfurt in 1734.

104. Cf. Jan van Ruusbroek, *Werken* (Amsterdam, 1934), II:6, *Van den Gheesteliken Tabernakel* (p. 336). Oetinger slightly altered and abbreviated the passage which he quoted from the Gottfried Arnold translation. See note 10.

105. Probably Johann Arndt (1555-1621), the author of *True Christianity*. See note 133.

106. Source reference in Ehmann, p. 107. In Oetinger's *Gespräch im Reich der Todten* ...(1761), p. 3, there is general reference to this work in Herrnhut.

107. A book about Job, published in Esslingen, 1748.

108. Published in 1761 (n.p.). Oetinger's comparison between New England churches and the Moravian congregations is of interest at this point. See Ehmann, p. 118.

109. Jonas Korte, a book salesman, published his "Reise nach dem gelobten Land" in 1743. Ehmann, p. 113, remarks that no trace of the invitation can be found in the first edition of Korte's book and that the second edition of 1751 is unknown to him. The 1743 edition I was able to check does, however, refer in the preface to a learned Magister (without mentioning his name) which could well have been Oetinger.

110. Published in Leipzig in 1735. Ehmann describes the book, pp. 125ff. It is a combination of several translations and Oetinger's own ideas about separatism.

111. Johann Adam Steinmetz (1689-1763), abbot of the Bergen monastery and chief superintendent of duchy Magdeburg. Oetinger was supposed to have become Steinmetz's secretary. But this did not materialize. See Ehmann, p. 135.

112. Ehmann thinks that the "sectarians" were probably the Gichtelians, followers of Johann Georg Gichtel (1638-1710), radical critic of the Lutheran church, later in his life in Amsterdam head of nonchurch Christians. In 1682 Gichtel issued the first complete edition of Jakob Böhme's works.

113. Dr. Kämpf, originally a pastor in the Alsace, but compelled to give up his pastorate in 1716 because of his separatist views, studied medicine and in 1719 became a hospital physician in Zweibrücken. Highly gifted and influential, he was able to hold his position for many years, even though he belonged to the Inspired. Finally dismissed in 1734, he moved to Hesse-Homburg where in 1736 he opened a famous medical school. Oetinger was one of his students.

114. Beate Sturm (1682-1730), active in the care for the poor and lonely in Stuttgart.

115. Cf. note 18.

116. The Karaites are a Jewish sect, founded 761-62 A.D. At the turn of the century about 5500 members were still known to exist, chiefly in Russia.

117. Cf. note 76.

118. Here follows in Ehmann a passage about Dr. Kämpf which we inserted earlier according to Hamberger.

119. Cf. note 110.

120. In 1753 Oetinger published in Stuttgart *Das wichtigste in der Kirchen-Historie, nämlich das, woraus das Ius publicum divinum hervorleuchtet.* By *ius publicum divinum* Oetinger understood that hidden activity of God in history whereby God directs the divine kingdom to prevail in the final elimination of the kingdoms of the world. For this divine right he appealed especially to Deut. 32:34 and interpreted the meaning of history in the light of Rev. 12. He concludes the volume with an extended reference to Bengel.

121. Ehmann inserts: "after about three quarters of a year" (p. 139).

122. Only at this point does Hamberger insert, in an extended footnote, the introduction to the autobiography which appears in Ehmann, pp. 1-5. Our edition, pp. 145-150.

123. Cf. note 31.

124. Stephen Schulze was a member of the Institutum Judiacum in Halle.

125. The word Oetinger uses here is "Idiot," according to Ehmann, p. 140. Sentence missing in Hamberger.

126. In June, 1737.

127. Oetinger here uses the plural "Bücher," since the book contains a combination and translation of three biographies (Cf. note 110) Because it deals with the possibility of a corruptness of the established church and criticizes blind obedience towards it, the church authorities were not pleased with it.

128. A "Repetent" is an instructor in the Tübinger Stift (see note 45).

129. Oetinger's wife, Christiane Dorothea Linsenmann, was born in Urach. They were engaged while Oetinger was "Repetent" in Tübingen and married April 22, 1738 in Urach. Ten children were born of this marriage, six of them dying early. After having been a widow for fourteen years, Mrs. Oetinger died December 26, 1796, in Sindelfingen at the home of her daughter, wife of the pastor Joh. Ferd. Seiz.

130. Cf. note 13.

131. Zinzendorf at that time preached in Hirsau, and Oetinger had the sermon printed. See Ehmann, p. 142f.

132. This was printed as a part of the work referred to in note 108.

133. Johann Arndt (1555-1621), son of a pastor in Ballenstedt. Initially studied medicine and after recovery from a serious illness studied theology. Gained new insights by reading Bernard of Clairvaux, Johann Tauler, Thomas à Kempis, the *Theologia deutsch*, and Martin Luther. Pastor in Badeborn near Ballenstedt, later in Quedlinburg, Braunschweig, and Eisleben. Then chief superintendent in Celle. His book *True Christianity* became the most widely read devotional work of Protestantism. One of the better known sayings of Arndt is: "Christ has many servants, but few followers."

134. Valentin Weigel (1533-1588), pastor in Zschopau until his death. Strongly influenced by the mysticism of the *Theologia deutsch* and Johann Tauler. His works posthumously published. His mystical ideas condemned as heresy by the prevailing theology. The objective word of God does not avail anything if the inner word does not cause it to become clear and take its place, as it were.

135. Johann Oechslin (1677-1738), 1701-1707 one of the "Repetenten" in the Tübingen Stift, during his later years court chaplain in Stuttgart.

136. Johann Reinhard Hedinger (1664-1704), court chaplain of Duke Eberhard Ludwig since 1699. Like Johann Andrews Hochstetter (see note 35) promoter of Pietism.

137. Ehmann reports that Karl Heinrich Rieger (1726-1791) expressed himself somewhat more moderately: the Holy Spirit accompanied him always up to the conference room, but in front of the door he would leave him (p. 148). - Rieger, after holding various positions in the Württemberg church, was consistory councilor.

138. Jane Leade (1623-1704), representative of English mysticism, student of Jakob Böhme who experienced revelations and visions, and co-founder of the "Philadelphian Society" (cf. note 92).

139. Christian Gottfried Schmoller died in 1707.

140. Beat Ludwig von Muralt of Bern wrote *Lettres sur les Anglais et sur les Français*, new ed. by O. von Greyerz and E. Ritter, 1897.

141. Lukas Osiander, Jr. (1571-1638), 1623 wrote "Theologisches Bedenken, welcher Gestalt Johann Arnds Bücher des genannten Wahren Christentums anzusehen."

142. Ehmann (p. 150) records that the letter got lost, but tries to reconstruct it from other still available materials.

143. Emanuel Swedenborg (1688-1772), in London in 1745 experienced visions. 1749-1758 in eight volumes published his alleged revelations in the form of an interpretation of Genesis and Exodus.

144. Ferdinand Olivier Petitpierre, pastor in Les Ponts (Neuenburg) since 1755. Died in 1790.

145. Cf. note 109.

146. A book dealing with catechetical instruction to the major parts of Luther's Catechism, published in Tübingen in 1762. See Ehmann, p. 176.

147. *Theologia emblematica* was for Oetinger a theology that concerned itself with the great symbols and metaphors of biblical thought, for example, the "woman clothed with the sun" of Rev. 12.

148. Alchemy was usually understood as the presumed art of changing base metals, such as lead or copper, into silver or gold by so-called transmutation. The alchemists were mainly searching for the white and the red tinctures. The white tincture was supposed to change the base metals into silver, whereas the great or red elixir (also called the red lion) was to change them in turn to gold. A trace of the preparative covered with wax had to be cast on liquid lead, tin, zinc, or copper. The great elixir, also called "the philosopher's stone," was not only supposed to change metals, but also, in a dissolved and diluted form, to heal diseases and to prolong life. Leibniz and many other seventeenth- and eighteenth-century philosophers were as much interested in alchemy as was Oetinger.

149. Those well versed in alchemy.

150. Raimundus Lullus (1235-1316), theologian, mystic, and poet, widely influential in the Middle Ages, also influenced Leibniz.

151. The text may be rendered into English as follows: "The living body (a) we dissolve in Apollonian fire, / so that what was stone may become spirit. / And out of its innermost depth we gain the gold / which purifies the sick metals from the dirt of the mother. / After we have separated the bones from the seed (b) which belongs to the birth, / we then wash in water what is related by blood. / Out of this originates a bird (c), colorfully decorated (d), / after it has turned brightly white it flies towards heaven. / Then, in a new fire, we separate its wings, / which are dyed with milk (e) and sprinkle them with its milk. / The remainder we nourish with blood, / until the grown-up bird stands the fierceness of the fire. / 'Three times great Hermes' (f) says accordingly that the bird / of wisdom gets burned (g), and in the whole world he does not have a father."

The key concepts call for a brief interpretation. (a) The main presupposition of alchemy was the existence of one basic substance, the *prima materia*, which continues to develop and change. (b) 'Seed' was one of the alchemist terms for *materia*. (c) For the alchemists, the *materia* is a *myrionymus*, a thing with a thousand names. It is called *Mondkraut* (moonplant), white and red lily on a green stem, snake and dragon, the bird of Hermes, etc. The various stages or degrees of heating the stone preparative are called: black raven, white eagle, white swan, white dove, red salamander, red lion, peacock's tail, etc. (d) According to the alchemists, nothing attains perfection unless it has first perfected its colors. (e) 'Milk' is the alchemistic word for mercury. (f) Hermes Trismegistos (*thrice-greatest*) is a mythical figure. The *Tabula smaragdina* ascribed to him was the standard work of alchemy. Alchemy is therefore also called the *hermetic art*. (g) In the second-last line of the Latin text "morsi" seems to be a truncated word. Perhaps it should be read *morderi (mordere*—to bite, hurt, burn, scorch), which would render the meaning: the bird of wisdom is born in pure fire, without earthly procreation.

152. The son of Oetinger, Joh. Fr. Oetinger, in his diary reports that the writer was the Danish poet Ludwig Holberg (1684-1754).

153. Published in 1753 in Tübingen.

154. Published in 1753 in Stuttgart.

155. Anthony Ashley Cooper, third Earl of Shaftesbury (1671-1713), English politician and philosophical writer at the begirming of the Enlightenment.

156. Published in 1765 in Stettin. Tr. into German by Julius Hamberger and published in 1852 in Stuttgart. Oetinger wrote his autobiography in 1762 or 1764. Thus the *Theologia ex idea vitae deducta* was not as yet printed.

157. Both were published in "*Beihilfe zum reinen Schriftverstand...*" in 1777 (n.p.).

158. Published in 1753 in Heilbronn.

159. Cf. Note 98.

160. Lutz, Count of Castell (1707-1772), for many years in correspondence with Oetinger.

161. Johann Ludwig Fricker (1729-1766), pastor in Württemberg, the most gifted among Oetinger's followers. In 1760 he visited the revival groups in the Rhineland where he exerted a considerable influence.

162. Franz I (1745-1765).

163. Oetinger stayed in Weinsberg 1752-1759, during which time he had to suffer personal calumny in regard to his family. Through the schoolteacher and the maid of the Oetingers rumors were spread about his wife and daughter. Accused of immoral relationships with a young teacher who gave piano lessons in the parsonage, the accusations proved unwarranted. Oetinger himself was also attacked because of his alchemistic studies.

164. Initially Oetinger called it an *attempt* at a biblical dictionary. It appeared attached to a collection of sermons (the so-called *Weinsberger Predigtbuch*) in Tübingen in 1759. This first form of the biblical dictionary is much shorter and thus more incomplete than the 1776 dictionary. Cf. Note 11.

165. Short meditations about the epistles which were added to the *Weinsberger Predigtbuch*. Cf. Note 164.

166. See 1 Tim. 1:20; 2 Tim. 2:17; 4:14.

167. The same Scripture references as in note 166.

168. Only Hamberger brings this sentence.

169. Published in Frankfurt and Leipzig. The first part appeared in 1759, the second and third part in 1761. Oetinger understood the Golden Age as the millenium.

170. Published in Frankfurt and Leipzig in 1762.

171. Cf. Note 108.

172. Uncle of the hymnwriter Chr. Karl Ludwig von Pfeil.

173. Published in Tübingen in 1761.

174. Cf. Note 170.

175. This work must have gotten lost in manuscript form, according to Ehmann, p. 283.

176. Ehmann, p. 283, quotes the volume and page reference.

177. Oetinger's autobiography according to its earliest edition, that of Immanuel Kolb of 1818 (and also in the other one Kolb edited in 1849) ends at this point. What follows is a later addition. Hamberger remarked at this point in his 1845 edition: "This is the end of Oetinger's autobiography which he wrote in his sixtieth year. What follows had to be pieced together and brought into order from very unclear notes written down at a later time and which were to a large extent unusable because of their meager content." Ehmann comments briefly on these notes: "One cannot help being deeply and sadly moved in examining the last notes of the autobiography which ends in a haphazard notebook. Thoughts float past him like dream visions which he cannot hold on to and bring into a framework. He puts down words and crosses them out in order to put down different ones and to cross out those because he cannot find the connecting link to join them, like a child who can only stammer words piecemeal." Our text continues to follow Ehmann.

178. About this stay in Herrenberg Oetinger writes: "On Sundays we have gatherings, and I teach the people to be good house-fathers, but also good servants and maids; since there are enough Christians who speculate, but few who practice Jesus' rule in Matth. 7: 12," "So whatever you wish …".

179. Published in Frankfurt and Leipzig in 1765. Authorship of this book (also about Swedenborg) caused him considerable trouble when it was discovered. Cf. Note 184.

180. Philipp Mattäus Hahn (1739-1790), 1764 pastor in Onstmettingen, 1770 in Kornwestheim, and 1781 in Echterdingen. Worked intensively with cell-groups in his congregations promoting well-founded insight and true discipleship. Hahn was not only an excellent theologian and minister, but also a great mathematician. Invented the cylinder escapement for pocket watches, promoted tool making, and was a builder of astronomical clocks. Goethe, Lavater, and other great men of his day were in contact with him.

181. In 1766 Oetinger became prelate in Murrhardt (prelate is the same as "Propst" in position, but is always tied to a particular place). This position included membership in the Landschaft (the Württemberg congress of that day), where he opposed various abuses in the administrative board and demanded the release and reinstatement of Johann Jakob Moser as legal advisor. Cf. Note 68.

182. "Serenissimus," the same as "His Highness," was commonly used for the duke who in this case was Karl Eugen of Württemberg.

183. See Ehmann, p. 290, for the content of the two letters.

184. See Ehmann, p. 291ff. for the particulars of the controversy.

185. Cf. Note 181.

186. Duke of Württemberg, 1795-1797.

187. Princess Antonia (1613- 1679), daughter of Duke Johann Friedrich of Württemberg, studied Hebrew and concerned herself especially with the cabala. She had placed in the church near the Deinach mineral springs a painting depicting the most important teachings of Jewish philosophy. Oetinger wrote a book about the painting, published in Tübingen in 1763. The Deinach (or Teinach) altarpiece has become important for feminists in the 20th century because it depicts 94 female figures from the Bible as they approach Christ and, besides a shadowy background with Father, Son, and Holy Spirit, it shows in the center a female trinity in bright colors. See Elisabeth Moltmann-Wendel and Jürgen

Moltmann, *Humanity in God* (New York: Pilgrim Press, 1983), pp. 46 and 48.

188. See Ehmann, p. 297 and pp. 687-693.

189. As the correspondence between Oetinger and Swedenborg indicates, Oetinger asked pointed questions all along about the new system. See especially Ehmann, p. 693.

190. See Ehmann footnote, p. 301. Oetinger slightly exaggerated here.

191. See Ehmann, pp. 749ff. There is a contradiction between the place of publication mentioned in Ehmann's text (Halle) and the Ehmann bibliographical reference, which lists Frankfurt and Leipzig as places of publication. Messerer, the publisher, was actually in Schwäbisch-Hall, so that Halle might be a misprint anyway.

192. Cf. Note 170.

193. Published in 1771.

194. Published in Frankfurt in 1772.

195. Guillaume Postel (1510-1581), French Roman Catholic mystic, with contacts to Protestants and also radicals, such as Schwenkfeld. Cf. Note 66.

196. Johann Salomo Semler (1725-1791), 1752 professor of theology in Halle, introduced rationalism at Halle. Known for criticism of the biblical text and the history of the canon.

197. Cf. Note 181.

198. Father of the famous Stuttgart pastor, C. A. Dann.

199. Published in 1772.

200. The coherence of the argument breaks down at this point in the various available texts. See Ehmann, p. 335, about the fragmentary, dreamlike character of Oetinger's last entries. We conclude with the important points of the argument.

201. Oetinger's reference here is to the word of Newton, *Vacuum est sensorium Dei*. See Ehmann, p. 315.

202 Cf. Note 11.

203. Johann Gerhard Hasenkamp (1736-1777), headmaster of the Gymnasium in Duisburg since 1766. Deeply influenced by Bengel and Oetinger, a friend of Gerhard Tersteegen and Samuel Collenbusch. Together with Collenbusch, he developed a strange doctrine of sanctification which was inspired by the visions and revelations of the somnambulistically inclined Dorothea Wuppermann. Cf. Note 204.

204. Dorothea Wuppermann (1747-1816), married to pastor Friedrich Wilhelm Elbers of Lüttringhausen, Cf. note 203.

205. Hamberger (p. 110) points out that the poet Christian Friedrich Schubart during his long and severe captivity on the Hohenasperg came to acknowledge the truth of the Christian faith especially through Oetinger's writings, and that Johann Friedrich Oberlin in his parish in the Alsace was led away from his early rationalism only through Oetinger.—The last work which Oetinger still edited himself was *Versuch einer Auflösung der 177 Fragen aus Jakob Böhm*, published in 1777.

206. Johann Friedrich Oetinger died in 1784. It was assumed that he was the author of the funeral sermon for his father (Hamberger, p. 97). Ehmann (p. 336) corrects this.

BIBLIOGRAPHY

Arndt, Johann. *True Christianity*, tr. and ed. Peter Erb. New York, 1979.

Arnold, Gottfried. *Unparteiische Kirchen-und Ketzerhistorie*. Frankfurt, 1699.

Barnes, Robin Bruce. *Apocalypticism in the Wake of the Lutheran Reformation*. Stanford, CA, 1988.

Beach, Waldo. *The Christian Life*. Richmond, VA, 1966.

Bengel, Johann Albrecht. *Abriss der sogennanten Brüdergemeinde in welchem die Lehre und die ganze Sache geprüfet*. Stuttgart, 1751.
_____. *Gnomon Novi Testamenti*. Tübingen, 1742.
_____. *Erklärte Offenbarung Johannes*. Stuttgart, 1740.

Benz, Ernst. *The Mystical Sources of German Romantic Philosophy*, tr. Blair R. Reynolds and Eunice M. Paul. Allison Park, PA, 1983.
_____."Ecumenical Relations between Boston Puritanism and German Pietism: C. Mather and A.H. Francke," *Church History*, 20, 1951, pp. 28-55.

Beyreuther, Erich. *Zinzendorf und die Christenheit*. Marburg, 1961.
_____. Geschichte der Diakonie und Inneren Mission in der Neuzeit. Berlin, 1962.

Bonhoeffer, Dietrich. *Life Together*. New York, 1954.

Bornkamm, Heinrich. *Mystik, Spiritualismus und die Anfänge des Pietismus im Luthertum*. Giessen, 1926.

Brecht, Martin, ed. *Geschichte des Pietismus*, Vols. 1 and 2. Göttingen, 1993, 1995.
_____. and Jörg Sandberger. "Hegels Begegnung mit der Theologie im Tübinger Stift," *Hegel-Studien* 5 (1969), 49ff.
_____. "Vom Pietismus zur Erweckungsbewegung," *Blätter für württembergische Kirchengeschichte* 68/69 (1968/1969), 370.

Brown, Dale W. *Understanding Pietism*. Grand Rapids, MI, 1978.

Cicero. *De Re Publica, De Legibus*, tr. Clinton Walker Keyes. London, 1928, II, 418.

Deppermann, Klaus. *Der hallesche Pietismus und der preussische Staat unter Friedrich III. (I.)*. Göttingen, 1961.

Dorner, I. A. *Geschichte der protestantischen Theologie*. München, 1867.

Durnbaugh, Donald F. *European Origins of the Brethren*. Elgin, IL, 1958.

Ehmann, Karl Chr. Eberh. *Friedrich Christoph Oetinger's Leben und Briefe als urkundlicher Commentar zu dessen Schriften*. Stuttgart, 1859.
_____. (Oetinger) Sämmtliche Schriften. 2. Abth., Bd. 6 (Stuttgart, 1858-64), 29-30.

Erb, Peter C., ed. *Pietists: Selected Writings*. New York, 1983.

Fenelon, François de Salignac de la Motte. *Des aventures de Telemaque*. 1699.

Fogel, Robert William. *The Fourth Great Awakening and the Future of Egalitarianism*. Chicago, 2000.

Francke, August Hermann. *Pietas Hallensis, or an Abstract of the Marvellous Footsteps of Divine Providence*. London, 1707, second edition.
_____. *Der Grosse Aufsatz*. Otto Podczeck, ed. Berlin, 1962.

Friedenthal, Richard. *Luther: Sein Leben und seine Zeit*. München, 1967.

Fulbrook, Mary. *Piety and Politics: Religion and the Rise of Absolutism in England, Württemberg and Prussia*. New York, 1983.

Gawthrop, Richard. *Pietism and the Making of Eighteenth Century Prussia*. New York, 1993.

Gehrlich, Fritz. *Der Kommunismus als Lehre vom tausendjährigen Reich*. München, 1920.

Geiges, R. "Die Auseinandersetzung zwischen Chr. Fr. Oetinger und Zinzendorf," *Blätter fur württembergische Kirchengeschichte* 3/4: 1935 and 1/2: 1936.

Goeters, Wilhelm. *Die Vorbereitung des Pietismus in der Reformierten Kirche der Niederlande biz zur labadistischen Krisis*. Leipzig, 1911.

Greschat, Martin, ed. *Orthodoxie und Pietismus*. Stuttgart, 1982.

Gruen, Willi. *Speners soziale Leistungen und Gedanken. Ein Beitrag zur Geschichte des Armenwesens und des kirchlichen Pietismus in Frankfurt a.M. und in Brandenburg-Preussen*. Würzburg, 1934.

Gruenberg, Paul, ed. *Hauptschriften Philipp Jakob Speners*. Gotha, 1889.
_____. Philipp Jakob Spener. Göttingen, 1905, II.

Hauck, Wilhelm-Albert. *Das Geheimnis des Lebens*. Heidelberg, 1947.

Heppe, Heinrich. *Geschichte des Pietismus und der Mystik in der reformierten Kirche, namentlich der Niederlande*. Leiden, 1879.

Herpel, Otto, ed. *Friedrich Christoph Oetinger: Die heilige Philosophie.* München, 1923.

Herzog, Frederick. "August Hermann Francke: Francke's Conversion," in *Mid-Stream*, 8, 3, Spring 1969, 41-49.
_____. "Diakonia in Modern Times: Eighteenth-Twentieth Centuries," in *Service in Christ: Essays Presented to Karl Barth on his 80th Birthday.* Ed. By James I. McCord and T.H.L. Parker. London: Epworth, 1966, 135-150.

Hinrichs, Carl. *Friedrich Wilhelm I. Koenig in Preussen.* Hamburg, 1941.
_____. "Der Hallische Pietismus als politisch-soziale Reformbewegung des 18. Jahrhunderts," in *Preussen als Historisches Problem.* Berlin, 1964.
_____. *Preussentum und Pietismus*: Göttingen, 1971.
_____. "Pietismus und Militarismus im alten Preussen," in *Archiv für Reformationsgeschichte*, 49, 1, 2(1958), 270-323.

Holl, Karl. "Luther und das landesherrliche Kirchenregiment," in *Gesammelte Aufsätze zur Kirchengeschichte.* Tübingen, 1932, I, 339ff.
_____. *Die Bedeutung der grosser Kriege für das religiöse und kirchliche Leben innerhalb des deutschen Protestantismus.* Tübingen, 1917.

Irwin, Joyce. "Anna Maria Van Schurman: From Feminism to Pietism," in *Church History*, 46 (March 1977), pp. 48-62.

Kanzenbach, Friedrich Wilhelm. *Orthodoxie und Pietismus.* Gütersloh, 1966.

Knorr von Rosenroth, Christian, ed. *Cabbala Denudata*, 1677.

Kramer, Gustav. *August Hermann Francke: Ein Lebensbild.* Halle, 1880.

Kupisch, Karl. *Vom Pietismus zum Kommunismus.* Berlin, 1953.

Labadie, Jean de. *La Reformation de l'Eglise par le Pastorat, contenue en deux lettres pastorales.* Pt. I, Middelburg, H. Smidt, 1667.

Lang, August. *Puritanismus und Pietismus.* Neukirchen, 1941.

Langen, August. *Der Wortschatz des deutschen Pietismus.* Tübingen, 1954.

Lehmann, Hartmut. *Pietismus und weltliche Ordnung in Württemberg vom 17. bis zum 20. Jahrhundert.* Stuttgart, 1969.

Leube, Hans. *Die Reformation in der deutschen lutherischen Kirche zur Zeit der Orthodoxie.* Leipzig, 1924.

Lewis, A.J. *Zinzendorf the Ecumenical Pioneer.* London, 1962.

Lovelace, Richard F. *The American Pietism of Cotton Mather.* Grand Rapids, MI, 1979.

McCord, James I. and T. H. L. Parker, eds. *Service in Christ: Essays Presented to Karl Barth on his Eightieth Birthday.* London, 1966.

McLoughlin, William G. *Revivals, Awakenings and Reform.* Chicago, 1978.

Muralt, Beat Ludwig von. *Lettres sur les Anglais et sur les Français,* ed. O. von Greyerz and E. Ritter, 1897.

Nagler, Arthur Wilford. *Pietism and Methodism.* Nashville, 1918.

Nigg, Walter. *Das Ewige Reich.* Erlenbach-Zürich, 1944.

Oetinger, Friedrich Christoph. *Selbstbiographie. Genealogie der realen Gedanken eines Gottgelehrten,* ed. J. Roessle, Metzingen, 1961.

_____. *Biblisches und emblematisches Wörterbuch dem Tellerischen Wörterbuch und Anderer falschen Schrifterklärungen entgegengesetzt.* 1776.
_____. *Inquisitio in sensum communem et rationem.* Tübingen, 1753.
_____. *Gespräch im Reich der Todten.* 1761.
_____. *Das wichtigste in der Kirchen-Historie, nämlich das woraus das Ius publicum divinum hervorleuchtet.* Stuttgart, 1753.

Osiander, Lukas, Jr. *Theologisches Bedenken, welcher Gestalt Johann Arnds Bücher des genannten Wahren Christentums.* 1623.

Piepmeier, Rainer. "F. C. Oetinger" in *Orthodoxie und Pietismus,* ed. M. Greschat, 373-390.

Pinson, Koppel S. *Pietism as a Factor in the Rise of German Nationalism.* New York, 1934.

Ritschl, Albrecht. *Geschichte des Pietismus.* 3 vols. Bonn, 1880.

Ruerup, Reinhard. *Johann Jakob Moser, Pietismus und Reform.* Wiesbaden, 1965.

Sachse, Julius Friedrich. *The German Pietists of Provincial Pennsylvania.* Philadelphia, 1895.

Sattler, Gary R. *God's Glory, Neighbor's Good: A Brief Introduction to the Life and Writings of August Hermann Francke.* Chicago, 1982.

Saxby, T. J. *The Quest for the New Jerusalem, Jean De Labadie and the Labadists, 1610-1744.* Dordrecht, 1987.

Schmid, Heinrich. *Die Geschichte des Pietismus.* Nordlingen, 1863.

Schmidt, Kurt Dietrich. "Labadie und Spener," in *Zeitschrift für Kirchengeschichte,* 46, 1928, 566.

Schmidt, Martin. *Pietismus*. Stuttgart, 1972.

Schneider, Robert. *Schellings und Hegels schwäbische Geistessahnen.* Würzburg-Aumühle, 1938.

Schubert, Hans von. *Grundzüge der Kirchengeschichte*. Tübingen, 1921.

Seneca. *Ad Lucilium Epistulae Morales*. London 1917.

Spangenburg, August Gottlieb. *Idea fidei fratrum*. 1779.

Stein, K. James. *Philip Jakob Spener: Pietist Patriarch*. Chicago, 1986.

Spener, Philipp Jakob. *Pia Desideria*, ed. Kurt Aland and Theodore G. Tappert. Philadelphia, 1964.

Stoeffler, F. Ernest. *The Rise of Evangelical Pietism*. Leiden, 1965.
_____. German Pietism During the Eighteenth Century. Leiden, 1973.

Walker, Mack. *Johann Jakob Moser and the Holy Roman Empire*, Chapel Hill, NC, 1981.

Walzer, Michael. *The Revolution of the Saints*. Cambridge, MA, 1965.

Wallmann, Johannes. *Philipp Jakob Spener und die Anfaenge des Pietismus.* Tübingen, 1970.

Weber, Max. *Die protestantische Ethik*, München, 1965.

Winter, Eduard. *Halle als Ausgangspunkt der deutschen Russlandkunde im 18. Jahrundert*, Berlin, 1953.

Winter, Gibson. *The New Creation as Metropolis*. New York, 1963.

Yeide, Harry Jr. *Studies in Classical Pietism: The Flowering of the 'Ecclesio-' la,'* New York, 1997.

Zuck, Lowell H., ed. *Pia Desideria: Six Proposals in Consolidation and Expansion,* Vol IV of *Living Theological Heritage of the United Church of Christ.* Cleveland, 2000, 230-240.
_____. "Cotton Mather and German Pietism," *Historical Intelligencer*, Fall 1982, 11-16.